W9-DGB-389

Why do thousands of people across North America volunteer their time, creativity and energy to raise funds through relief sales to benefit Mennonite Central Committee's worldwide relief and development work?

Volunteers put Christian love into action as they rise early to prepare bread dough, fire the charcoal for barbecued chicken or stir a cauldron of ham and bean soup. MCC volunteers have opened their eyes to the needs in the world. They are supported by their faith and motivated by the biblical passage, *"Suppose there are brothers and sisters who need clothes and do not have enough to eat. What good is there in your saying to them God bless you! Keep warm and eat well, if you do not give them necessities of life" (James 2:15-16)*

Planning for sale day is year-long work involving monthly meetings, delegating, recruiting and follow-up. The day of a relief sale is a joyful occasion as each person does their part, accomplishing humble tasks with thoughtful care; giving their best time and talents.

Relief sales are celebrations of community.
These are happy times, reminiscent of family and neighbors working together at harvest, helping raise a barn or sharing the task of spring housecleaning. Volunteers experience camaraderie and fellowship through the activities of the day.
In their giving, volunteers receive.

Volunteer participation has undergirded Mennonite Central Committee work for 75 years. The organization is dependent on the good efforts of thousands of volunteers. They are essential to the work of caring for people who are suffering. Through your purchase at relief sales you too become an essential part of ministry, "in the Name of Christ."

John A. Lapp
Executive Director
Mennonite Central Committee

Spice for Living: Love

*This "recipe"—contributed by Sally Reddecliff, of Johnstown, Pennsylvania—
is a fitting beginning for this book.*

*Don't keep Love locked up in a cupboard.
Put a big pinch of it in everything you cook.*

What Does MCC Really Mean by Marie Nussbaum

MCC — *Mennonite Central Committee*

MCC — *Much Caring and Consideration for others and unselfishness.*

MCC — *Many caring couples who give love, time and energy to build God's
kingdom in a practical way.*

MCC — *More concentrated concern for those who are in need. Men and
matrons constructing cupboards, houses and other buildings.*

Merry, chubby chums who befriend other cultures.

Middle-aged characters cultivating corn, beans and other crops.

Mainly contentious crowds going forth to many different parts of the earth.

Modernizing crude crank shafts and imparting technology.

Materials — coveralls — and cows given in the name of Christ.

Ministering cordially and continually.

MCC — *My constant commission to bring glory to God by all my actions.*

— *Submitted by Leila Muff, Minot, North Dakota, Relief Sale*

Treasured Mennonite Recipes

Series II

published in cooperation
with Mennonite Central Committee

Fox Chapel Publishing
Box 7948, Lancaster, PA 17604

©1996, Fox Chapel Publishing Co. Inc.

ISBN #1- 56523-028-0
Publisher: Alan Giagnocavo
Project Editor: Grace Palsgrove
Recipe Editor: Beverly J. DeWitt

Cover illustration by Pam McKee, "Inklinations", Romansville, PA
Interior Design and Layout by Chuck Golding
Cover Design by Robert Altland
Special thanks to Brenda Wagner, Mennonite Central Committee.
Printed in the United States of America

All rights reserved.

How does the sale of this cookbook benefit MCC?

Because we really believe in the work that MCC accomplishes, Fox Chapel Publishing has set up an arrangement whereby MCC raises funds without any risk or financial investment.
We do everything, collect recipes from volunteers, edit, write the stories, design the book and pay for printing and binding the finished books. Immediately upon publication, we tithe the print run by giving at no cost ten percent of the books printed to MCC for sale through its Relief Sale Committees. We also market the book ourselves through book and gift stores.
As of this writing, 21,000 copies of the first book - Treasured Mennonite Recipes are in print. 2100 copies donated free to MCC have raised over $25,000. Extra copies sold beyond the tithed copies that the committees buy and re-sell earn them a 60% profit. (i.e. a $12.95 book earns MCC $7.77 in profit). Thank you for your support by buying this cookbook. Over the life of this project we hope to raise more than $100,000 for MCC.

❖ *Contents* ❖

Appetizers & Dips	1
Soups	6
Main Dishes & Casseroles	26
Poultry	26
Beef	34
Pork	46
Meat-Filled Pastries	55
Dairy & Vegetarian	60
Side Dishes	66
Vegetables	75
Salads & Dressings	80
Snacks	93
Jams, Jellies & Fruit Butters	95
Pickles, Relishes & Sauces	98
Beverages	110
Yeast Breads & Rolls	114
Quick Breads, muffins & Coffee Cakes	132
Crullers, Fritters & Doughnuts	139
Pancakes	145
Pies & Tarts	150
Cakes & Cupcakes	162
Cookies, Squares & Bars	174
Desserts	202
Candies	214
Relief Soap Making	216

Publisher Foreword

This cookbook is born of caring and compassion. One of the most obvious traits that develop after one commits to following Jesus is a deep sense of concern for others. We begin to reach out to help not only our family and friends but even total strangers.

But how can we really help others? The truth is that helping others in an effective, authentic way is often difficult.

Some time ago, I spent a semester studying both poverty law and international development at a secular university. The courses left me cold and uninspired. I realized how a Christian approach to helping others based on mutual respect, brotherhood and compassion is very different from an approach that is based largely on pity, guilt and a modern form of noblesse oblige.

That experience left me with a new appreciation for the work of Mennonite Central Committee.

Through intensive personal work at the grass roots level in countries around the world, MCC has been consistently effective in meeting peoples short and long term needs.

From humanitarian relief in Ethiopia and Bosnia, to developing businesses and farms for long term self-sufficiency in Africa and Asia, MCC is bringing healing to troubled countries and permanently lifting people out of poverty.

One of the strengths of MCC is its ability to use every day skills and abilities of volunteers in creative ways. This book is a celebration of the traditions and history of this one type of volunteer enthusiasm — the Relief Sales.

If you've never attended a Relief Sale — don't delay! Read through the sale locations and dates and plan your trip now. A Relief Sale combines the best elements of an auction sale, family reunion and bazaar. It is my hope that this book will serve to recognize the volunteers who together spend 1000's of hours each year to organize a relief sale and to encourage you to attend as many as possible.

Finally, I would like to dedicate this book to the memory of the late Reverend Vernon Leis of Tavistock, Ontario. Vernon taught me much about faith and caring in both word and deed.

Alan Giagnocavo
Publisher

 Treasured Mennonite Recipes

How This Book Was Written

This book is a companion volume to *Treasured Mennonite Recipes #1* published in 1992. The first volume contained recipes gathered by the New Hamburg, Ontario Relief Sale Committee.

Treasured Mennonite Recipes Volume Two is a compilation of the histories of the 38 MCC relief sales held throughout North America as well as some of the favorite recipes of the people who make these events successful fund-raisers.

Based on the success of the first volume which has raised over $25,000 for MCC to date, we planned an all-new second volume that would feature such recipes, sales history and events from the area and its volunteers.

Grace Palsgrove, former Lifestyle editor of the *Lancaster Intelligencer*, was given the task of contacting each sale committee to collect recipes, photos, history and anecdotes. Working together with Brenda Wagner (Constituency Ministries, MCC) Grace was able to pry loose lots of delicious recipes and fascinating information from each of the 38 relief sales.

The chairmen of the various sales were contacted initially through a letter and then with subsequent telephone calls or further correspondence to ask their help in gathering their stories.

As is usually the case, the volunteers who work so hard at the sales are also busy working. People took time out of their busy schedules to research their sales, contact cooks, and gather photographs — or found someone who could — to contribute to this cookbook because proceeds from its sale will go directly to MCC for the same end they work so hard to fulfill — to feed the hungry.

With this goal in mind, everyone was cooperative. Some of the information was previously published. Others sent extremely detailed, type-written texts. Still others jotted their information in a note and some even shared their stories over the telephone. However received, all of the stories reveal a great commitment to a most worthy cause.

Special thanks for recipe editing to Beverly DeWitt — an editor with formidable skill in organizing recipes and catching omitted steps often taken for granted in family recipes.

Directory of Mennonite Relief Sales — United States

Here is a listing of all current Relief Sales. For further information contact:

Mennonite Central Committee
704 Main St.
Box 500
Akron, PA 17501

State	City	Date
California	Fresno	First Saturday of April
Colorado	Rocky Ford	Third Saturday of October
Illinois	Arthur	Fourth Saturday of August
Illinois	Peoria	Third Friday and Saturday of March
Indiana	Goshen	Fourth Weekend of September
Indiana	Montgomery	Second Saturday of July
Iowa	Iowa City	Memorial Day Weekend
Kansas	Hutchinson	Second Saturday of April, (unless Easter Weekend, then First)
Michigan	Fairview	First Saturday of August
Missouri	Harrisonville	Second Saturday in October
Nebraska	Aurora	First Saturday of April, (Unless Easter Weekend, then Second)
North Dakota	Minot	First Saturday of April
Ohio	Kidron	First Saturday of August
Oklahoma	Fairview	Always the Friday and Saturday after Thanksgiving
Oregon	Albany	Second Saturday in October
Pennsylvania	Gap	Second Saturday of August
Pennsylvania	Harrisburg	First Saturday of April, (Unless Easter Weekend, then Second) A very large sale!
Pennsylvania	Johnstown	Fourth Thursday, Friday and Saturday of October
Pennsylvania	Lancaster	Second Thursday of March Selling livestock and hay
New York	Bath	Last Saturday in July
South Dakota	Sioux Falls	Fourth Friday of August
Texas	Houston	First Saturday of November
Virginia	Fisherville	Last Saturday of September
Washington	Ritzville	First Saturday in October
Wisconsin	Jefferson	Second Saturday of August

 Treasured Mennonite Recipes

Directory of Mennonite Relief Sales — Canada

State	City	Date
Alberta	Tofield/ Coaldale	July 17-18 Weekend
British Columbia	Black Creek	
British Columbia	Clearbroo	September 19 Weekend
British Columbia	Kelowna	September 26 Weekend
British Columbia	Prince George	October 3 Weekend
Ontario	Black Creek	September 19 Weekend
Ontario	Guelph	February 20 Weekend Sells mostly cattle
Ontario	New Hamburg	May 30 Weekend A very large sale!
Manitoba	Brandon	August 15 Weekend
Manitoba	Morris	September 19 Weekend
Saskatch- ewan	Hague	June 13 Weekend' Sells mostly grain and farm supplies
Saskatchewan		Saskatoon May 29-30 Weekend

For further information, you can write to the provincial MCC Headquarters listed below:

MCC Ontario
50 Kent Ave.
Kitchener, Ont. N2G 3R1

MCC British Columbia
31872 S. Fraser Way
Bos 2038
Clearbrook BC V2T 3TB

MC Saskatchewan
600 45th Street West
Saskatoon, Sask. S7L 5W9

MCC Alberta
76 Skyline Crescent NE
Calgary, Alta. T2K 5X7

MCC Manitoba
134 Plaza Drive
Winnipeg, Man. R3T 5K9

75 Years of Service in the Name of Christ

In 1920, Mennonite villages in Russia and the Ukraine sent four representatives to their brothers and sisters in North America asking for help during war and famine. Seven Mennonite conferences and relief organizations united to send food and other aid. At meetings in July and September of that year, Mennonite Central Committee (MCC) was formed.

MCC sent three relief workers to Russia in September 1920. The first MCC feeding operations began March 16, 1922; at their peak 43,000 rations were served daily. Fifty Fordson tractor-plow outfits, sent in 1922, were MCC's first development project.

Six weeks after the tractors and plows arrived in the Ukraine more than 4,300 acres of land had been plowed.

Today, 75 years later, MCC continues this tradition with programs that provide strength for today and hope for a brighter tomorrow.

Since 1920 more than 12,000 people have served in one-, two - and three-year MCC assignments overseas and in North America. Currently more than 900 MCC workers serve in some 50 countries. MCC workers help increase crop yields, construct irrigation systems; teach English, Bible, math and other subjects; encourage communities to form savings and loan groups; promote forestry; administer relief programs and perform many other tasks.

MCC in 1995 continues its ministry "In the name of Christ" as an expression of Christian love for the poor. As a Haitian MCC staff member observed, "Our vision is not just health and agriculture, but also to share our faith that God is with the people."

— From Celebrate, Reflect, Recommit, MCC, 1995

The Mennonite Relief Sales

Mennonites have a unique way of combining fellowship with charity at relief sales. These events — which usually center around an auction of quilts, crafts, and even livestock — are significant to the Mennonite communities in which they are held.

Volunteers work year-round on the planning and people congregate from miles away on the day of the sale. Auction bidders raise the prices of everything from exquisite handcrafted furniture to loaves of bread. The money paid rarely reflects the true value of the goods. The people at these sales are buying something more intangible; they are reaching out to fellow human beings. They take the opportunity of these sales to witness their faith in Christ.

Those who donate items to be sold, too, do their part for relief. They lovingly stitch quilts, bake foods, create crafts, and donate heirlooms. And somehow that love shows through on sale day to draw a financial commitment from the bidders and buyers to the advantage of the world's disadvantaged.

Those who attend relief sales come to share food, friendship, and the hope that they can do their part to support the Mennonite Central Committee (MCC), which has about 1,000 persons in service in more than 50 countries around the world in agriculture, community development, education, peace work, economic and technical development, health and social services.

In 1995, 38 relief sales are planned in North America. In 1994, sales raised $4,541,788 to help these missions in 50 locations worldwide.

While helping the causes of MCC, relief sales are special events of the large Mennonite family. And like any family, no matter the culture, food seems to be a central part of special events, holidays, and other celebrations. Many people cannot wait to taste the raisin fritters served at the sale in Fresno, Calif., or the freshly pressed apple cider at the MCC Fall Festival in Albany, Ore. They carry the memory of the delicious Chicken Brunswick Stew of Fisherville, Va., throughout the year in anticipation of next year's sale and the chance to eat their favorites once again.

Now you don't have to wait. Bring a little flavor and celebrate at home the fellowship experienced at the events that help MCC accomplish so much where it's so desperately needed.

In this second volume of Treasured Mennonite Recipes find out about the 25 relief sales in the United States and the 13 sales in Canada and notice how they have evolved through the work of the people who make them a growing success every year.

Chronology of North American Relief Sales

1948 — Gap Relief Sale, Gap, Pennsylvania

1957 — Pennsylvania Relief Sale, Harrisburg, Pennsylvania

1959 — Illinois Mennonite Relief Sale, Peoria, Illinois

1962 — Arthur Mennonite Relief Sale, Arthur, Illinois

1966 — Ohio Mennonite Relief Sale, Kidron, Ohio

1967 — Ontario Mennonite Relief Sale, New Hamburg, Ontario

1967 — Northern Michigan Relief Sale, Fairview, Michigan

1967 — Virginia Relief Sale, Fisherville, Virginia

1967 — Morris MCC Relief Auction Sale, Morris, Manitoba

1967 — Black Creek Pioneer Village Relief Sale, Black Creek, Ont.

1968 — West Coast Mennonite Sale for World Relief, Fresno, Calif.

1968 — Mid-Kansas Relief Sale, Hutchinson, Kansas

1968 — Michiana Mennonite Relief Sale, Goshen, Indiana

1970 — Saskatoon Mennonite Relief Sale, Saskatoon, Saskatchewan.

1970 — Clearbrook Mennonite Relief Sale, Clearbrook, B.C.

1974 — Missouri MCC Relief Sale, Harrisonville, Missouri

1975 — MCC Alberta Relief Sale, Coaldale, Tofield, Didsbury, Alta.

1976 — Rocky Mountain Mennonite Relief Sale, Rocky Ford, Colorado

1977 — Oklahoma Mennonite Relief Sale, Fairview, Oklahoma

1978 — Mennonite Country Auction, Ritzville, Washington

1978 — MCC Quilt Auction and Relief Sale, Johnstown, Pennsylvania

1979 — Nebraska Mennonite Relief Sale, Aurora, Nebraska

1980 — Upper Midwest Relief Sale, Minot, North Dakota

1980 — Iowa Mennonite Relief Sale, Iowa City, Iowa

1980 — Food Grains Bank Sale, Hague, Saskatchewan

1981 — Pennsylvania Heifer Relief Sale for MCC, Lancaster, Pa.

1981 — Daviess County Relief Sale, Montgomery, Indiana

1982 — Ontario Heifer Sale, Guelph, Ontario

1982 — Prince George Mennonite Relief Sale, Prince George, B.C.

1983 — Bath MCC Relief Sale, Bath, New York

1984 — MCC Oregon Fall Festival, Albany, Oregon

1985 — Brandon Relief Sale, Brandon, Manitoba

1987 — Black Creek MCC Relief Sale, Black Creek, British Columbia

1987 — Minn-Kota Country Auction and Fair, Sioux Falls, S.D.

1988 — Okanagan Valley Fall Relief Sale, Kelowna, British Columbia

 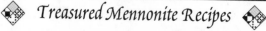

1990 — Texas Mennonite Relief Sale, Houston, Texas
1992 — Wisconsin MCC Relief Sale, Jefferson, Wisconsin
1994 — Winnipeg MCC Relief Sale, Winnipeg, Manitoba

Just as the relief sales have evolved over the years, so have many of our diets. Because of the raised consciousness toward our diets, this second volume also highlights many light and healthy recipes the contributors offered to share. These low or lower fat dishes are signified with a ♥.

Histories

MCC Alberta Relief Sale

Five people from southern Alberta Mennonite congregations met in the home of Jake and Herta Janzen of Coaldale on April 25, 1975 to begin the MCC Alberta Relief Sale.

More planning meetings were held, interest and enthusiasm were aroused, and funds were raised beforehand so that the entire amount raised

Dr. Howard Stutzman of La Junta, Colo., displays a 50-cent necktie that brought $410.50 to the Rocky Mountain Relief Sale in Rocky Ford, Colo.

In 1991, 100 members of the Kansas Mennonite Men's Chorus presented the Friday evening program. A member of the chorus, Orlando Penner of Hillsboro, Kansas, thought he needed a coat and tie for the evening performance. He purchased an average necktie at a thrift shop in Rocky Ford for 50 cents.

During the rehearsal, he realized he didn't need a tie after all, so he took it off and laid it by his side. Somehow the tie ended up on the director's stand. The director called for the auctioneer and the tie was purchased for $10.50. The buyer put it up for auction after the program, and it brought $30.

The buyer then took it back for Saturday's auction. After being purchased and resold four times, the final tally was $360.50, including the Friday evening income. However, the buyer brought the tie back to the 1992 auction. It was offered twice and brought $50. Altogether the 50-cent necktie has resulted in $410.50 for relief.

- Submitted by Paul Isaak. (Photo by Beryl Isaak)

This wagon and a quilt were on display in a local shopping mall and generated a great deal of public interest in the 1992 Clearbrook Relief Sale. Dr. Arthur Jones of Maple Ridge donated the antique 1905 McLoughlin two-passenger, one-horse carriage, which was re-finished in oak by the Golden Agers of the Clearbrook Community Centre and others. The wagon contributed $12,000 through its auction to the remarkable total of $307,000.

(Photo by Gerry Harms)

on the day of the sale could be forwarded to MCC, a practice that has continued.

Everyone gets a chance to participate at a variety of booths. From the original Friday evening open house to only view sale items and to visit over a cup of coffee and home-baked cinnamon buns, the sales have increased to include an auction and brisk selling at all booths both Friday evening and Saturday.

Relief sales have been held in Coaldale every second year since 1975. At the 10th sale in 1993, a 12-minute commemorative video was produced to help with promotion for future sales.

When the sale is not held at Coaldale, the location moves to Tofield and most recently to Didsbury in 1994.

One of the important benefits of relief sales is the fine spirit of cooperation for a worthy cause. One Hutterite Colony has donated all the pancake mix for every sale. Coaldale has always donated the use of its excellent facilities, while a non-Mennonite auctioneering firm has donated equipment and staff.

Long-term, dedicated personnel have worked on the sale committees in

Coaldale, according to Herta Janzen, Alice Klassen and Anne Neufeld, who share Coaldale's story here.

Support for the sales comes from many people. Young children who were introduced to the sale years ago are now active participants.

Through the years many interesting items have been donated and sold. For the first sale, the Coaldale Mennonite Church Men's Club assembled a Dutch windmill which sold for $2,400. In this and successive years, quilts have always been prominent items at the auction — the highest one going for $3,100 in 1993.

The first sale went beyond the organizers' wildest expectations in that $63,000 was raised. In 1991 the highest figure of $162,600 was reached. Every item, large or small, whatever it sold for, was important to help raise more than $1 million from the 10 sales held in Coaldale since 1975.

According to Henry Nachtigal, former chairman of the sale in Tofield, the first sale was held at the Tofield Curling Rink and Skating Rink in 1984. Three sales have been held there so far and the next one is slated for 1996. About 1,000 to 1,200 people attend the sale that features all kinds of items. "We advertise it as relief help for needy people. That's the draw. It's not just for Third World countries," Nachtigal explained, adding that people get together to visit and look forward to eating ethnic foods and buying crafts and quilts.

Meals are also popular at the sale in Tofield. One year, 700 people arrived for breakfast. In 1992 the Tofield sale raised more than $100,000.

The recreation center in the central location of Didsbury was the site of the sale for the first time in 1994. The committee worked for two years to prepare for its first sale which was the 100th anniversary of the first Mennonite settlers in Didsbury from Ontario. Chairman Henry Goerzen's wife, Erna, explained that the sale celebrated 100 years of community. She added that a lot of volunteer work is contributed from the community, Mennonite and non-Mennonite alike.

About 3,000 people attended the Didsbury sale. Food sales brought in much of the proceeds. The big ticket items were purchased mostly by Mennonite people. "Many have not yet come to realize this is not a bargain basement," Mrs. Goerzen explained. "It's a donation for relief." Everything from pie socials to fashion shows help raise money for expenses.

Black Creek MCC Relief Sale

The Black Creek MCC Relief Sale has been held since 1987 in this central location on Vancouver Island in British Columbia, which probably makes it the westernmost of all the sales.

The sale is held in mid-May as a one-day event hosted by the Vancouver Island Mennonite churches from Port Hardy, Campbell River, Gold River, Black Creek, Courtenay, Nanaimo, and Saanich.

The event has outgrown the local church yards and is now held at the Black Creek Recreation Facility. Traditional foods, crafts, auctions, plant sales, and entertainment are all part of the venue. The community supports the sale, which raises awareness of the relief work of MCC.

Clearbrook Mennonite Relief Sale

Relief sales have been a resounding success in British Columbia since the first on Sept. 12, 1970, when approximately 5,600 people crowded Matsqui Fairgrounds near Clearbrook. Donated auction items totaled 4,000 and most were sold by mid-afternoon. According to excerpts of "Footprints of Compassion, the History of MCC B.C. 1964-1989," edited by Helen Grace Lescheid, approximately $20,754 was raised; cash donations of $1,500 were received.

For the first successful event, Jacob R. Rahn lead the relief committee which conducted 16 planning meetings and three regional banquets to raise money for expenses.

The next year the sale was moved to the Chilliwack Fair Grounds, where it stayed for 16 years. The third sale in 1984 raised $23,542 which was used for an educational program in Laos.

In 1988, the sale returned to Clearbrook to offer a more central location and more than 10,000 people took part.

Once a month during the previous year the 12-member relief sale committee has planned and prayed for this event. All expenses are covered by the proceeds from four banquets held in Chilliwack, Abbotsford, and Vancouver. All items to be sold are donated. Services rendered, including auctioneering, are voluntary. The total in 1988 was $176,000.

In 1992, $307,000 was raised at the sale. Many people look forward to buying home-baked goodies, which are usually sold out by 10 a.m., according to Helen Harms. The bake sale alone in 1992 totaled $14,296.69.

In 1994, about 12,000 people attended the event that 1,000- plus volunteers ran. A 1994 relief sale in Abbotsford, British Columbia, is part of the Fraser Valley sale, and will become the new location of the combined efforts of Clearbrook and Abbotsford, according to Edward Janzen of MCC BC.

Okanagan Valley Fall Relief Sale

In March of 1987, the Kelowna MCC Store Committee introduced the idea of doing its own sale. By August of 1987, planning was under way for a 1988 fall sale. An auctioneer was found from one of the churches and committees were formed.

The first members secured the use of the Boardwalk Convention Center in Kelowna for September 24, 1988. The sale items included home-baked goods, crafts, used goods, sausage, SELFHELP crafts, and quilts.

The second sale was held on September 9, 1989 at the much larger Kelowna Curling Rink and $10,500 was sent to MCC BC.

The third sale was again held at the Kelowna Curling Rink on September 8, 1990 and more than $17,750 was raised. In 1991 the relief sale took on a new approach with an international food banquet and craft and bake sale held at an evangelical church gym. This took a lot less physical labor and planning, according to the present chairman, Ed Rempel. The net proceeds were more than $23,000 that year and the same style of event was planned for 1992.

With a new Board of Representatives appointed from the Okanagan and area churches in 1993, the sale was reinstated. Baked goods, crafts, sausage and the food fair ideas were featured and on November 20, 1993, a full house was seen at the First Mennonite Church. The sale raised $6,500. On September 11 a banquet was held and more than $8,900 was raised to bring a total of $15,400 to MCC BC.

The 1994 sale held at the Willow Park Church, had about three times the room. This year they saw a decline in the number of donated items and only brought in just under $7,000.

Prince George Mennonite Relief Sale

The Prince George Relief Sale in British Columbia started small, but it has grown into something quite large in the past 13 years.

Wendy Herring, Frances Willms, and Jake Penner began the first sale that brought in about $4,000. Now the sale raises about $35,000 and in 1994 had to be moved to the Prince George Civic Center, where the 18,000-square-foot facility has enough room to house all of the booths and the 10,000 or so people who attend.

Vera Campbell, who has been the SELFHELP Crafts coordinator for 11 years now, says about 200 volunteers work on the sale which features a special lunch, a home-baked goods table, produce, crafts, garage sale, and good-and-used clothing.

Held on a weekend in October, a portion of the Prince George sale is earmarked for a special MCC project. In 1994, funds were sent to Rwanda relief and a mine detection project in Laos. Taking advantage of a new $1 coin with a loon on it, which Canadians call a "loonie," a "Loonie Barrel" was created from a beer barrel and a sign was put on it that read "Feed the Hungry in Rwanda." The proceeds from this barrel were sent to hungry children in Rwanda.

Some patrons come just to buy the farmer's sausage of which they sell 3,000 pounds during the event.

The sale opens an hour early for senior citizens and handicapped patrons and the youth group of the Westwood Mennonite Brethren Church help those who need it to get around the sale in wheelchairs.

The costs of the event — including $2,000 rent for the hall — are paid in advance through soup suppers during the year.

Advertising in the church bulletin begins in August. Members of the congregation are asked to save bags, get their closets cleaned out and make donations. A different coordinator was chosen every year, but now the post is held for two years for a smoother transition.

West Coast Mennonite Sale for World Relief

The initiative for an annual West Coast Mennonite Sale and Auction for World Relief began with the West Coast Mennonite Relief Committee who first discussed the idea in 1966. According to an article by Kevin Enns-Rempel in the Mennonite Brethren Historical Society of the West Coast Bulletin and submitted by Kathy Heinrichs Wiest, relief sale publicity chair, the committee appointed MCC West Coast Director Norman Wingert to explore the possibilities and he was soon joined by Otto Jost of Reedley who was asked to organize the event.

An initial planning meeting drew only about a dozen interested people, but enthusiasm spread quickly. The Richland Packing Co. facility was chosen as the site and the date was set for April 20, 1968. By the fall of 1967 people began bringing items to Reedley.

The day of the sale began at 6 a.m. with a sausage and pancake breakfast for the workers.

Throughout the day, eight auctioneers worked the crowd of some 5,000 people. The event was, by any standard, a great success. A Ford tractor brought $900, evidently the highest price paid for a single item that day. Demand for Portzelki (raisin fritters) was such that several women worked at home to supplement those made at the sale. The rummage sale netted almost $3,000. About 150 quilts and blankets were sold at an average of $40 each. Net proceeds were $17,600.

Subsequent sales followed in the successful tradition and raised phenomenal amounts of money for an all-volunteer effort. Net proceeds for the 1970 sale increased to $19,000; by 1975 the quilt auction alone brought in that amount. In 1976 net proceeds passed the $50,000 mark; in 1980 they exceeded $100,000. The 1991 sale brought in a record $220,000. Since 1968 the sale has netted about $3 million for MCC.

The West Coast Sale has diversified and grown in other ways. Volunteers have created features such as a book sale, international craft shop, classic car show, and a variety of ethnic food booths that add to the festive atmosphere.

Hundreds of church people have responded to the growing need for volunteers to flip hamburgers, tend booths, set up shops, count proceeds, and fill the myriad other jobs that must be done to make the sale a success.

With the success, though, came problems, the most pressing being ad-

equate space and facilities. As early as 1974 the Relief Sale Committee raised the issue of alternative sites. In 1982 the sale made the move to its current location on the campus of Fresno Pacific College.

Rocky Mountain Mennonite Relief Sale

Rocky Mountain Mennonite Relief Sale is held the third Saturday in October at the Arkansas Valley Fairgrounds, Rocky Ford, Colorado.

The sale began in 1976 through the persistence of Ella Bickel and Valera Riemenschneider, members of the Rocky Ford Mennonite Church.

Rickshaw rides are one of many fascinating features at the Rocky Mountain Relief Sale in Rocky Ford, Colo.
(Photo by Paul Isaak)

After reading about relief sales in other states, they had a vision to sponsoring one in Rocky Ford. They approached the Women's Missionary and Service Commission in the congregation. Initial response was "we are too small for that" and "there would be too much work." However, their request to present the idea to the Church Board was affirmed.

According to records, Ella Bickel met with the board in March, 1976, with the request "that the ladies of the church sponsor a MCC relief sale, possibly in October." Request was granted.

A May planning meeting included not only the women of the church, but also men from the church and representatives from the Mennonite churches in La Junta and Cheraw. The decision was made to sponsor a sale that "would be a uniquely Colorado sale."

The first sale was held at Rocky Ford Mennonite Church on October 23, 1976. The church building and an adjacent vacant lot were used.

Ella Bickel tells how the group felt after the sale: "We were busy cleaning up after the sale. We had to get the church ready for Sunday morning. Treasurer Derald Brenneman came around asking us to guess how much we made. We had no idea how much had come in. When he told us that the total was $7,674, we were so excited we weren't tired anymore. We felt our work was worth it."

Other Mennonite churches in Colorado and from the Rocky Mountain Mennonite Conference became involved. In 1980, the sale was moved to the Arkansas Valley Fairgrounds.

The third Saturday in October was selected as the permanent date, with Friday used for set up. Now, meals are served, a program is presented, and some booths are open for sales on Friday evening.

Sale receipts have increased almost every year, according to Paul Isaak, 1994 chairman. In 1984, gross receipts reached $41,034. The 1992 total was $86,033. And in 1994, the sale reached a record $101,447. One quilt brought $4,200.

Thirty Mennonite churches are involved. In 1992, 30 Colorado towns and 11 other states were represented. A record has been reached in six of eight years since 1984.

Illinois Mennonite Relief Sale and Arthur Mennonite Relief Sale

John Roth took the idea of having a relief sale in Illinois like one he read about in Pennsylvania to family members and then suggested it in the October 1958 issue of "The Missionary Guide."

At first, according to "Love in Action, The Story of Thirty Illinois Mennonite Relief Sales" by Steven R. Estes, edited by Donald F. Roth and Ruth C. King Roth, John Roth received a lukewarm response. When he finally spoke with the Rev. Roy C. Bucher at the Inter-Mennonite Ministers' Fellowship meeting, Roth and his idea were rejuvenated. The two ministers and laymen worked on the plans.

In December 1958, church representatives from central Illinois congregations met to organize. More than 400 items were donated and ranged from farm equipment to quilts. The first sale became a reality on March 21, 1959 at the Central Illinois Aberdeen-Angus Breeders' Association Sale Pavilion, Congerville, Ill.

About 800 people bid generously at the auction. The net proceeds amounted to $4,795.71.

After it was decided to have a second sale in 1960, Roth and Yordy solicited the help of the Arthur Mennonite Church and other congregations in southern Illinois. The amount of donated items doubled and about 1,000 people attended the sale which sent $4,100 to MCC. A third sale was planned for March 11, 1961, but Roth decided if the proceeds did not increase, it would be the last. More than 1,100 items were auctioned. With donations and food sales, $5,201 was sent to Akron.

The work at Congerville encouraged people in Arthur to hold their own sale. On February 17, 1962, $2,000 was raised in the Arthur Sale Barn and forwarded to Congerville. The Authur auction moved to the larger Bontrager Building in 1965 and 1966, back to the Arthur Sale Barn in 1967-68 and then to the Moultrie-Douglas County Fairgrounds in 1970. It began sending the proceeds directly to MCC after 1966. It is now held in late August or early September. Both

Sale participants take a look at the quilts that will soon be on the auction block at the 1990 Michiana Relief Sale in Goshen, Ind.

(Photo by Steve Echols, Elkhart, Ind.)

Illinois sales have continued a cordial relationship; organizers share equipment and support each others' efforts. And both sales continued to grow.

The Illinois Mennonite Relief Sale was receiving crowds of about 3,000 and moved to Exposition Gardens in Peoria. By 1981, 20,000 people were attending the event run by 1,500 to 2,000 volunteers. Features grew, too.

The work of John Roth, who died in 1969, continues with his nephew Donald F. Roth as general secretary.

Daviess County Relief Sale

The Daviess County Relief Sale in Montgomery, Ind., started in 1981 for the Haiti Mission and Relief Fund.

Over the years sales have raised between $30,000 and $63,000. From 1986 to 1992, the proceeds were divided in thirds — to Christian Aid for Romania, Jesus to the Iron Curtain and to MCC. In 1993, the sale board began keeping 20 percent for local missions.

Quilts are the biggest auction items and bring from $300 to $1,200 each.

Auctioneer John Swartzendruber calls for bids on a quilt done by the Sunnyside Church women for the Iowa MCC Relief Sale in Iowa City. The quilt sold for $750.

(Photo by Frank and Ada Yoder)

The furniture sale also draws a large crowd, with a grandfather clock leading the way. Food starts being served at 6 a.m.

Michiana Mennonite Relief Sale

The annual Michiana Mennonite Relief Sale is held the fourth Saturday of September at the Elkhart County Fairgrounds, Goshen, Indiana, attracting approximately 50,000 people from across the country.

Folks travel from as far as California to bid on quilts and antiques, dine on a smorgasbord of foods and shop. Others attend a large auction of quality new and used items.

In the middle of the late '60s, it was decided that with the help of volunteers, the first Michiana Mennonite Relief Sale would be organized.

The primary goal was to support relief efforts of MCC. The first sale was held in 1968 and $50,000 was contributed to MCC. The two largest revenue producers in 1968 (and still true today according to Steve Schrock, who contributed this information) were the quilt auction and food. Women's activities, crafts, antiques, and new and used manufactured articles have also grown into major attractions. The dollars sent to MCC increased each year, peaking in 1989 at $495,000. Since then, the sale has maintained an annual contribution of $450,000 to $490,000. From 1968 to 1994, almost $8 million has been forwarded to MCC.

The largest addition to the sale since 1987 is the House Against Hunger, which is built with much volunteer labor and many donated materials and sold on or near sale day.

The Michiana sale is a success because of all of the donated items and time, the proximity to large metropolitan areas, and support from local Mennonites and non-Mennonites.

An 11-member board governs the sale. Each board member is elected for a three-year term. During sale month the board meets almost weekly. The meeting after the sale is a time for evaluation, suggestions for the next sale and making certain all financial records are in order.

The sale is a splendid focus for fellowship and cooperation between the Mennonite and Amish churches. The sale also provides an opportunity for many to use skills in work benefitting the relief program as well as to give witness to our Lord.

Iowa Mennonite Relief Sale

The first Iowa MCC Sale was held in April 1980 at the Washington Fair Grounds in Washington, Iowa.

As the sales grew, it became necessary to move to larger facilities at the Recreation Center on the University of Iowa campus in Iowa City, then to the Johnson County Fairgrounds. The present arrangement has given the people from the Iowa churches an opportunity to contribute toward the global needs of the world through MCC.

They realize, though, that because of their geographic location and the population densities of their state, the Iowa sale may never be the largest. However, from 1980 to 1994, $1,444,000 have been forwarded to MCC.

Mid-Kansas MCC Relief Sale

The first relief sale in Kansas was held on April 8, 1968 in Hillsboro after about a year of preparation. And in 25 years the Mid-Kansas MCC Relief Sale developed into the largest money-raising sale, bringing in $525,000 in 1993.

From Jake Daum, a 94-year-old man who raised almost $9,000 in 1992 through a 61-mile cattle walk from Hillsboro to Hutchinson, to Sunday school children donating about $10,000 in coins, the community bands together to do its part.

Although Kansas has a large Mennonite population, the Kansans attribute their success to strong leadership. According to LaVern D. Stucky, president, in the 1994 "Feed the World's Hungry Children," a booklet passed out during the sale, "Early on, our people decided that the event was to be more than just an auction with a food tent attached. It was to be a celebration of who we are as people... Our craftsmanship is exposed through the items sold at the auctions and the House Against Hunger. Our rural roots are exposed through the Cattle Walk; our frugality through the Penny Challenge; our social nature

---

through the Fellowship Meals; our concern for others through the selling of imported SELFHELP Crafts; our heritage through the foods we serve and sell. Perhaps the most notable tribute to the vision of those early leaders was the effort to find a home for the sale that was conveniently located and would provide space to grow."

Vice President Howard Kaufman said in 1994 volunteers made more than 19,000 vereneki and more than 7,000 Bohna Berroggee for food lines. The House Against Hunger was auctioned for $133,000, and $29,000 was raised during a 58-mile, three-day walk against hunger. One walker alone collected $10,050.

Brandon Relief Sale

In early 1985 representatives of Mennonite congregations in Western Manitoba met to organize a relief sale for the western part of the province. For some years, southern and eastern Manitoba Mennonites had been conducting relief sales in Morris, but the distance kept many western residents from participating. Fewer than 5,000 Mennonites in western Manitoba are scattered over 15,000 square miles in approximately 20 congregations.

The first sale was conducted in August 1985 at the United Commercial Travellers hall and grounds in Brandon, a centrally located city of 45,000. Members of most congregations contributed crafts, produce, meats, baked goods, miscellaneous items for sale and auction, and ethnic Mennonite food for meals. The sale resulted in proceeds of $30,000 for MCC.

For the following five years the sale was conducted in the larger Riverview Curling Club and continued to produce reasonable profits. Even these facilities however were found to be crowded and subject to disruption by inclement weather; a hot day drove buyers away from the outdoor auction ring, and a rainy day drove them away all together.

In 1991 the sale was moved to the Manitoba Room of the Keystone Centre, which is large enough to accommodate the entire sale. Each committee is allotted sufficient space to display the goods in separate areas. A pancake and sausage breakfast and a noon meal are served on a second level of the complex.

In its first 10 years, $239,800 has been forwarded to MCC. The aim for future sales is to reach the non-Mennonite community, and to present the work of MCC.

Morris MCC Relief Auction Sale

The Morris Relief Sale in Manitoba, Canada, began in 1967. Small at first, with proceeds equalling $2,500, the event has grown every year. A couple of years in the 1970s passed without a sale, but in 1980 the location was changed to Morris at the Stampede grounds and the date was set at the third Saturday of September.

The sale committee is made up from the congregations of approximately 30 area churches. Morris is the center of the 40- to 50-mile radius of these churches.

The auction block is outside for the hardware, furniture, and implements. Quilts are auctioned inside the recreation center.

More than 5,000 people attend. The post sale receipts have amounted to $1,377,317 as of 1994.

More than 200 volunteers are involved. MCC Manitoba also provides a computer and staff for the accounts and to prepare the financial statement.

Winnipeg MCC Relief Sale

Until the creation of a relief sale in 1994, the only thing Mennonites in Winnipeg did together was sing and play baseball in a church league.

The 40 Mennonite churches in Winnepeg came together in the late 1980s to organize the 12th Assembly of the Mennonite World Conference, held there in 1990.

Art DeFehr, co-owner and president of Palliser Furniture, one of Winnipeg's largest industries, was troubled by this and felt a sale could be organized in a city with so many Mennonites. In 1989 he offered to underwrite the expenses of the first sale through his family's foundation. Because many people were occupied with the World Conference at the time, it was agreed to wait a year.

For around two years, small group meetings brought together people interested in organizing a sale. From early on it was agreed that while inter-Mennonite cooperation was important, another goal was reaching out so non-Mennonites would feel welcomed. Education about hunger and poverty would be an essential part of the sale.

By 1992 enough people had come together to make sale planning a reality. In June 1994 the first sale was held at The Forks, a popular Winnipeg meetingplace at the confluence of the Red and Assiniboine rivers. More than $50,000 was raised.

Northern Michigan Relief Sale

The first Northern Michigan Relief Sale at Fairview, Michigan, was held on May 6, 1967. Because MCC has been an important part of the Fairview congregation since the times of Civilian Public Service and through the years of Pax (alternatives to serving in the military during wars), when the idea came to have a relief sale to support MCC, the church was very supportive even though the community was small and rural and no large cities were nearby.

According to Bill Esch, chairman, the support of Mennonite congregations in northern lower Michigan and the Upper Peninsula made the growth

This handmade train, donated to the Northern Michigan Relief Sale in Fairview, was created by Ora Troyer, who was 90 years old at the time. The train had a light and a bell.
(Photo by Bill Esch)

possible. Growing pains included a search for another location, finally deciding to stay at Fairview, and realizing that even quality-made items sometimes do not bring their true value. The early years included adding a variety of shops, SELFHELP Crafts, and food.

Some have continued and some have been dropped but all have been a part of the vision. A generation of children have grown up not knowing a summer without the sale and the responsibility of the work will soon fall on their shoulders.

Missouri MCC Relief Sale

In November 1974, in rural Cass County, Missouri, Sycamore Grove had its first relief sale. The Fall Harvest Festival, as it was then called, started as a mission project for New Trikes Training School, Camdenton, Missouri.

The original sale was an auction with crafts, fresh produce, canned goods and baked goods that raised $614.14.

Women displayed quilts and comforters on a clothesline hung between the trees. The average paid for quilts was $175; $25 for comforters. Currently, churches and individuals from Missouri and Arkansas donate the quilts and comforters.

Over the years, attractions have been added, including a pancake and sausage breakfast, Friday night barbecue with a music program, a craft booth, SELFHELP Crafts, plants and produce.

Within several years of the sale starting at Sycamore Grove, Harrisonville Mennonite Church began contributing. Then other churches throughout Missouri and Arkansas joined.

Nebraska Mennonite Relief Sale

Many people in the Henderson, Nebraska, community for some years wished to have a relief sale. Many attended the Kansas sale. Eventually a committee was set up. Unable to find proper facilities in Henderson, the committee approached the County Fair Grounds Board in Aurora.

The Nebraska MCC Relief Sale in Aurora was realized in 1979 and at first fit in one building. According to former Board member Henry Klieiver, who now works between the Fair Board and MCC, by 1981, proceeds were $104,000 and have increased every year. Because the sales became so crowded for eating, green houses were set up. In 1983 the Mennonites tore down an old building and a new building was constructed, which housed the quilt auction. In 1991 a livestock auction was added and brought $8,000. Quilts and excellent woodwork items are also a draw. Non-Mennonite people donate items and there is great cooperation in setting up.

Rod Kennel and Cornelia Kleiver work in a gazebo Rod made as a focal point for the Nebraska MCC Relief Sale where board members gave out information about MCC and the sale.

Bath MCC Relief Sale

In the early 1980s some Mennonite families who had moved to

---

northern Pennsylvania and southern New York from Lancaster County, Pennsylvania, began to envision having a relief sale. A committee was formed and the first sale was held in August 1983 at the Bath (New York) Fair Grounds.

With the power of 12 small churches scattered over a large area, there is a lot of work for everyone. Mildred Weaver, Bath resident and relief sale volunteer, said the sale is held on the last Saturday of July and it is amazing how people from the community who have no connection to the churches realize it is a good project and want to get involved.

Upper Midwest Relief Sale

The Upper Midwest Relief Sale was started in 1980. The Casselton, North Dakota, congregation wondered if its church could hold a relief sale and soon realized it was too big a job for one small church.

People were contacted from Mennonite, Mennonite Brethren, and General Conference churches in North Dakota, Minnesota, Montana, and Wisconsin. The sale has representation from approximately 15 churches. The first three years the sale was held in Fargo, then in Minot, North Dakota.

Ohio Mennonite Relief Sale

Ford Berg from Kidron, Ohio, first conceived the idea of having a relief sale when he moved to Morgantown, Pennsylvania. That first

Til's homemade ice cream is always popular on those sweltering August relief sale days in Kidron, Ohio.

sale was held on a Morgantown farm in 1957, and brought $4,500. The idea spread to Illinois and Kansas. Their successes prompted a committee in Ohio to set up a sale.

The first Ohio sale was held June 25, 1966 at Central Christian High School. The committee stressed the importance of bringing good-quality items so the auction would produce a favorable image. All food and merchandise were donated.

More than 100 churches sponsor the Ohio Mennonite Relief Sale which is held on the first Saturday of August. It includes Amish, Apostolic, Brethren, Mennonite, and Conservatives in Ohio and western Pennsylvania. The two main attractions are the 125 or so Mennonite and Amish quilts and the wooden items sold simultaneously in separate auctions.

About 20,000 attended the 1994 sale that features a free hayride shuttle service to facilitate parking, a "Run for Relief" five-kilometer loop, and sweets in the Swiss pantry.

The record sales for the past 29 years came in 1993 with $213,000 from the auction and an additional $160,000 for the House Against Hunger built in Kidron. Each year volunteer labor and many donated materials are used to build the house. Total receipts for the 1994 sale were more than $200,000.

One person described the sale as "a huge family gathering."

Oklahoma Mennonite Relief Sale

The Oklahoma Relief Sale originated in 1977. The sale, which has been held on the fairgrounds of Fairview, Oklahoma, since its beginning, is held on the weekend after Thanksgiving. It nets approximately $90,000 each year. A lot of food booths, arts and crafts, flowers, and dried fruit and peanuts are big draws to the sale. Friday night is an open house.

A feature quilt, a collective effort of 41 churches, is auctioned each year. Members of each church embroider and donate one block that reflects a designated theme. One year it brought $2,700 at auction.

Black Creek Pioneer Village Relief Sale

Black Creek Pioneer Village, Downsview, Ontario, is a historic village museum just inside the northern boundary of metropolitan Toronto. In 1967, the concept of a relief sale inspired the museum's curator, Russell Cooper, who invited MCC in Kitchener to hold a sale at the village's annual Fall Festival. MCC contacted the Women's Missionary Service Committee to organize this project. With three weeks notice Gladys Grove and Stella Reesor called on friends and local churches to contribute time and effort for the Fall Festival on the third Saturday of September 1967.

For the first festival there were pies, sandwiches, baked goods, and a quilting demonstration. After the one-day event, left-over food was sent to the Yonge Street Mission and $1,300 was sent to MCC.

In 1968, after three weeks of preparation, the same amount of money was sent to MCC. Cooper wanted a relief sale every year as part of the village's Fall Festival. As a result of his interest, a committee was formed in 1969 and a partnership with the village established.

Cooper visited several sales in Pennsylvania and brought many ideas and special requests to the committee. The quilt auction was started in 1971 and has generally contributed about 40 percent of the funds. Subsequently a variety of additional foods and several craft demonstrations have been included. Music with a Christian message has been added.

Since those first few years the Black Creek Pioneer Village Relief Sale has brought in participants from many Toronto area churches.

Although the number of visitors seemed relatively constant at near 5,000, the annual donation increased every year to more than $50,000 at the end of the 1980s. Since then, the combined effects of recession and lower attendance have reduced the contributions but the range of the relief sale efforts and contributions continues to increase.

Ontario Heifer Sale

Orton Bauman began the Ontario Heifer Sale in 1982 at Brubaker's Sales Arena in Guelph where he worked part time. Bauman managed to have more than 100 head donated. The facilities and the auctioneers' time were also donated. Between $100,000 and $125,000 (Canadian) is raised each year, from the auction and cash donations, according to the current chairman Joel Snyder, who took the position after Bauman's sudden death in the late 1980s. As of 1993, 1,543 head were sold for $1,384,435 and $141,870 in cash donations were collected for a total of $1,526,305 (Canadian) for world relief. In 1994, the sale added another $122,000 (Canadian). And the Canadian government sometimes matches the proceeds three or four times through the Canadian International Development Association.

About 250 people from all walks of life attend the sale. Although the majority are farmers, some people just come to satisfy their curiosity or to give donations to help others in need.

"We get heifers donated by non-Mennonites and some buyers are as well," says Snyder. "So we get money from outside the Mennonite Church." He added that people are happy to donate when they hear it is for relief.

Ontario Mennonite Relief Sale

The idea to have a relief sale was brought to Ontario by Dr. J.W. Fretz of Kansas, who came to Waterloo to become president of Conrad Grebel College.

At the Oct. 5, 1966 meeting the questions were how to organize for it and

 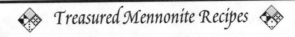

how best to proceed with it. Dr. Fretz stressed mission, using the abundance of resources, and having everything possible donated. The group elected officers. It was also decided that the sale be on May 27, 1967.

This group then contacted other interested people. Prior to the event a number of people visited the Pennsylvania sale and got the idea for fresh strawberry pies. They also visited the sale in Peoria, Illinois.

The first Ontario Mennonite Relief Sale, initiated by 38 volunteers, netted $34,286.25, through the sale of such items as live rabbits for $1.50 each, a sea shell for 50 cents, a bag of fertilizer for $3 and an oxen harness for $18.75. It is held in New Hamburg, Ontario, in a small town outside Kitchener in Waterloo County.

Since 1967 thousands of volunteers have sewn quilts, barbecued chicken, baked pies, fashioned crafts, and cooked and baked their way to a successful festival that hosts 40,000 visitors and have raised more than $6 million. In 1990, $450,000 was donated directly to MCC. The sale income for the May 28, 1994 sale amounted to $286,500.

The strength of the relief sales in Ontario for 28 years has been the involvement of hundreds of people, before and during the sale, and in the fact that this volunteer effort is overhead free, because costs are covered through other donations.

MCC Oregon Fall Festival

The MCC Oregon Fall Festival has its roots in an Oregon State Fair booth. John Willems of Albany, Oregon, and others continued to operate the MCC Testimony and Witness Booth for about 10 years. SELFHELP Crafts were sold in increasing quantities from the second year of the booth until, during the last two or three years at the fair, it was necessary to use two booth spaces.

Considering the number of volunteers and hours needed during the 10-day fair, the profits from the booth did not seem to warrant the time investment. Coordinators decided to form a formal board and, in 1984, the first MCC Oregon Fall Festival was born on the Richreall Fairgrounds in Polk County.

A new location at the Linn County Fairgrounds in Albany helped increase the majority of activities under one roof from 1986. And a silent auction has been held several of the years. Income has grown from $23,000 the first year to about $74,000 in 1992 from the sale put on by more than 300 volunteers from 35 to 40 churches in Oregon.

Gap Relief Sale

The Gap Relief Sale held in the Paradise Sales Barn in Paradise, Pennsylvania, is the oldest relief sale in North America. The first sale in 1948 was held at Leon Summers' farm in Lancaster County, Pennsylvania, hosted

---

primarily by the Maple Grove district churches, according to an excerpt taken from a letter to MCC Heifer Sale volunteers from James W. Shenk, MCC East Coast director in 1988. (It has been said, though, that the first MCC relief sale was held on a farm near Reedley, California, in 1992.) The location was selected to be near Old Order Amish who participated from the beginning. The first sale of household items, baked goods, a few quilts, and some outdated farm equipment brought in $3,000. In 1984 the sale moved to an auction barn near Intercourse, Pennsylvania.

In 1994, two Houses Against Hunger were built in Gap. One was started in 1993 and completed and sold in 1994. The first one was built in 1991.

MCC Quilt Auction and Relief Sale

October 1993 was the 15th anniversary of the MCC Quilt Auction and Relief Sale at the Richland Mall in Johnstown, Pennsylvania. Although quilts are the main theme, many other handcrafted items are donated and the bidding is fun to watch.

Volunteers enjoy demonstrating their quilting and auction items for three days in the mall. Because the facility is open from 9 a.m. to 9 p.m., this makes long days for many of the women involved. Sometimes they've had poor weather to contend with, making traveling to and from the event treacherous. By vote, the groups decided to hold the auction every other year instead of annually.

Pennsylvania Heifer Relief Sale

The first Pennsylvania Heifer Relief Sale for MCC was held March 5, 1981, at the Guernsey Sales Barn in Lancaster, Pennsylvania, with 80 donated head of Holstein heifers, and service-age bulls. Breeder associations donated semen and other farm products, including hay, straw, firewood, and more.

The sale has become an annual event on the second Thursday in March. In 1987 the sale site changed to the Mel Kolb Inc. Sales Arena in Lancaster.

During December and January, 25 men make contacts with dairy farmers for a donation of a heifer. Life records are provided for the identification of the animal to be put into a catalog for sale time. The animals are tested according to state regulations for shipment.

Students help the day before and on the day of the sale to move cattle. Food is provided by the Pennsylvania Relief Sale food committee. According to Wilmer G. Kraybill of Elverson, Pennsylvania, sales manager, the 1994 sale was the 14th sale since 1981 that 1,000 head went through the auction, which along with beef animal sales, business ads in the catalog, donations, and prayer, generated $1 million for MCC.

Pennsylvania Relief Sale

The Pennsylvania Relief Sale in Harrisburg, Pennsylvania, began as a congregational project of the Zion Mennonite Church on Saturday, March 30, 1957 on the Ralph Hertzler farm, one-half mile south of Morgantown, Pennsylvania. With a tentative goal of $2,000, the sale grossed $4,500.65 with $200 in expenses. It then grew to become the Tri-County Relief Sale, representing Berks, Chester and Lancaster counties.

Ford Berg, pastor of the Zion Mennonite Church, had a conviction that something should be done for relief. Berg proposed to the church council that every member of the Mennonite churches donate $10 for relief purposes. Council agreed with the idea, but the first pastor Berg visited said his members couldn't afford the donation. Berg returned to his home congregation and proposed the relief sale.

That work of the staff and planning committees has been well rewarded by the attendance of large crowds of people.

After only five years, visitors from four states attended the sale and according to an article published in the New Holland (Pennsylvania) Clarion, $5,600 was raised from about 1,000 buyers. The sale had to be moved to Harrisburg in 1977 because the Morgantown facilities were not able to handle the crowds. The Pennsylvania Relief Sale donated $390,501 in 1994, which included the sale of a house for $105,000.

Food Grains Bank Sale

Since 1980 the Food Grains Bank Sale has been held in Hague, Saskachewan. Started by Dave Buhler and Cornie Derksen, for the last 12 to 13 years it has been located on the Peter Hiebert farm.

William K. Wiebe, the present chairman who has been on the committee for ten years, says the sale is on a farm and many of the items sold are farm-related. A dairy cow sale is a highlight of the event, with twenty or more donated head. A committee of fifteen couples, from farmers to businessmen, work on the sale.

About 1,000 people attend the sale that features everything from crafts to cows. All costs are covered prior to the sale, so 100 percent of the proceeds are sent for relief work.

Saskatoon Mennonite Relief Sale

In 1970, Irma Balzar from Rosthern, Saskatchewan, who was then chairperson of the Auxiliary of MCC Saskatchewan approached Fred Peters, executive director of MCC Saskatchewan, to request he call a meeting with representatives from the various conferences to see if a relief auction could be held.

Balzar had attended a relief auction in Ontario, the only one being held in Canada at the time, to see what and how it was being done. The first sale in Saskatoon was held in June 1970 where $20,000 was raised. An annual auction sale has been held in Saskatoon ever since, and has grown tremendously both in auction items and ethnic Mennonite foods served.

The 23rd annual sale was held May 28, 1992 where an all-time high of $91,200 was raised.

In recent years the sale has been expanded to Friday night and Saturday. On Friday, the young people serve a supper. There is a preview of auction articles, as well as some sales. Various musical groups also entertain. Saturday morning starts with a pancake breakfast, as well as the "Menno Mile," a 5-kilometer event which has nearly 300 participants of varying ages.

The auction of quality handcrafted goods begins at 9:30 a.m. The food booths have also expanded over the years.

In recent years, a garage is built on site through the donations of businesses and is used for cooking and then is auctioned and moved to its location.

Sunday schools have become involved in "Power Pennies" by collection coins for a month prior to the sale and bringing them to fill a large jar. An MCC project is picked, so the children know where the money is going.

Since 1970, the people in Saskatoon and surrounding areas have raised more than $1 million.

Minn-Kota MCC Country Auction and Fair

Minn-Kota MCC Country Auction and Fair is held in Sioux Falls, South Dakota, in the Sioux Falls Arena. In 1992, people from 17 states and provinces were represented. The quilt and woodwork auctions are a big part of the sale but Laotian egg rolls, made by members of a Laotian Mennonite church established in 1992, have found their niche.

In spring 1986, Mennonite churches in southern Minnesota and South Dakota received letters inviting their participation in a relief sale and requesting them to send delegates to the first meeting in April to discuss the fall 1987 event. More than 30 people attended that meeting and Sioux Falls was chosen to be the site for the sale because it is the largest city in this area.

At the July meeting, constituents agreed that they did not know the talents of the group well enough to vote intelligently for officers. It was decided that an executive committee representing Minnesota and South Dakota and serving staggered terms would be appointed the first round to handle official business and also a sale chairman would be appointed and reviewed annually. With advice from the executive committee, the sale chairman would select a sale committee which would be responsible to plan details for the sale. MCC regional representatives for the Northern Tier of Central States who knew the Minnesota and South Dakota constituency, Edie and Larry Tschetter were asked to prayerfully select the first officers who would represent a variety of skills needed.

With a year and a half to plan and prepare for the first sale, the proceeds

Buyers turn their attention to a wooden table at the Texas MCC Relief Sale in Houston.

far surpassed most expectations. It was held at the W.H. Lyon Fairgrounds with concession rights being purchased from the concessionaire and the fairgrounds; two succeeding sales were held there with good working relationships with the fairground personnel. When the concessionaire for the Sioux Falls Arena changed hands, the new management met with the officers of the sale and to negotiate for homemade, ethnic concessions to be served during the sale. For the fifth sale in 1991, the concessionaire donated the equivalent to the rental fee.

A primary constituency of generous farmers have donated several cattle and 40 hogs for processing each year for food preparation and sales in booths as well as sold packaged from a frozen meat booth. While women have been busy quilting beautiful quilts, making a variety of other needlework items, and preparing food, the men have made wood items from grandfather clocks to cedar chests. The highest price paid for an item as of 1991, was a quilt which sold for $3,200. Each year, all expenses have been paid by donation, thus allowing 100 percent of the sale proceeds to be sent to MCC.

Texas MCC Relief Sale

The fifth annual Texas MCC Relief Sale was held November 12, 1994 and raised about $23,600. A little more than half of the money came from the quilt auctions.

The sale began in 1990 and is held on the grounds of the Houston Mennonite Church and the adjacent Terrace Methodist Church.

Seven churches in Texas work on the sale. Each church takes turns running the different booths. Scattered Mennonite and Amish groups in Texas send baked goods, crafts, and other support. Quilts have been donated from as far away as Hawaii. The auction has averaged about 40 quilts each year.

The sale features a craft area within the church. The quilt auction is held under the Methodist church's large, covered pavilion. A tent is set up with SELFHELP crafts and a couple from Dallas run a woodworking booth, doing while-you-wait personalized woodworking.

On the Sunday after the sale, people who have come from all over the state (and out of state, too) participate with special music at a Songfest. "Potluck to go" follows this service.

Food booths are in abundance. The bake sale table, usually filled with pies and breads, always sells out quickly.

In 1994, after a potluck, they held a craft party, which they hope to make an annual event. Women in the church always make a group quilt for the sale, too.

Virginia Relief Sale

The Virginia Relief Sale began as Augusta Relief Sale on a farm in Augusta County, Virginia. The first planning meeting was held January 23, 1967 for those interested in raising funds for world-wide relief administered through MCC.

The first sale in September 1967 netted $6,394. After seven years the sale outgrew the farm and in 1974 was moved to Expoland in Fisherville, Virginia. It was renamed Virginia Relief Sale in 1980 to include statewide involvement of more than 1,000 persons. The sale is held annually on the last Saturday of September. The 1991 sale netted $120,000.

The event features auctions of quilts, art work, and other donated items, as well as food.

Mennonite Country Auction

Each year the Mennonite Country Auction is held on the first Saturday in October at the Menno Mennonite Church grounds west of Ritzville, Washington. Visitors from 80 Washington towns and from out of state gather to buy crafts and auction items, as well as form long lines for food.

The steering committee is made up of Menno and Warden churches' members. In the spring, the publicity chairperson mails a letter to Washington and Idaho Mennonite congregations inviting them to support and participate. Letters are also mailed to individuals who have sent special items for the auction.

Pre-sale fund-raisers are planned. In the early years there were pie socials and auctions. More recently, rest stops are set up on the highways where travelers are asked for donations for cookies and lemonade. A bike-a-thon started in 1993 has helped buy a 40-foot semi-trailer and a walk-in freezer.

The auction is a way to express Christian compassion for those who are less fortunate. The idea to have a relief sale at Menno Church came about when the Christian Enrichment Committee was planning programs. Under their direction, the first Menno Mennonite Church MCC Relief Sale and Auction was held on September 23, 1978, and consisted of an auction and eight booths, including pony rides. Total receipts were $7,300.

The next year, the Steering Committee increased the hours of the sale and the total rose to $16,200. In 1980 a Youth Booth was added and the sale was held in mid-September. Despite a steady heavy rain a great crowd still generated $21,813.

A silent auction was added in 1982, but the farm economy was falling so attendance fell and the total receipts fell to $22,127.

The sale continued to grow. In 1983 and '84 receipts reached nearly $30,000. The sale date became permanent in 1983 and the cider stand was opened that year. In 1985, the name Mennonite Country Auction was used on all letters and flyers for the first time. The auction was included in the Washington State Department of Tourism calendar. The name drew an interest and increased attendance by non-Mennonites gave the opportunity to witness "In the name of Christ."

The sale has grown over the years to a full-day event with 21 booths. In 1993 receipts totalled $72,993.

Wisconsin MCC Relief Sale

The vision to have a sale in Wisconsin was first presented in late 1990 by Richard Wildermuth, a first-generation Mennonite who also holds membership in an Evangelical Lutheran church in the American congregation.

Wildermuth, originally from Illinois, was familiar with the Peoria sale. The idea in Wisconsin met with some opposition, however Richard perservered and the first sale was held August 8, 1992 at the Jefferson County Fairgrounds 4-H Activity Center in Jefferson, Wisconsin.

The first sale consisted of an auction, lunch stand and SELFHELP Crafts, and sent $9,200 to MCC. Twenty percent of the net proceeds are distributed locally.

The sale committee is committed to holding a sale every year on the second Saturday of August. According to Wildermuth, the Wisconsin Mennonite Relief Sale and Benefit Auction chairman, the volunteers represent approximately one-fifth of the 750 Anabaptists (excluding Old Order Amish) living in Wisconsin as of 1994.

Vietnamese Spring Rolls

Hundreds of spring rolls are prepared and sold each year at the Oregon MCC Fall Festival in Albany. The Bounthanh Syravong family spends many hours preparing the spring rolls. Volunteers help "Boonie" and family fry and serve these tasty rolls on sale day!

1 package (8 oz) bean thread
    noodles
1 pound very lean, coarsely
    ground pork (preferably
    ground at home)
1 cup minced onion
1 cup finely shredded carrot
2 cups shredded jicama
1 teaspoon sugar
1 teaspoon MSG
1 tablespoon fish sauce
1/4 teaspoon salt
1 1/2 teaspoons coarse black
    pepper
4 dozen egg roll wrappers
Oil (for frying)

Make the Filling:
Soak bean thread noodles in warm water for 30 minutes. Drain. Cut into 1-inch sections. (You should have about 1 1/2 cups.)

In a large bowl, combine noodles with remaining ingredients (except egg roll wrappers and oil). Using both hands, mix filling until well blended. Set aside.

Wrap the Rolls:
Place egg roll wrappers on a smooth surface. Drop 1 heaping tablespoon of filling 1 inch from lower edge; shape filling into a 3-inch-wide roll. Fold bottom edge of wrapper over filling, roll once, then fold in both side edges. Finish rolling (loosely, because the filling will expand during cooking) to form a neat cylinder. Wrap rolls carefully, taking care not to tear the wrappers. (Holes let the filling drop out during cooking.) Set finished rolls on a platter, seam side down, to seal the seam.

Fry the Rolls:
In a large, nonstick frying pan, heat oil over medium-high heat until very hot but not smoking (360°F). Put a few rolls in the pan, folded edge down so the rolls won't open during cooking. Leave a little space between rolls. Using tongs or long chopsticks, turn rolls occasionally and fry until light golden brown all over. Watch carefully so they don't overcook or get too brown.

Line a large bowl with several layers of paper towels. Transfer cooked rolls to bowl, leaning them upright against rim of bowl to drain.

Makes about 4 dozen

Ham Balls

Balls:
1 to 1 1/2 pounds ground ham
1 to 1 1/2 pounds ground beef
2 eggs, beaten
2 cups bread crumbs
1 cup milk
Salt and pepper to taste

Sauce:
1 1/2 cups brown sugar
1 tablespoon dry mustard
1/2 cup vinegar
1/2 cup water

Mix together ingredients for ham balls. Form into about 25 small balls. Place in a roaster. Mix together sauce ingredients. Pour over ham balls. Cover and bake at 350°F for 2 hours.

Sharon Yoder
Pleasant View Mennonite Church,
Goshen, Indiana

Baked Ham Balls

Sauce:
6 cups brown sugar
6 teaspoons dry mustard
3 cups vinegar
3 cups water

Balls:
6 pounds ham, ground
9 pounds pork, ground
12 eggs, beaten
6 cups milk
12 cups bread crumbs

To prepare sauce, mix ingredients together and heat to dissolve sugar. To prepare ham balls, mix ingredients well; form into small balls. Place in baking pans; pour sauce over. Bake at 325°F for 1 1/2 to 2 hours or until done. Baste frequently.

Makes 80 balls

Martha Tschetter, Freeman, South Dakota
Minn-Kota MCC Relief Sale,
Sioux Falls, South Dakota

Amish-Style Deviled Eggs

These eggs are always very popular at potlucks. A washed Styrofoam egg carton makes the perfect carrying case to transport them to the get-together.

1 dozen eggs
2 tablespoons mayonnaise
1 heaping tablespoon yellow
  mustard
4 ounces chopped olives
Dash salt and pepper

Bring a large pan of water to a boil; then turn off heat. Prick the end of the shell of each egg and drop gently into the hot water. Cover and let sit for 20 minutes. Pour out water; rinse eggs in cold water. Peel.

Halve eggs and remove yolks, placing them in a medium bowl. Mash yolks. Mix in mayonnaise, mustard, olives, and salt and pepper. Stuff eggs with mixture.

Brunetta Lloyd Martin
Houston Mennonite Church, Texas

Corrine Hanna Diller of Houston, Texas, is an enthusiastic supporter of the Texas MCC Relief Sale. In 1993 and 1994, she has made five quilts plus wall hangings to be auctioned. The woman who has sewn all of her life, though, was diagnosed with arthritis in 1982 and subsequently could not do any hand sewing. When the relief sale started up, Corrine says she asked a lot of "why" questions to God.

After her first two machine-made quilts, she resolved to try and find someone to hand-quilt a top. She then recruited more people. Corrine feels her contribution of finding others to quilt for the relief sale is God's way of answering her questions.

"God has told me that if I had been able to sew anything I wanted, I would have made one quilt a year, and been satisfied with that," Corrine writes in a letter. "Instead, I'm recruiting people all over the country, getting more people involved, and having five times as many quilts up for auction."

She says she realizes that she could never serve as a missionary or relief worker, but she can still do something significant to support the work these people do.

At the time of the 1994 sale, Corrine already had three quilts in the works for the '95 sale. She says she's always looking for more people to hand-quilt for the Texas sale and those who do get their name in the auction book for their labor. Corrine can be contacted at 8443 Sonnerville Drive, Houston, TX 77080-3638.

Cheese Ball

1 package (8 oz) cream
   cheese
1 jar (5 oz) Kraft Old English
   sharp processed cheese
   spread
1/2 teaspoon Worcestershire
   sauce
1/4 teaspoon garlic salt
1/2 cup chopped English
   walnuts

Bring cheeses to room temperature. Mix until
well combined. Stir in Worcestershire sauce
and garlic salt. Form into a ball. Roll in
chopped nuts.

Nila Kauffman
Pleasant View Mennonite Church,
Goshen, Indiana

Apple Dip

8 ounces cream cheese,
   softened
3/4 cup brown sugar
1/4 cup granulated sugar
2 teaspoons vanilla

Mix all ingredients well to blend. Serve with
raw apple slices.

Mrs. Kenneth (Christine) Folkers,
Flanagan, Illinois
Salem Evangelical Mennonite Church,
Gridley, Illinois
Illinois Mennonite Relief Sale, Peoria

Ham Dip

2 cups ground ham
1 package (8 oz) cream
    cheese
1 cup sour cream
1/2 cup salad dressing
2 green onions, chopped
    with tops
1/2 teaspoon seasoned salt
1 loaf French or round rye
    bread

Mix all ingredients (except bread). Refrigerate until ready to serve.

Cut top third off bread. Hollow out loaf, leaving a 1-inch-thick shell. Cut up removed portion of bread into 1-inch cubes; set aside.

When ready to serve, toast bread shell in 400°F oven for 3 minutes. (This keeps dip from soaking into bread shell.) Place ham dip in shell. Serve with reserved bread cubes and vegetable sticks.

Variation: Thaw 1 package (10 oz) frozen chopped spinach; drain well. Mix into ham dip.

Ardith Epp, Henderson, Nebraska
Nebraska Mennonite Relief Sale, Aurora

"The Best You Ever Had" Dip

2 packages (8 oz each) cream
    cheese
4 tablespoons milk
1 cup sour cream
1 jar (15 oz) chipped beef,
    shredded
2 tablespoons chopped
    onion
2 tablespoons chopped
    green pepper
1/2 cup chopped nuts
1/4 teaspoon pepper

Mix cream cheese and milk. Stir in remaining ingredients. Place in small ovenproof casserole dish and bake at 350°F for 15 minutes.

Serve warm with crackers, chips, or vegetables.

Virginia Gindlesperger, Johnstown, Pennsylvania
MCC Quilt Auction and Relief Sale, Johnstown

Cabbage Cheese Soup

2 tablespoons butter
1 cup chopped onion
4 cups chopped cabbage
1 cup sliced celery
2 cups diced potatoes
1 can (13 oz) chicken broth
1 teaspoon salt
1/4 cup butter
1/4 cup flour
1/4 teaspoon paprika
1/4 teaspoon pepper
4 cups milk
1 1/2 cups shredded cheddar
    cheese
Dash dillweed

Melt the 2 tablespoons butter in a large saucepan; add onion and saute until soft. Add cabbage, celery, potatoes, chicken broth, and salt. Cover, bring to a boil, reduce heat, and simmer until vegetables are tender (about 20 minutes).

Meanwhile, melt the 1/4 cup butter in a 4-quart saucepan. Blend in flour, paprika, and pepper. Remove from heat; then stir in milk. Heat to boiling, stirring, and boil 1 minute. Remove from heat and add cheese, stirring until it melts.

Add vegetables and their liquid to cheese mixture. Return soup to stove and warm over low heat. Sprinkle dillweed over top before serving.

Makes 10 to 12 cups

Lena Sala, Hollsopple, Pennsylvania
MCC Quilt Auction and Relief Sale,
Johnstown, Pennsylvania

Chicken Borscht

Paul Isaak of Rocky Ford Mennonite Church, Rocky Ford, Colorado, says he usually makes a big kettle of this borscht and freezes the leftovers in meal-size containers.

1 chicken
10 cups water
1 1/2 teaspoons salt
3 cups diced potatoes
3 cups diced carrots
3/4 cup onion
3 cups cooked tomatoes
6 cups shredded cabbage
6-10 peppercorns
3-4 bay leaves
4-6 whole allspice
Chicken bouillon to taste

Cook chicken in salted water until tender. Remove skin and debone chicken. Cut up meat and set it aside.

Skim fat off broth. Add potatoes, carrots, and onion. Cook until almost tender. Add reserved chicken, tomatoes, and cabbage. Place peppercorns, bay leaves, and allspice in cheesecloth bag or spice holder; add to soup. Simmer until cabbage is tender.

Remove spices. Add chicken bouillon to taste. (The bouillon provides the salt.)

Notes: If a thinner soup is desired, add more water. For additional taste, add a few drops of vinegar to each portion after ladling it into the bowl.

Serves 8 to 10

Rocky Ford MCC Relief Sale

Borscht

The women affiliated with the Saskatoon Relief Auction in Saskachewan, Canada, make 15 to 20 gallons of this borscht, which is served at the annual relief sale.

A 2-pound soup bone
2 quarts cold water
2 carrots, chopped (optional)
1 medium head cabbage, chopped fine
2 medium potatoes, cubed
1 medium onion, minced
1 teaspoon salt
Half a star aniseed (optional)
1 small bay leaf
10 whole allspice
1 1/2 tablespoons chopped parsley
Bunch dill
1 to 1 1/2 cups whole tomatoes
Cream (optional)

Bring soup bone and water to a boil. Simmer briskly for at least 1 1/2 hours, adding more water as it boils away, to keep the broth at 2 quarts.

Add vegetables (except tomatoes) and seasonings. Cook until vegetables are done (20 to 30 minutes). Then add tomatoes and bring just to the boil.

If desired, add cream just before serving.

SERVES 6 TO 8

Hilda Patkau, Clavet, Saskachewan

Borscht

At the Kelowna, British Columbia, Relief Sale, five 20-gallon cauldrons of this borscht were prepared at the auction site. The stock was made the night before and the vegetables cut up. The morning of the sale, cooking started about 6 AM. The soup was ready by about 9:30, and bowls were selling briskly by 10 AM. About 300 one-liter containers were also sold to attendees who wanted to take the goodness home.

50 pounds bones and meat (pork and beef)
Water
Fresh dill and parsley, tied in large bunches
12 pounds onions, chopped or sliced
1 bunch celery, chopped or sliced
5 pounds carrots, chopped or sliced
5 bell peppers (preferably red), cored, seeded, and chopped or sliced
3 cans (48 oz each) tomato soup
100 ounces tomato juice
50 ounces (or less) ketchup
2 cups (or less) salt
2 tablespoons crushed chilies
25 pounds potatoes, chopped or sliced
22 pounds cabbage, chopped or sliced
100 ounces fresh tomatoes

In a 20-gallon cauldron, boil bones and meat in water with big bunches of dill and parsley for 3 hours. Remove everything from cauldron, separating stock from meat and bones and discarding herbs. Clean cauldron and return stock to it. Separate meat from bones, and cut up or shred into bite-size pieces. Reserve meat.

To stock in cauldron, add onions, celery, carrots, peppers, and seasonings (tomato soup, juice, ketchup, salt, and chilies). Cook until vegetables are partly done. Then add potatoes, next cabbage, and finally tomatoes.

When vegetables are tender, return cut-up meat to cauldron. Cook until heated through.

MAKES 20 GALLONS

Anni Giesbrecht, Kelowna

Borsch

This recipe is from the book Mennonite Favorites, MCC Relief Sale Recipes.

1 gallon soup stock (see
    instructions)
1 cup minced onions
1 cup diced carrots
1 cup cubed potatoes
1 medium cabbage (about 2
    lbs), shredded
1 green pepper, cored,
    seeded, and diced
4 stalks celery, diced
1 can (16 oz) tomato juice
1 can (16 oz) tomato soup
A small sprig each dill and
    parsley
1/2 teaspoon paprika
Salt to taste

To make soup stock, place 3 to 4 pounds bones with some meat in a large kettle. Cover with 1 gallon water, and simmer for about 3 hours. Remove bones from stock. Separate meat from bones, chop, and set aside to add to soup later.

Add remaining ingredients to stock. Cook until tender, adding meat toward end of cooking time.

SERVES 10

Submitted by Helen Harms, Aldegrove, British Columbia

Borcht

Half a chicken or a beef
    soup bone (or roast)
2 quarts water
1 medium onion
1 tablespoon salt
Pinch pepper
Parsley leaves
1 bay leaf
A few potatoes
Small head of cabbage
1/2 cup cream
1 small can whole tomatoes
    or tomato sauce

Cook chicken (cut it up) or beef bone in water with onion, salt and pepper, parsley, and bay leaf for at least 45 minutes. Dice potatoes and cabbage; add to pot. Cook briskly until vegetables are done. Add cream and tomatoes and it's ready to serve. The flavor is even better the next day.

*Irene Penner, Corn, Oklahoma
Oklahoma MCC Relief Sale, Fairview*

Chicken Corn Soup

This recipe by the late Rhoda Petersheim was used at the Pennsylvania Relief Sale, Harrisburg. Women from the Zion Mennonite Church, Birdsboro, and from Martindale Mennonite Church made the soup at the MCC processing plant at Akron. The recipe was contributed by Irene Zimmerman, assistant food chairman of the sale.

A 6-pound stewing chicken
1 pound extra-fine noodles
3 packages (10 oz each) frozen corn
1 medium onion, chopped
1 tablespoon chopped parsley
Pinch saffron
2 teaspoons Accent seasoning
1/2 teaspoon black pepper
Salt (to taste)
4 hard-boiled eggs, chopped

In enough water to cover, cook chicken until tender. Remove meat from bones, chop, and return to broth.

Add remaining ingredients (except eggs), along with more water if needed. Bring to a boil, reduce heat to low, and cook 45 minutes, watching carefully so that soup does not scorch.

Remove from heat; stir in chopped eggs and serve.

Storage note: Let cool, *uncovered*, in a cool place for about an hour. Cover and refrigerate; keep very cold.

Makes 10 quarts

Mennonite Bean Soup

This recipe can be ready to serve for potluck after Sunday worship service.

2 cups assorted dried beans
1 3/4 quarts water
1 ham bone
1 onion, chopped
3 stalks celery, chopped
3 carrots, chopped
4 cups canned tomatoes
Salt and pepper (to taste)

On Saturday evening, soak the beans in the water. Transfer to a crockpot before bedtime. Turn pot on low.

Sunday morning, add remaining ingredients to pot. Take crockpot along to church, and plug it in before Sunday School. Soup will be ready following worship service.

Relief Sale Recipe
Houston Mennonite Church, Texas

Waiting is a big part of making perfect bean soup at the Northern Michigan Relief Sale in Fairview. These two cooks wait for the soup to cook in the converted milk bulk tank behind them.

(Photo submitted by Bill Esch)

Bean Soup

200 pounds beans
7 bunches celery, diced
9 pounds carrots, diced
60 pounds potatoes, diced
25 pounds ham, diced
3 gallons whole tomatoes
4 cans tomato juice
4 jars (28 oz each) barbecue
    sauce
10 jars ham base
4 ounces black pepper
2 pounds dry onions
15 five-gallon pails water

Wash beans. Put in cooker with 7 five-gallon pails water. Add celery, carrots, potatoes, and ham. Make sure the water covers all this, adding more if necessary. Cook 2 hours.

Add tomatoes, juice, barbecue sauce, ham base, pepper, and dry onions. Add a few more pails water if needed. Continue cooking, adding water as needed and stirring occasionally, for about 6 hours more. Raise or lower heat of cooker as necessary to keep soup cooking.

Michigan Avenue Mennonite Church, Pigeon
Michigan Relief Sale, Fairview

Ham and Bean Soup

The now-late Sadie Weaver prepared this soup for the Pennsylvania Relief Sale when it was held in Morgantown. When the sale moved to Harrisburg, Mrs. Weaver gave the food committee the recipe. Florence Detweiler, of Mechanicsburg, asked ladies from the churches in her area to make the soup, which she now sells at the annual sale. Women from the Petra Fellowship also make the bean soup to serve the Friday before the sale.

4 pounds large navy beans
4 pounds picnic ham,
    chopped fine
1 onion, minced
4 stalks celery, chopped
2 carrots, sliced on cabbage
    cutter
Salt, pepper, onion salt, and
    garlic salt (to taste)

Soak beans overnight. Add remaining ingredients, plus enough water to make 10 quarts of soup. Bring to a boil, reduce heat, and simmer until beans are soft (about 2 hours).

MAKES ABOUT 10 QUARTS

Dutch Potato Soup

This soup is prepared in quantity for sale at the Pennsylvania Relief Sale in Harrisburg. The contributor indicates that this recipe serves four--or two if the diners are farmers!

2 cups diced potatoes
1/2 cup diced onion (op-
    tional)
3 cups water
1 teaspoon salt
1 cup chopped celery
1/2 cup grated carrot
1 quart milk
2 tablespoons butter
3 hard-boiled eggs, chopped
1 tablespoon chopped fresh
    parsley

Bring potatoes, onion, water, and salt to a boil; simmer briefly. When potatoes are partially cooked, add celery and carrot. In a separate saucepan, heat milk. Add to soup mixture when potatoes are soft. Stir in butter, eggs, and parsley just before serving.

Irene Zimmerman, Brownstown, Pennsylvania

Chili

12 1/2 pounds ground beef
1 gallon cooked beans (chili,
    kidney or a mixture)
2 gallons tomato juice
Brown sugar
Chili powder
Minced onion
Salt and pepper (to taste)

Brown ground beef. Place in large electric roaster along with remaining ingredients.

Fay Kliewer
Nebraska MCC Relief Sale, Aurora

Chili Soup

Twenty-three women each made a batch of this chili soup from 5 pounds of hamburger. All of the soup was sold in two days at the 1992 Minn-Kota Relief Sale in Sioux Falls, South Dakota.

30 pounds hamburger
2 large onions, chopped
    (more if desired)
2 large cans tomato soup
1 1/2 gallons chili beans
    with sauce
1 1/2 gallons kidney beans
1 gallon tomatoes, chopped
2 large cans tomato juice
3 packages chili seasoning
2 tablespoons salt
Chili powder to taste

Brown hamburger. Drain off fat. Add remaining ingredients. Bring to a boil, reduce heat, and simmer to enhance the flavor until ready to serve.

MAKES ABOUT 9 GALLONS OR 96 1 1/2-CUP SERVINGS

Mrs. LeRoy D. Hofer, Dolton, South Dakota

Grene Schauble Suppe (Green Bean Soup)

This big seller at the Mennonite Country Auction and MCC Relief Sale in Ritzville, Washington, has been featured since 1982. About 25 gallons are consumed.

6-7 quarts chunked potatoes
7-8 quarts green beans (fresh or frozen)
7 cups chopped onions
1 quart sliced (or grated) carrots
5 teaspoons salt
Clump of summer savory 1 inch thick and 4 inches long (wrapped and tied in cloth)
6 pounds boneless ham, cut in 1/2-inch cubes
5 cups sour cream

Cover potatoes, beans, onions, carrots, salt, and savory with water. Bring to a boil.

Add cubed ham, reduce heat to a simmer, and cook until vegetables are tender.

To keep sour cream from curdling when added to soup, first ladle several cups of the hot broth into the sour cream; mix well. Then stir sour cream into soup. Remove from heat.

Makes 5 gallons

Green Bean Soup

The first green beans of the summer always go into a soup. Serve this soup with fresh bread for a wholesome meal.

1 1/2 to 2 pounds ham bones and meat
4 or 5 sprigs summer savory
2 cups diced potatoes
4 cups cut green beans
1 teaspoon salt
2 tablespoons ham base
2 cups sour cream

Place ham bones and summer savory in cooking pot. Cover with water and cook about 2 hours. Remove ham from bones; chop meat and return to pot. Add potatoes, beans, salt, and ham base; cook until vegetables are tender. Just before serving, stir in sour cream.

Serves 8

Ardith Epp, Henderson, Nebraska
Nebraska MCC Relief Sale, Aurora

Vegetable Soup

4 pounds beef
25 quarts tomato juice
1 pound barley
30 pounds potatoes
14 pounds baby lima beans
14 pounds peas
14 pounds carrots
6-8 quarts green beans
8 medium heads cabbage
30 large onions
6 bunches celery
12 pounds corn
2 1/4 cups salt
2 1/4 cups sugar

Cook beef in plenty of water until tender; remove from broth and cut into small pieces; reserve. Add tomato juice and barley to beef broth; cook until barley just begins to get tender. Clean all vegetables and cut into small pieces. Add to soup pot along with salt and sugar. Cook until vegetables are tender.

MAKES ABOUT 30 GALLONS

Kathryn L. Suter
Virginia Relief Sale, Fisherville

Vegetable Soup

Evelyn Buller of Henderson, Nebraska, prepared this soup for the soup supper at the first Nebraska MCC Relief Sale, held in Aurora in 1982.

4 pounds chuck roast, cubed
3 packages chicken backs
    and necks (cook in water
    to make broth)
A 1-pound cabbage, shredded
3 cups diced carrots
4 medium onions, diced
6 cups diced celery
5 pounds diced potatoes
6 cups tomato juice
6 cans (15 1/2 oz each) green
    beans
4 cans (15 oz each) dark red
    kidney beans
1 cup pearl barley
    (quick-cooking)
1 package soup macaroni
Onion soup mix
Cream

Boil chuck in plenty of water with some parsley, peppercorns, bay leaves, half a clove garlic, basil, thyme, rosemary, and celery leaves. Meanwhile, in separate pot, cook chicken in plenty of water. When both meats are tender, remove from broth. Set chuck aside; discard chicken skins and bones. Strain broth, discarding seasonings.

In very large kettle, combine beef and chicken broths. Add chuck and remaining ingredients. Cook until tender. At serving time, stir in some onion soup mix and cream.

Mrs. Eichelberger's Hamburger Vegetable Soup

3 cups water
4 beef bouillon cubes
3 peeled carrots, cut up
2 medium potatoes, cut up
1 cup cut-up celery
2 medium onions, cut up
1/2 cup cut-up green pepper
1 pound ground beef
1 teaspoon Kitchen Bouquet
1 teaspoon salt
1/2 teaspoon pepper
1 bay leaf
1/8 teaspoon dried basil
    leaves
1 can (16 oz) stewed toma-
    toes (or substitute
    tomato juice)

Bring water and bouillon cubes to a simmer; stir to dissolve cubes. Add carrots, potatoes, celery, onions, and green pepper to broth; simmer.

Meanwhile, brown ground beef, draining off any fat. Add browned meat and remaining ingredients to soup pot. Cover and simmer until vegetables are tender.

Note: This soup is a good way to use up leftover vegetables. Add them to the soup near serving time, allowing enough time for them to heat through.

MAKES 6 GENEROUS SERVINGS

Mrs. Roger (Lavonne) McGuire, Morton, Illinois
First Mennonite Church, Morton
Illinois MCC Relief Sale, Peoria

Cabbage Beef Soup

1 pound beef with bone
2 quarts water
2 tablespoons salt
2 parsley roots
2 bay leaves
1 teaspoon dill or dillweed
6 cups shredded cabbage
1 medium or large onion, cut
    up
2 cups sliced carrots
5 cups cubed potatoes
1 quart whole tomatoes or
    tomato soup

Cover beef with the water. Add salt, parsley roots, bay leaves, and dill. Cook until meat is almost done.

Then add cabbage, onion, carrots, and potatoes. (Add more water if necessary to cover vegetables.) Simmer slowly until vegetables are almost tender.

Then add tomatoes and heat to boiling. Serve plain or with cream.

Note: This soup is very good reheated; it gives the flavorings more time to blend.

SERVES 8

Mary B. Duerksen, Mountain Lake, Minnesota
Minn-Kota MCC Relief Sale, Sioux Falls,
South Dakota

Broccoli-Cauliflower-Cheese Soup

3 chicken bouillon cubes
3 cups water
1/2 cup diced celery
1/2 cup diced green pepper
1/2 cup diced carrots
1/4 cup diced onion
1 cup cauliflower, cut into
    flowerets
1 cup broccoli, cut up
6 cups milk
1/2 cup melted butter
1/2 cup flour
1 cup cubed Velveeta cheese

In soup kettle, dissolve bouillon cubes in water. Add celery, green pepper, carrots, and onion. Cook until partly tender. Then add cauliflower and broccoli. Cook until all vegetables are tender.

Add milk to soup; heat but do not boil. Meanwhile, in separate saucepan, blend together butter and flour; cook until frothy but not browned. Off heat, blend a little of the soup broth into the butter-flour mixture to thin it. Then add it to soup kettle, stirring until well blended.

Add cheese. Heat soup gently, stirring to prevent sticking, until cheese melts. Do not let soup boil.

Ruby Waltner, Marion, South Dakota
Minn-Kota MCC Relief Sale, Sioux Falls, S. Dakota

Zucchini Soup

2 tablespoons chopped
    shallots or onions
1 clove garlic, minced
2 tablespoons butter
1 teaspoon curry powder
1 pound cleaned, unpeeled
    zucchini, chopped
1 3/4 cups chicken broth (or
    water plus 3 chicken
    bouillon cubes)
1/2 cup coffee cream
1/2 teaspoon salt (optional)

In heavy saucepan, saute shallots and garlic in butter until soft but not browned. Add curry powder, zucchini, and broth. Cook 10 to 20 minutes, stirring to keep from burning.

When zucchini is tender, transfer soup to blender container and blend (in batches if necessary). Stir in cream. Taste, and add salt if desired. Serve hot with croutons or cold with chives.

SERVES 2 TO 4

Cleva Waltner, Freeman, South Dakota
Minn-Kota MCC Relief Sale, Sioux Falls, S. Dakota

Wild Rice Soup with Chicken Dumplings

The recipe for this family favorite of the Siemenses in Winnipeg, Manitoba, was given to Susana Siemens by her son, who is a chef. She has scaled the recipe to family portions.

Soup:
1 cup wild rice
1/4 cup butter
2 cups finely diced carrots
    (see *Note*)
2 cups finely diced celery
1 large onion, finely diced
1/3 cup oil
1/2 cup flour
3 cups cream or whole milk
5 cups chicken stock
Salt and pepper (to taste)

Dumplings:
1 cup ground chicken pieces
1 or 2 eggs
Salt and pepper

Precook the wild rice (it will take about an hour). Set aside.

Melt butter in a heavy frying pan. Add carrots, celery, and onion; saute. Set aside.

In a large stock pot, make a white sauce with the oil, flour, and cream. Add the chicken stock, whisking until smooth. Add sauteed vegetables. Cook until vegetables are tender (about 15 minutes), stirring soup and watching it carefully so it doesn't burn. Season to taste.

Add reserved wild rice and simmer a few minutes more.

Meanwhile, make dumpling mixture: In a blender, blend chicken until very fine. Add eggs and seasonings.

Shortly before serving, drop dumpling mixture by teaspoons into the soup. Simmer a few minutes until dumplings cook through.

Note: Dice the vegetables very fine--into 1/4-inch pieces.

MCC Manitoba Relief Sale

Meatball Soup

Soup:
1 medium onion, sliced
2 stalks celery, sliced
1 grated carrot
4 potatoes, peeled and cubed
1 bay leaf
Salt and pepper
2 1/2 quarts water
1/2 cup sour cream

Meatballs:
1 pound ground beef
1 egg
1 small onion, chopped
1 small potato, grated
Salt, pepper, and chopped
    parsley

In a large stock pot, cook vegetables, potatoes, bay leaf, and seasonings in water until just beginning to get tender.

Meanwhile, mix ingredients for meatballs. Form into balls and drop into the soup. Continue boiling for 20 minutes; then reduce to a simmer.

When ready to serve, remove from heat and stir in sour cream.

Susana Siemens, Winnipeg, Manitoba
MCC Manitoba Relief Sale

Plumi Moos

Three ladies' groups each make one recipe of this moos at home and bring it chilled to the Saskatoon Relief Auction in Saskachewan, Canada. Between 50 and 60 gallons of the moos are served by the bowl or sold in jars to take home.

3 cups cut-up mixed dried
    fruits
4 quarts water
1 1/2 cups sugar
4 tablespoons cornstarch
1 package cherry-flavored
    gelatin

Cook fruit in the water until very tender. (Or, soak fruit overnight; then just bring to a boil the next day.)

Mix sugar with cornstarch; stir in enough water to make a thin paste. Add paste to hot fruit mixture, letting it cook a few minutes to take away the starchy taste.

Remove from heat; stir in cherry-flavored gelatin.

MAKES 1 GALLON

Hilda Patkua, Clavet, Saskatchewan

Pluma Mose

Three volunteers from the Bethesda Church prepare about 40 gallons of this soup for the Nebraska MCC Sale in Aurora. Soaking the fruit the night before helps cut down on preparation time.

2 1/2 pounds prunes
3 pounds raisins
1 stick cinnamon
3 gallons water
5 cups sugar
3 1/2 cups flour
1 teaspoon ground cinna-
    mon
3 cups cream
4 cups milk
1/4 cup white vinegar

Soak fruit and cinnamon stick in water overnight. The next morning, bring fruit to a boil and cook about 5 minutes. Then drain the fruit broth into a 5-gallon kettle, reserving the cooked fruit. Bring broth to a rolling boil.

Meanwhile, mix sugar, flour, cinnamon, cream, and milk until smooth. When fruit broth reaches boil, add this mixture to it. Cook 5 minutes. Pour over cooked fruit. Stir in vinegar.

To cool moos, stir mixture well every hour until cooled.

SERVES 80

Ann D. Friesen, Henderson, Nebraska

Pluma Mos

Fifty gallons of this fruit soup were eaten at the 1992 Nebraska MCC Relief Sale at Aurora.

3 pounds seedless raisins
2 pounds pitted prunes
3 gallons water
4 1/2 cups sugar
1 teaspoon cinnamon
Scant 4 cups flour
4 cups milk
2 1/2 cups sweet cream
2 tablespoons white vinegar

Wash and drain raisins. Soak raisins and prunes overnight in the water.

The next morning, cook fruits in soaking water. When done, remove fruits to a 5-gallon bucket. Bring fruit broth to a full boil.

Meanwhile, with a mixer, combine sugar, cinnamon, flour, milk, and cream. Add to boiling broth and cook, stirring constantly, until mixture thickens. Pour over reserved cooked fruit. Stir in vinegar.

Let cool, stirring occasionally to keep skin from forming on top.

MAKES 5 GALLONS

Mrs. Jacob (Sarah) Rempel, Henderson, Nebraska

The city of Fresno has recognized the contribution of Mennonite quilters with an exhibit of Mennonite Quilts at the city's Metropolitan Museum of Art in 1990.

In 1992 the quilt auction at the West Coast Sale for World Relief received its highest price ever for a single quilt made by West Coast quilters. The cross-stitched top was made by Alma Goossen of Reedley who makes two quilt tops each year for Reedley's Mennonite Quilt Center quilters. Her son, Virgil, was determined to have the quilt and finally got it at $5,300 after a fierce bidding battle with another relative in the audience, according to Kathy Heinrichs Weist, sale chairperson.

Plumamousse

This fruity soup is served at the verenika dinner at the West Coast Mennonite Sale and Auction for World Relief. Verenika are made in four all-day verenika factories in three church kitchens. The verenika are served at three fund-raising dinners in January, February, and March, as well as on the day of the sale. This recipe, submitted by Kathy Heinrichs Wiest of Kingsburg, California, is from the 1949 cookbook published by the Missionary Society of Reedley Mennonite Brethren Church. It was submitted for that cookbook by Mrs. G. B. Huebert.

1 cup dried prunes
3/4 cup raisins
3 heaping tablespoons flour
1/2 cup sugar
3/4 cup cream or canned milk
2 cups milk
1/2 teaspoon cinnamon (optional)
1 tablespoon vinegar (optional)

Cook prunes in 3 cups of water until well done. Mash the prunes; then add raisins and 2 more cups of water. Cook a little longer.

Mix flour and sugar together; blend in cream. Stir the paste into hot fruit mixture. Add milk and bring to a boil. (Adding the optional cinnamon and vinegar improves the flavor.)

Makes about 1/2 gallon

Pluma Moos

This fruit soup is sold in half-cup containers at the Minn-Kota Relief Sale in Sioux Falls, South Dakota. It's usually prepared in 1-gallon batches in various homes and then delivered to the food chairman, who takes it to the sale.

1 1/2 cups dried prunes
1 1/2 cups dried apricots
1 1/2 cups raisins
Cinnamon stick 1 to 1 1/2
    inches long
4 quarts water
1 cup sugar (or less, to taste)
1/4 to 1/2 cup flour
1/2 cup cream
3/4 cup milk

Soak dried fruits and cinnamon stick overnight in the water. The next morning, cook fruit in soaking water until soft (simmering 30 minutes to 1 hour).

Mix together sugar, flour, cream, and milk to form a paste. Very slowly add to the hot fruit. Simmer 10 minutes more, or until thickened. (Mixture will thicken more as it cools.) Cool.

Note: If you do not want a creamy moos, substitute same amount of water for the cream and milk.

Makes 1 gallon

Cleo Friesen, Mountain Lake, Minnesota

Cherry Moos

This special cherry moos is also sold at the Minn-Kota Relief Sale in Sioux Falls.

1 quart sour cherries (pitted)
    and juice
1 quart water
6 tablespoons flour
1 1/2 to 2 cups sugar
1 cup sweet cream
1 quart milk

In a 5- or 6-quart saucepan, bring cherries (and their juice) and the water to a boil. Meanwhile, make a paste of the flour, sugar, cream, and milk. When cherries are boiling, stir in paste; bring to a boil again. Cook, stirring and watching carefully to prevent burning, until mixture thickens. Serve hot or cold.

Makes 1 gallon

Cleo Friesen, Mountain Lake, Minnesota

♥ Herb Shaker

Sally Ann Reddecliff, of Johnstown, Pennsylvania, suggests replacing your salt shaker with an herb shaker. Try this mixture on some of the main dishes in this section.

To make the seasoning blend, thoroughly combine 1 tablespoon of each of the following:

Garlic powder
Basil
Marjoram
Thyme
Onion powder
Parsley flakes
Freshly ground white or
    black pepper
Paprika

 ## ◆ POULTRY ◆

Chicken-Filled Shells

2 cups cubed cooked
    chicken
1 cup cooked peas
1/2 cup mayonnaise
1/3 cup finely chopped
    onion
1 package (16 oz) jumbo
    shells, cooked and
    drained
1 can (10 3/4 oz) condensed
    cream of mushroom
    soup
1/2 cup water

Mix together chicken, peas, mayonnaise, and onion. Stuff into shells. Arrange shells in a single layer in a baking dish. Stir soup and water together. Pour over stuffed shells. Cover with aluminum foil and bake at 325°F for 25 minutes.

Virginia Gindlesperger, Johnstown, Pennsylvania
MCC Quilt Auction and Relief Sale, Johnstown

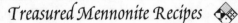

Chicken and Dressing Casserole

A 3- to 4-pound chicken
2 cans (10 3/4 oz each) cream
    of mushroom soup
1 medium onion, diced
3/4 teaspoon poultry season-
    ing
Salt and pepper to taste
20 slices dried bread, cubed
Chicken broth
2 eggs, beaten

Cook chicken; remove meat from bones. Combine meat and mushroom soup; set aside. Combine onion, seasoning, salt, pepper, and bread cubes with enough broth to moisten. Spread half the dressing over bottom of a 13x9-inch baking pan. Add chicken mixture. Add beaten eggs to remaining dressing; spread over top of casserole. Bake at 350°F for 45 minutes.

Jo Ann Swearengin
Missouri MCC Relief Sale, Harrisonville

♥ Chicken-Bean Casserole

1 box croutettes stuffing mix
1 can (14 1/2 oz) French-cut
    green beans
2 to 3 cups cooked diced
    chicken or turkey
1 package (2 oz) slivered
    almonds (optional)
1 can (10 3/4 oz) cream of
    chicken soup
1 cup chicken broth or milk

Spread half the package of croutettes over bottom of a casserole. Spread drained beans over. Layer with chicken and almonds. Mix soup with broth or milk; pour over ingredients in casserole. Cover with remaining croutettes. Bake at 350°F for about 1 hour.

SERVES 6 TO 8

Rita Ann Graber, Freeman, South Dakota
Minn-Kota MCC Relief Sale, Sioux Falls,
South Dakota

♥ *Plou (Chicken and Rice)*

This recipe, brought to this country in the late 1800s and passed down through generations of the Jantzens in Beatrice, Nebraska, is a favorite at family picnics.

1 large chicken
3 quarts water
1 tablespoon salt
1 1/2 teaspoons allspice
1 onion, diced
2 tablespoons shortening
2 cups uncooked rice
4 cups chicken broth
4 carrots, sliced
1/4 teaspoon pepper

Cook chicken in the water, with the salt and allspice, until tender. Remove chicken from bones and cut into small pieces. Saute onion in the shortening. Add rice, chicken broth, carrots, and pepper. Simmer for 1 1/2 hours. (Do not overcook. The rice should stay crumply.)

SERVES 6 TO 8

Gretl Jantzen
Nebraska MCC Relief Sale, Aurora

Baked Chicken with Rice

1 whole chicken
1 1/2 to 2 cups uncooked rice
1 can (10 3/4 oz) tomato soup
1 can (10 3/4 oz) cream of
    mushroom soup
2 cups water
Salt (to taste)

Cut up chicken and brown in frying pan. In a roaster, combine rice, soups, water, and salt; stir well. Place chicken pieces on top. Bake at 350°F for 1 1/4 to 1 1/2 hours.

SERVES 5 TO 6

Edie Tschetter, Freeman, South Dakota
Minn-Kota MCC Relief Sale, Sioux Falls,
South Dakota

Chicken-Broccoli Casserole

1 cup uncooked rice
1 package (20 oz) frozen
    broccoli
1 jar (16 oz) Cheese Whiz
    process cheese sauce
1 can (10 3/4 oz) cream of
    chicken soup
3 cups deboned chicken
Buttered bread crumbs

Cook rice; cook broccoli and drain. Combine; then mix in cheese sauce, soup, and chicken. Put into a buttered 13x9-inch baking pan. Top with crumbs. Bake at 350°F for 45 minutes to 1 hour.

Mary Glanzer, Freeman, South Dakota
Minn-Kota MCC Relief Sale, Sioux Falls,
South Dakota

♥ Chicken Vegetable Casserole

2 cups cut-up cooked
    chicken
2 cans (10 3/4 oz each) cream
    of mushroom soup
1 can (8 oz) water chestnuts
1 small can mushrooms
1 bag (16 oz) California
    mixed frozen vegetables
1 tablespoon finely chopped
    onion
4 ounces Cheddar cheese

In a casserole dish, mix together all ingredients in order given. Bake at 350°F, covered, for 1 hour. Then uncover and bake 15 to 20 minutes longer.

SERVES 8

Mrs. Arthur (Beverly) Carlson, Odin, Minnesota
Minn-Kota MCC Relief Sale, Sioux Falls,
South Dakota

Quick Saucy Chicken Casserole

3 cups cut-up cooked
   chicken
2 cans (10 3/4 oz each) cream
   of mushroom soup
1 box frozen mixed veg-
   etables
1 teaspoon poultry seasoning (optional)
1/2 teaspoon garlic salt
2 cups Bisquick baking mix
1 1/2 cups milk
1 teaspoon parsley
1 cup shredded Cheddar
   cheese

Mix chicken, soup, mixed vegetables, and
seasonings. Spread over bottom of a
13x9x2-inch baking dish. Stir together
Bisquick and milk. Pour over chicken mixture. Spread cheese and parsley over top of
casserole. Bake at 450°F for 30 to 35 minutes.

Serves 8 to 10

Lena Sala, Hollsopple, Pennsylvania
MCC Quilt Auction and Relief Sale, Johnstown

Festive Mexican Chicken

1 can broth
1 can cream of chicken soup
1 can cream of mushroom
   soup
Cooked chicken
1 medium onion, diced
1 package corn chips,
   crushed
2 cups shredded Cheddar
   cheese
Chopped black olives and
   red peppers, for garnish

Mix together broth and soups; set aside. Cut
up chicken and spread over bottom of a
13x9-inch baking pan. Top with layers of
onion, then crushed chips, and then cheese.
Pour soup mixture over all. Top with olives
and peppers. Bake at 350°F for 20 to 30
minutes.

Jean Shaw
Missouri MCC Relief Sale, Harrisonville

Chicken Casserole

2 cups diced cooked chicken
1 package (7 oz) elbow
    macaroni (uncooked)
1/4 pound grated Cheddar
    cheese
2 cans (10 3/4 oz each) cream
    of mushroom or celery
    soup
2 cups milk *or* half milk and
    half chicken broth
Half a green pepper, minced
1 small can pimientos,
    chopped
1 cup finely chopped celery
4 hard-cooked eggs, coarsely
    chopped
1 small onion, minced

Combine all ingredients; refrigerate overnight. Bake at 350°F for 1 hour.

Mrs. Charles Kreider, Sterling, Illinois
Science Ridge Mennonite Church
Illinois MCC Relief Sale, Peoria

Chicken-Macaroni Casserole

2 cups uncooked elbow
    macaroni
2 cups diced cooked chicken
    or turkey
1 package (8 oz) Velveeta
    process cheese spread
2 cans (10 3/4 oz each) cream
    of chicken soup
2 cups milk
4 diced hard-cooked eggs

Mix all ingredients together. Place in casserole, cover, and refrigerate overnight. Remove from refrigerator 1 hour before baking. Bake at 350°F for 1 hour.

Nila Kauffman
Pleasant View Mennonite Church
Indiana MCC Relief Sale, Goshen

♥ *Chinese Chow Mein Dinner*

Chow Mein:
1 small onion, diced
Vegetable oil
1 head cabbage, shredded
2 cans bean sprouts, drained
2 cans (4 oz each) mush-
   rooms
2 stalks celery, diced
2 cups cooked, cut-up
   chicken or beef
Chinese pea pods (optional)

Fried Rice:
1 cup diced celery
1 cup diced carrots
1 cup peas
1 tablespoon margarine
1 1/2 to 2 cups cooked rice
1 pound bacon, diced and
   fried

To make chow mein, saute onion in oil. Add remaining ingredients and simmer about 1/2 hour.

To make fried rice, cook celery, carrots, and peas together in a little water until soft; drain. Season with salt and pepper as desired. Melt margarine in a skillet. Combine all ingredients in skillet, mix well, and simmer about 1/2 hour.

Mrs. Lonnie (Linda) Ulrich, Metamora, Illinois
Linn Mennonite Church
Illinois MCC Relief Sale, Peoria

Chicken Brunswick Stew

Preparing this recipe, which is cooked in an open kettle, is an all-day affair. It was contributed by Bid Lloyd, the son of Dewey and Beamer White Lloyd, for the Virginia Relief Sale, in Fisherville. Mr. Lloyd notes that Brunswick Stew should be thick enough to eat with a fork. He also cautions that the kettle has to be stirred regularly from beginning to end to keep the stew from sticking.

100 pounds whole chickens
**30 pounds onions, peeled
 and diced beforehand**
**100 pounds potatoes, peeled
 and diced beforehand**
12 gallons tomatoes
12 gallons butter beans
1 box (1/4 oz) red pepper
2 pounds salt
1 box (8 oz) black pepper
**12 gallons whole-kernel corn
 (white or yellow)**
4 pounds butter

Starting around 6 A.M., put chickens and enough water to cover in a large open kettle. Cook until meat falls off bones; pick bones out of meat and broth. Then add potatoes and onions--and some water if the stock is thickening too fast. (Add only a little water at a time.) When potatoes are cooking well, add the tomatoes. Drain liquid from butter beans into a kettle and save it. (You may need to add more liquid to the stew later.) Add drained beans after pot begins to boil again. Add the box of red pepper, and 1 pound of the salt. Let mixture cook until about 4 P.M., adding the black pepper and the remainder of the salt about mid-afternoon. Drain corn and add to kettle at 4:00. At 4:30, add the butter. Cook, stirring constantly, until 5 P.M., when the stew should be ready.

MAKES 50 GALLONS /RECIPE CAN BE CUT TO SIZE AS DESIRED

◆ BEEF ◆

Best Ever Stew

2 pounds chuck or round
    steak, cut in cubes
2 tablespoons oil
3 medium onions, cut in
    chunks
3 carrots, cut in chunks
4 stalks celery, cut in chunks
3 or 4 potatoes, cut in chunks
1 tablespoon tomato paste
3 tablespoons flour
2 to 3 cups beef broth
Salt and pepper to taste

Brown meat in oil in heavy ovenproof pan; remove and set aside. Add vegetables to pan, along with a little more oil if needed; brown slightly. Stir in tomato paste, flour, and broth; season with salt and pepper. Return meat to pan and cook on top of stove until sauce is thickened. Then bake in a 325°F oven for 2 hours, or until beef is tender.

Hint: To store the remainder of the can of tomato paste, drop tablespoons of the paste onto waxed paper; freeze. Store frozen paste in a small plastic bag--ready for use the next time you make stew.

Lena Sala, Hollsopple, Pennsylvania
MCC Quilt Auction and Relief Sale, Johnstown

Swiss Steak

This main dish is served at the Oregon MCC Fall Festival workers' appreciation dinners--by special request. The ingredients below make a family-size meal.

3 tablespoons fat
2 pounds round steak (1 inch
    thick)
1/2 cup flour
1 1/2 teaspoons salt
1/4 teaspoon pepper
1 can (10 3/4 oz) cream of
    mushroom soup
1 soup can water

Melt fat in skillet. Cut steak into serving-size pieces and roll/dredge in a mixture of the flour, salt, and pepper. Brown steak on both sides; transfer meat to a baking dish or roaster. Combine mushroom soup and water; pour over steak. Cover and bake at 350°F for 1 1/2 hours.

SERVES 8

Adella (Stutzman) Gingrich, Albany, Oregon

Juicy Meat Loaf

A favorite at the Minn-Kota Relief Sale annual kick-off dinner, this main course will satisfy the heartiest of appetites.

1 1/2 pounds ground beef
1/4 pound ground pork
1/4 cup finely cut onion
1 cup quick-cooking or
    regular rolled oats
2 teaspoons salt
1/4 teaspoon pepper
1/2 teaspoon dry mustard (or
    2 1/2 teaspoons prepared
    mustard)
1/4 cup catsup
1 beaten egg
1 cup water or milk

Mix all ingredients thoroughly. Pack into a 9x5-inch loaf pan. Bake at 375°F for 1 to 1 1/2 hours. Slice and serve garnished with parsley sprigs.

Note: To make enough meatloaf for a crowd, multiply the ingredients by 10 or 15. Mix well and pack firmly into 13x9-inch baking pans. Cut into serving-size pieces *before* baking to make serving easy. Bake at 375°F for about 1 1/2 hours.

Martha Tschetter, Freeman, South Dakota

Layered Meat Loaf

1 1/2 pounds ground beef
3/4 cup uncooked rolled oats
1 egg, beaten
1/4 cup chopped onion
1 1/2 teaspoons salt
1/4 teaspoon pepper
1/4 teaspoon oregano
2 teaspoons parsley flakes
1 cup tomato juice
1 1/2 cups cooked sliced
    carrots
2 cups mashed potatoes
2 tablespoons grated cheese

Combine beef, oats, egg, onion, seasonings, and tomato juice. Pack into microwave-safe 8-inch-square pan. Bake in microwave about 10 minutes, testing to see that meat is set in center. Spread carrots over meat; then spread mashed potatoes evenly over carrots. Sprinkle with cheese. Return to microwave and bake 5 minutes more.

Lisa Kauffman
Pleasant View Mennonite Church, Goshen,
Indiana

Barbecued Meatballs

These saucy meatballs are served at the kick-off meal for the Minn-Kota Relief Sale in Sioux Falls, South Dakota.

Meatballs:
3 pounds ground beef
1 can (12 oz) evaporated
    milk
1 cup rolled oats
1 cup cracker crumbs
2 eggs
1/2 cup chopped onion
1/2 teaspoon garlic powder
2 teaspoons salt
1/2 teaspoon pepper
2 teaspoons chili powder

Sauce:
2 cups catsup
1 cup brown sugar
1/2 teaspoon liquid smoke
    (or to taste)
1/2 teaspoon garlic powder
1/4 cup chopped onion

To make meatballs, combine all ingredients (mixture will be soft). Shape into walnut-size balls. Place meatballs in a single layer on waxed paper-lined cookie sheets; freeze until solid. Store in bags in freezer until ready to cook.

To cook, place frozen meatballs in a 13x9-inch baking pan. Combine all sauce ingredients, stirring until sugar is dissolved. Pour sauce over meatballs. Bake at 350°F for 1 hour.

MAKES ABOUT 80 MEATBALLS

Ladonna Waltner, Marion, South Dakota

People line up to buy bulk meats at the Illinois Mennonite Relief Sale in Peoria.

Saure Klops (Sour Meatballs)

Most Mennonites like to flavor their foods with vinegar. If you like vinegar, you'll enjoy this favorite, from the Nebraska MCC Relief Sale Cookbook, of the family of Rogena (Friesen) Jantzen, of Plymouth, Nebraska.

Meatballs:
2 pounds ground beef
2 eggs
2 teaspoons salt
1/2 teaspoon pepper
1 cup cracker crumbs (rolled fine)
1 cup water (scant)

Sauce:
5 cups water
12 allspice
4 bay leaves
Salt
Flour
Cream
4 teaspoons vinegar
2 level teaspoons sugar

Mix all meatball ingredients together. Form into balls a little bigger than a golf ball. To cook, bring the 5 cups water to a boil; add allspice, bay leaves, and salt. Put in meatballs; boil 20 minutes. Then combine flour and cream to make a thickening paste. Pour this into meatball cooking liquid to thicken it like gravy. Add vinegar and sugar. Stir well. Serve with potatoes or noodles.

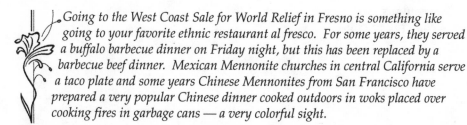

Going to the West Coast Sale for World Relief in Fresno is something like going to your favorite ethnic restaurant al fresco. For some years, they served a buffalo barbecue dinner on Friday night, but this has been replaced by a barbecue beef dinner. Mexican Mennonite churches in central California serve a taco plate and some years Chinese Mennonites from San Francisco have prepared a very popular Chinese dinner cooked outdoors in woks placed over cooking fires in garbage cans — a very colorful sight.

Hamburger Balls with Sweet-and-Sour Sauce

Balls:
1 pound ground beef
1/4 cup diced onion
Bread or cracker crumbs
2 eggs
1/4 cup milk
1/2 teaspoon salt
Dash pepper

Sauce:
6 tablespoons brown sugar
3 tablespoons cornstarch
5 tablespoons vinegar
1 1/2 cups tomato juice
1 1/2 teaspoons salt
3/4 cup cold water
1/2 cup chopped onion

Mix together all ingredients for hamburger balls. Mold into balls. Brown in a skillet. Then transfer to a casserole dish.

While balls are browning, prepare sauce. Mix all ingredients, bring to a boil, and simmer until thick. Pour sauce over hamburger balls in casserole. Bake at 350°F for 1 hour.

Mrs. Lonnie (Linda) Ulrich, Metamora, Illinois
Linn Mennonite Church
Illinois MCC Relief Sale, Peoria

Barbecue

This recipe for barbecue, shared by Carol Tschetter, of Freeman, South Dakota, is very popular at the Minn-Kota Relief Sale, in Sioux Falls.

10 pounds ground beef
4 cans (10 3/4 oz each)
    tomato soup
2 packages dry onion soup
    mix
1/2 cup catsup
1/4 cup prepared mustard
1 1/2 teaspoons salt
3 to 4 cups rolled oats

Mix together all ingredients very well. Place in large baking pan and bake at 350°F for 2 hours, stirring occasionally.

Sloppy Joes

20 pounds ground beef
2 cans (7 lb, 2 oz each)
   ketchup
2 cans (8 oz each) tomato
   sauce
1 cup mustard
1 pound brown sugar
5 ounces minced onion
5 ounces Worcestershire
   sauce
2 tablespoons salt
2 tablespoons pepper
3 tablespoons chili powder

Brown ground beef; drain well. In a large kettle, combine remaining ingredients; warm over medium heat. Add browned beef; heat thoroughly. Serve two scoops per bun.

Marcella Powers
Missouri MCC Relief Sale, Harrisonville

Taverns (Sloppy Joes)

One volunteer brings this tasty sandwich filling to the Minn-Kota Relief Sale, where four volunteers assemble and sell the sandwiches to eager customers. Five times the quantity in this recipe was prepared for the two-day sale, for a total of about 200 sandwiches.

4 pounds ground beef
Chopped onion (amount to
   suit taste)
Salt and pepper to taste
1 cup catsup
1 can (10 3/4 oz) tomato soup
1 can (10 3/4 oz) chicken
   gumbo soup
1 1/2 tablespoons chili
   powder
2 tablespoons vinegar
2 tablespoons brown sugar

Brown ground beef and onions together. Drain grease. Season to taste with salt and pepper. Add remaining ingredients; mix well. Bake in a 250°F oven for 2 hours.

Mrs. Leroy D. Hofer, Dolton, South Dakota

Haystacks

3 pounds ground beef
1 large jar (28 oz) Ragu
    spaghetti sauce
Crushed soda crackers
2 cups cooked rice
Shredded lettuce
Cut-up tomatoes
Chopped onion
Crushed corn chips
Sliced olives
Chopped walnuts
2 cans (10 3/4 oz each)
    Cheddar cheese soup
1 cup milk

Brown ground beef; drain. Add Ragu sauce. Place crackers, rice, lettuce, tomatoes, onions, chips, olives, and walnuts in separate containers. Combine soup and milk; heat. Diners layer ingredients on their plates.

SERVES 8

Ann Goossen, Beatrice, Nebraska
Nebraska MCC Relief Sale, Aurora

Cabbage Rolls

More than 2,500 of these cabbage rolls are sold at the Kelowna, British Columbia, Relief Sale. Helen Harms and Elsie Dyck both shared this recipe from Mennonite Favorites: MCC Relief Sale Recipes, a small cookbook that was created for the sale in that Canadian province.

About 15 cabbages
25 pounds meat
3 3/4 cups raw rice, cooked
12 eggs
6 onions
4 potatoes
17 tablespoons salt
2 to 3 tablespoons pepper

Sauce:
6 cups ground carrots
1 bunch celery, ground
6 onions, ground
6 green peppers, ground
Sugar to taste
6 cans (14 oz each) tomato sauce
2 cans (14 oz each) tomato paste
7 cans (14 oz each) tomato juice
7 1/2 tomato-juice cans (14 oz each) water

Freeze whole cabbages for at least a week for using. Remove from freezer 24 hours before using, to thaw. (Leaves come off beautifully and are easy to work with. This eliminates the need to steam cabbage.) Mix together meat; rice; and eggs, onions, and potatoes (which have been chopped fine in a blender or food processor). Season with salt and pepper.

Place meat mixture into cabbage leaves, fold, and secure. Brown cabbage rolls. (To brown large batches of cabbage rolls, place them in the oven on cookie sheets.) Then transfer to baking pans.

To prepare sauce, combine ground vegetables and saute in a little vegetable oil. Stir in sugar. Add liquids and bring to a boil. Pour sauce over cabbage rolls. (Pans can be prepared ahead and frozen at this point.) Bake at 350°F for 2 hours.

Makes about 225 cabbage rolls

♥ Imam Bayildi (Stuffed Eggplant)

Using lean ground beef in this Greek dish minimizes the amount of fat in this healthy main dish. This recipe also appears in the cookbook Mennonite Favorites: MCC Relief Sale Recipes, *prepared for the British Columbia Relief Sale.*

3 medium-sized eggplants
6 medium-sized onions,
    sliced thin
Vegetable oil
1 pound lean ground beef
5 medium-sized tomatoes
7 cloves garlic
Salt
Ketchup

Cut stems off eggplants; slice in half lengthwise. Scoop out and save eggplant pulp, leaving 1 to 1 1/2 inches of pulp attached to skin. Set aside.

Saute onions in a little oil until clear; then add beef. Chop and add 4 of the tomatoes, as well as the garlic. Season with salt. Simmer until most of the liquid has evaporated. Chop reserved eggplant pulp and add to sauce.

Fill eggplant shells with sauce mixture. Slice remaining tomato; place on top of shells. Place stuffed eggplants in a baking dish containing 1 inch of water. Dilute ketchup with water and pour over each shell. Bake, covered, at 350°F for about 1 hour.

Helen Harmes, Aldergrove, British Columbia

Dried Beef Hot Dish

1 can (10 3/4 oz) cream of
    mushroom or chicken
    soup
1 soup-can milk
1 1/4 cups grated Cheddar
    cheese
1/4 cup finely chopped onion
1/4 cup finely chopped green
    pepper
1 cup uncooked elbow
    macaroni
1 package smoked-type
    dried beef
2 hard-boiled eggs, cut fine
1 package frozen peas (optional)

Mix all ingredients (except peas) together. Put in a baking dish, cover, and refrigerate overnight. If desired, stir in the frozen peas immediately before baking. Bake at 350°F for 45 minutes.

SERVES 6

Mrs. Marian Gering, Freeman, South Dakota
Minn-Kota MCC Relief Sale, Sioux Falls,
South Dakota

Hamburger-Corn Bake

This casserole is one of the items served at the kick-off dinner for the Minn-Kota Relief Sale, in Sioux Falls, South Dakota.

1 1/2 pounds ground beef
1 onion, chopped
1 package (12 oz) medium
    noodles
1 can (12 oz) whole kernel
    corn
1 can (10 3/4 oz) cream of
    mushroom soup
1 can (10 3/4 oz) cream of
    chicken soup
1 cup sour cream
1/4 teaspoon pepper
3/4 teaspoon salt (optional)
1/2 teaspoon monosodium
    glutamate (optional)
1/4 cup chopped canned
    pimientos (optional)
2 cups soft bread crumbs
    mixed with 4 teaspoons
    melted butter (optional)

Brown ground beef with onions; drain. Cook noodles following package directions; drain. Mix all ingredients (except bread crumbs) together. Place in a casserole. If desired, top with buttered bread crumbs. Bake at 350°F for 1 to 1 1/2 hours.

Serves 10 to 12

Martha Tschetter, Freeman, South Dakota

Hamburger-Green Bean Casserole

1 pound ground beef
1 onion, chopped
Salt and pepper to taste
1 can (14 1/2 oz) green beans,
    drained
2 small cans (8 oz each)
    tomato sauce *or* 1 can (10
    3/4 oz) tomato soup
Mashed potatoes

Brown beef and onion; season to taste. Spread over bottom of baking dish. Layer beans over meat mixture. Pour tomato sauce over beans. Spread mashed potatoes on top of everything. Bake at 350°F for 30 to 40 minutes.

LaVerna Friesen, Freeman, South Dakota
Minn-Kota MCC Relief Sale, Sioux Falls, South Dakota

♥ Zucchini Casserole

1 pound ground beef
2 cups chopped tomatoes
2 cups grated or very thinly
  sliced zucchini
1 small onion, finely
  chopped
1/2 cup Minute rice
1/4 pound Velveeta process
  cheese spread, shredded
  or cut in chunks
1/2 cup bread crumbs

Brown beef in skillet; drain. Add tomatoes, zucchini, onion, and rice. Transfer half the mixture to a casserole dish. Spread cheese (keeping a little for the top) and bread crumbs over bottom layer. Cover with remainder of meat mixture. Bake at 350°F for 45 minutes, adding the reserved cheese to top of casserole when it's almost done.

Mary Kaufman, Johnstown, Pennsylvania
MCC Quilt Auction and Relief Sale, Johnstown

Impossible Cheeseburger Pie

1 pound ground beef
1 1/2 cups chopped onion
1/2 teaspoon salt
1/4 teaspoon pepper
1 1/2 cups milk
3/4 cup Bisquick baking mix
3 eggs
2 tomatoes, sliced
1 cup shredded Cheddar
  cheese

Heat oven to 400°F. Grease a 1 1/2-inch-deep 10-inch pie plate. Brown beef and onion; drain. Stir in salt and pepper. Spread meat mixture in pie plate. Beat milk, baking mix, and eggs until smooth (15 seconds in blender on high or 1 minute with hand beater). Pour over meat mixture. Bake 25 minutes. Immediately top with tomatoes and sprinkle with cheese; bake 5 minutes more.

MAKES 6 TO 8 SERVINGS

Lynette P. Frey, Sterling, Illinois
Science Ridge Mennonite Church
Illinois MCC Relief Sale, Peoria

Quick Italian Bake

1 pound ground beef or
   Italian sausage
1 cup chopped tomato
3/4 cup frozen peas
1/2 teaspoon Italian seasoning
1 cup Bisquick baking mix
1 cup milk
2 eggs
1 cup shredded mozzarella
   cheese

Heat oven to 400°F. Grease a 9-inch pie plate. Brown ground beef; drain. Stir in tomato, peas, and seasoning. Spread meat mixture in plate. Stir baking mix, milk, and eggs with a fork until blended. Pour over meat mixture. Bake 25 minutes, or until knife comes out clean. Sprinkle with cheese. Bake 2 to 3 minutes longer, or until cheese is melted. Serve with pizza sauce if desired.

Makes 6 to 8 servings

Florence Blough, Hollsopple, Pennsylvania
MCC Quilt Auction and Relief Sale, Johnstown

Delton Litwiller, co-chairman of the 35th annual Illinois Mennonite Relief Sale, reported in the "Mennonite Weekly Review" that more than 4,000 pounds of whole-hog sausage were consumed in the mile-long breakfast line from 5 a.m. to noon.

-- Love in Action News, MCC

◆ PORK ◆

Breakfast Casserole

The contributor, Sally Ann Reddecliff, of Johnstown, Pennsylvania, suggests serving this casserole for Sunday breakfast before church, with orange juice and fresh fruits.

1 pound sausage
**1/4 cup (half a stick) butter
  or margarine, melted**
6 slices bread
**1 1/2 cups shredded Cheddar
  cheese**
5 eggs
2 cups half-and-half
1 teaspoon dry mustard
1/2 teaspoon salt

Cook sausage; drain well and set aside. Place melted butter in 13x9-inch baking pan. Cut bread into small squares (remove crusts or not, as desired.) Spread over butter. Spread drained sausage over bread; spread cheese over top. Beat together eggs, half-and-half, mustard, and salt. Pour over ingredients in baking pan. Chill 8 hours or overnight. Bake at 350°F for 40 to 50 minutes.

MCC Quilt Auction and Relief Sale, Johnstown

Breakfast Bake

**16 slices white bread (crusts
  removed)**
8 slices deli ham
**Shredded mozzarella, Swiss,
  or American cheese**
6 eggs
3 cups milk
1/2 teaspoon onion salt
1/2 teaspoon pepper
1/2 teaspoon dry mustard
**1/2 cup (1 stick) butter,
  melted**
Cornflakes

Grease a 9x13-inch baking pan. Cover bottom of pan with 8 slices of the bread. Layer ham over bread; then layer cheese. Top with the remaining 8 slices bread. Beat together eggs, milk, onion salt, pepper, and mustard. Pour over layers in baking pan. Refrigerate overnight.

Remove casserole from refrigerator 1 hour before baking. When ready to bake, pour melted butter over casserole; top with cornflakes. Bake at 350°F for 1 1/4 hours. Let stand 10 minutes before cutting and serving.

Florence Blough, Hollsopple, Pennsylvania
MCC Quilt Auction and Relief Sale, Johnstown

Roast Pig

The Gap Relief Sale, in Pennsylvania, has a roast pig kick-off dinner on the Friday evening before the August sale. In 1991, the first year the idea was tried, volunteers roasted two pigs. Rolls and barbecue sauce were ready to make pork sandwiches to sell the next day--but turnout was so good on Friday night that there were no leftovers! The following year, volunteers roasted four pigs. According to Debbie Byler, of Gap, the pork is served with baked potato, vegetable, applesauce, pepper cabbage, roll and butter, cupcake, and a drink.

If you want to try this, allow plenty of time. It takes almost a night and a day to roast a 200- to 220-pound pig! You'll also need plenty of volunteers to remove the meat from the bones once the pigs are roasted. The Gap group cuts the meat into serving pieces and then keeps it warm in large electric roasters.

1 pig (200 to 220 lbs live weight)
60 pounds of charcoal
Optional: Enough sauerkraut or bread filling to fill the cavity of the pig

Use a regular pig roaster or two 55-gallon barrels cut in half and welded together. Start charcoal and let it burn until it gets gray. Then just keep adding charcoal as needed to keep the temperature even. Roast pig approximately 16 to 18 hours.

Makes 200 to 225 servings

Smoky Country-Style Ribs

4 pounds country-style ribs
Garlic salt
Fresh ground pepper
1 1/4 cup catsup
3/4 cup firmly packed brown sugar
1/2 cup chili sauce
2 tablespoons vinegar
2 tablespoons Liquid Smoke seasoning
1 tablespoon lemon juice

Sprinkle ribs with garlic salt and pepper. Combine remaining ingredients in medium saucepan; cook over medium heat for about 10 minutes, stirring occasionally. Keep warm. Place ribs, rib bones down, on a rack in a shallow roasting pan. Baste with sauce. Bake at 325°F for 1 1/2 to 2 hours, turning and basting with sauce every 30 minutes. Cut into serving-size portions. Heat remaining sauce and serve with ribs.

Serves 4 to 6

Alisa (Epp) Krehbiel, West Chester, Pennsylvania
Nebraska MCC Relief Sale, Aurora

Ham Loaf

3 pounds smoked ham
1 pound fresh pork
1 pound beef
2 cups bread crumbs
4 eggs, beaten
1 cup tomato juice

Sauce:
1/2 cup brown sugar
1/4 cup vinegar
1/2 cup pineapple juice

Grind together the ham, pork, and beef (or have butcher grind it together). Add bread crumbs, eggs, and tomato juice to meat; mix well. Form into loaves. Combine sauce ingredients and pour over loaves. Bake at 350°F for 1 1/4 hours. Baste with sauce mixture during baking.

Mildred Brenneman, Bloomington, Illinois
Bethel Mennonite Church, Pekin
Illinois MCC Relief Sale, Peoria

Chalupa

A 3- to 4-pound pork roast
1 pound (3 cups) dried pinto
    beans
1/2 cup chopped onion
4 to 5 cups water
1 1/2 tablespoons chili
    powder
1 teaspoon garlic salt
1 teaspoon cumin
1 teaspoon oregano
1 can green chilies

Mix together all ingredients. Place in a crockpot (slow cooker) and cook for 12 hours. Serve over taco chips with lettuce, tomato, onion, green pepper, Cheddar cheese, taco sauce, and sour cream.

Sherry (Epp) Thiesen, Henderson, Nebraska
Nebraska MCC Relief Sale, Aurora

♥ Black Beans Brazilian Style

The Mennonite Central Committee training program has brought many recipes to the homes of sponsors. This cultural exchange has added a nutritional factor as well. This recipe is from trainees Betti Harder, Alberto Kruger, Evaldo Warkentin, and Marvin Warkentin.

2 cups (about 1 pound) dried
    black beans
6 cups water
3/4 teaspoon baking soda
2 cups water
1 teaspoon salt
Smoked pork hock, bacon or
    bacon fat, or smoked
    sausage (for flavor)
2 cloves garlic, minced
1 medium onion, chopped
Half a green pepper,
    chopped (optional)
2 teaspoons oil, bacon fat, or
    butter
1 cup chopped tomatoes
1 tablespoon flour

Place beans in the 6 cups water with the soda; soak overnight. The next day, drain and rinse beans. Place in crock pot with the 2 cups water, the salt, and the meat. Cook about 2 hours, or until beans and meat are tender.

In a frying pan, saute garlic, onion, and green pepper (if used) in the oil. When onion is transparent, add tomatoes and cook until they are tender. Remove 1/4 cup of the vegetable mixture; combine with the flour. Return paste to frying pan; stir well. Mix vegetable sauce into beans. Serve with rice.

Lois Thieszen Preheim
Bethesda Mennonite Church, Henderson
Nebraska MCC Relief Sale, Aurora

♥ *Stir-Fry Pork*

1 can (14 1/2 oz) chicken broth
2/3 cup soy sauce
2 tablespoons sugar
3 tablespoons dry sherry
2 pounds lean pork, cut into
    thin strips
1/4 cup salad oil
3 medium carrots, cut into
    thin strips
2 cups diagonally sliced
    green onions
2 cups diagonally sliced
    celery
1 cup broccoli, cut into thin
    strips
1 cup sliced fresh mush-
    rooms
1 can sliced bamboo shoots,
    drained
1 can sliced water chestnuts,
    drained
3 tablespoons cornstarch
2 bags Success rice, cooked
    and drained

Combine broth, soy sauce, sugar, and sherry. Pour over pork and let marinate 1 to 2 hours. Heat oil in wok. Drain pork, reserving sauce; add pork to wok and fry until cooked. Remove pork from wok. Add carrots, onions, celery, and broccoli stems. Cook a few minutes. Add broccoli tops, mushrooms, bamboo shoots, and water chestnuts. Return pork to wok. Cook until vegetables are tender-crisp. Mix cornstarch into reserved marinade; add to wok. Cook until sauce boils and thickens slightly. Serve over cooked rice.

Alisa (Epp) Krehbiel, West Chester, Pennsylvania
Nebraska MCC Relief Sale, Aurora

Chinese Casserole

This is a favorite of the family of the Rev. Allan Miller, founder of Bethel Mennonite Church, in Pekin, Illinois.

3 to 4 pounds bulk sausage
1 large green pepper, diced
1 large onion, diced
3 cups diced celery
3 cups sliced fresh mush-
    rooms (optional)
1 cup raw rice
4 packages chicken noodle
    soup
8 cups water
1 cup slivered almonds
1 can (8 oz) water chestnuts,
    sliced and cut into thirds

Brown sausage; drain well on paper towels. Add green pepper, onion, celery, and mushrooms to sausage fat; saute lightly. In a large casserole, combine sausage and vegetables with remaining ingredients; mix well. Bake at 325°F, covered, for 40 minutes; uncover and bake 20 minutes more.

SERVES 16

Jill Belsley, Morton, Illinois
Illinois MCC Relief Sale, Peoria

Dutch Goose Casserole

2 cups cubed bread
2 cups diced cooked pota-
    toes
Dressing seasonings to taste
1 pound sausage, fried and
    cut up
1 egg, beaten
Milk

Combine bread, potatoes, seasonings, and sausage. Beat together egg and enough milk to moisten the dressing ingredients. Pour over casserole and toss to mix. Bake in a moderate oven for 30 to 40 minutes.

Mary Kaufman, Johnstown, Pennsylvania
MCC Quilt Auction and Relief Sale, Johnstown

Ham and Wild Rice Casserole

1 package (6 oz) Uncle Ben's long grain and wild rice
1 bag (20 oz) frozen chopped broccoli
2 cups (about 12 oz) cubed ham
1 1/4 cups shredded Cheddar cheese
1 can (10 3/4 oz) Cheddar cheese soup
1 cup mayonnaise or Miracle Whip salad dressing
2 teaspoons dry mustard

Cook rice following directions on package. Spread over bottom of 13x9-inch pan. Top with a layer of broccoli, then ham, and then 1 cup of the shredded cheese. Mix together soup, mayonnaise, and mustard. Spread over casserole. Sprinkle rest of cheese over top. Bake at 350°F for 40 to 45 minutes.

Sharon Dirst
East Peoria Mennonite Church
Illinois MCC Relief Sale, Peoria

Ham, Potato, and Cheese Casserole

1 medium onion, chopped
3 tablespoons chopped green pepper (optional)
1/4 cup (half a stick) butter or margarine
2 1/2 tablespoons flour
2 cups milk
Salt and pepper to taste
3 cups cooked cubed potatoes
3 cups cooked cubed ham
3/4 cup shredded cheese

Cook onion (and green pepper if desired) in butter for 5 minutes. Add flour and stir. Then add milk. Cook until thickened. Season with salt and pepper. Add potatoes and ham. Put in 2-quart casserole. Top with cheese. Bake at 350°F for 25 to 30 minutes.

SERVES 6 EASILY

Trella Harshberger, Johnstown, Pennsylvania
MCC Quilt Auction and Relief Sale, Johnstown

Ham and Noodle Bake

8 ounces noodles
3 cups cubed ham
1 medium onion, chopped
1 teaspoon salt
Dash pepper
1 can (10 3/4 oz) cream of
   chicken soup
1 1/2 cups milk
1 cup sour cream
1 cup grated cheese

Cook noodles following package directions; drain. Meanwhile, brown ham and onion; season with salt and pepper. Mix together soup, milk, sour cream, and cheese. Combine with noodles, ham, and onion in a casserole dish. Bake at 350°F for 30 minutes.

SERVES 6

Daphne Epp, Crete, Nebraska
Nebraska MCC Relief Sale, Aurora

Fettucini Casserole

8 ounces fettucini noodles,
   cooked
2 cups cubed ham
1/4 cup chopped onion
3 cups milk
1 cup sour cream
1 small carton dry-curd
   cottage cheese
Salt and pepper to taste

Mix together all ingredients in a casserole. Bake at 350°F for 30 minutes.

Deb Roth, Henderson, Nebraska
Nebraska MCC Relief Sale, Aurora

Auctioneers take bids for a bright quilt at the 1994 Nebraska Mennonite Relief Sale in Aurora.

(Photo by Fay Kliever)

♥ Barbecued Kraut

Kidron, Ohio, is a Swiss/German community and home to the Ohio Mennonite Relief Sale. This special way of preparing kraut is a favorite of many families in that community.

4 strips bacon, diced
Half an onion, sliced
1/2 cup brown sugar
1 can (8 oz) tomato sauce
Dash *each:* **A-1 steak sauce,**
    Worcestershire sauce,
    barbecue sauce
2 pounds sauerkraut,
    drained and rinsed

Brown diced bacon; drain grease. In mixing bowl, combine bacon with remaining ingredients; mix well. Transfer to crock pot and simmer on high setting for 3 hours.

◆ MEAT-FILLED PASTRIES ◆

Savilla's Beef-Vegetable Pasties

Many stories have sprung up around foods in Michigan. One of them has to do with the pasty, a meat-and-vegetable pie that originated in the mining districts of Britain. It immigrated along with the people to the Upper Peninsula of Michigan, where today it's still a favorite.

Cornishmen say that the miners stuffed the snugly wrapped and still-hot pasty into their shirts and it kept them warm on the long walk to the mine through the crisp morning air. Then, while the miners worked, the heat of their bodies kept the pasty warm until dinnertime.

Pasty recipes are as varied as are cooks. Savilla Handrich, of Germfask, Michigan, shared her personal favorite, a recipe that has been used at the Fairview Relief Sale.

Filling:
5 pounds pork sausage
14 pounds coarsly ground
    beef
30 pounds chopped potatoes
8 pounds chopped onions
3 pounds chopped carrots
3 bunches celery, chopped
5 chopped green peppers
Salt and pepper

Crust:
3 cups water
1/2 cup orange juice
10 eggs
2 cans (3 lbs each)
    butter-flavor Crisco
Salt
8 pounds flour

Cook filling ingredients until meat has lost all pink color and vegetables are tender.

For crust, mix together water, juice, and eggs. Mix in Crisco and salt, and then the flour. Roll out dough; cut into pieces. Stuff and seal; bake.

MAKES 100 PASTIES

Kraut Runza

These dough pockets filled with a meat-and-vegetable mixture are sold at the Country Auction and Relief Sale in Ritzville, Washington.

Filling:
64 pounds lean ground beef
18 gallons sauerkraut
32 heads cabbage
64 onions
2 large or 4 small cooked
　　hams, ground into
　　crumbles
1 cup salt
1 cup pepper
1 cup garlic salt

Dough:
4 packages dry yeast
3/4 cup sugar
4 teaspoons salt
25-pound sack of flour
3/4 cup margarine

To prepare filling, crumble ground beef and brown; drain off *all* liquid. Simmer sauerkraut; drain *very well*. Grind cabbages and onions in batches in a food processor; saute in a little margarine or butter until golden; drain completely. Blend all ingredients and seasonings together. Cool overnight.

Prepare 3 batches of the bread dough recipe.

Form 1/3 cup filling and put inside a round of flattened dough. Pinch shut. Bake at 350°F for 15 to 20 minutes.

Bierocks

Filling:
10 pounds ground beef
1 cup water
3 pounds chopped cabbage
    (use Crisco can
    heaping-full)
1 1/2 cups onion
3 tablespoons salt
1 tablespoon pepper
1 teaspoon garlic powder
1 cup flour

Dough:
1 quart warm water
1/2 cup sugar
1/2 cup shortening
1/2 cup powdered milk
1/3 cup yeast
Enough flour to make a
    sponge
5 eggs
1 1/2 teaspoon salt
About 10 cups flour

Cook meat with water until all red is gone. Then add remaining ingredients (except flour). Cook until cabbage is done. Add flour; stir until well mixed. Drain the meat to remove excess grease. Let filling cool before using.

To make dough, combine the warm water, sugar, shortening, and powdered milk in a blender. Pour into a mixing bowl, along with the yeast. Mix well with enough flour to make a sponge. Let rise until bubbles form. Add eggs and salt. Mix in enough of the flour (10 cups more or less) to the sponge to make a soft dough. Let rise until double in bulk. Punch down and roll out to form bierocks. Use 1/3 cup filling for each bierock.

New Hopedale Church, Meno; West New Hopedale Church, Ringwood; and Saron Mennonite Church, Orienta Oklahoma MCC Relief Sale, Fairview

Calzone

1 loaf frozen bread dough

Filling:
**1 cup grated Parmesan
   cheese**
**1 1/2 cups grated mozzarella
   cheese**
**1 pound ground beef,
   browned and drained**
1 1/2 cups sliced mushrooms
1/2 cup sliced black olives

Sauce:
**2 cans (8 oz each) tomato
   sauce**
1 clove garlic, minced
2 teaspoons sugar
1 teaspoon oregano
3/4 teaspoon basil

Thaw bread dough but don't let it rise. Roll out into a very long rectangle, big enough to cover the bottom and sides of a 13x9-inch pan plus enough to fold completely over the top. Fit dough into pan.

Mix together all filling ingredients. Pour filling into dough-lined pan. Cover with rest of dough rectangle and seal edges. Bake at 375°F for 20 minutes, or until golden.

While calzone is baking, combine sauce ingredients and heat. Cut baked calzone into squares; serve with sauce.

Note: Bread dough can also be divided into portions and formed and filled to make individual calzone.

*Tanya Ortman, Marion, South Dakota
Minn-Kota MCC Relief Sale, Sioux Falls,
South Dakota*

Samosa

These East Indian dough pockets can be made hot by adding 1/4 to 1 teaspoon of hot chili powder to the filling. The recipe is from Mennonite Favorites: MCC Relief Sale Recipes, *prepared for the Kelowna, British Columbia, Relief Sale.*

1 pound flour
1/2 pound butter
1 medium onion, chopped
1 pound minced meat
1/4 pound green peas
1 teaspoon garlic powder
1/2 teaspoon salt
1 teaspoon ground black
   pepper
1/4 teaspoon Anardana
1 pound vegetable oil

Make a hard dough from the flour, 2 tablespoons of the butter, and water. Pinch off small balls of dough and roll into 6- to 8-inch circles. Cut circles in half.

Fry onion in a little of the remaining butter until brown. Mix in minced meat and fry over medium heat. Add peas and seasonings; cook until moisture is absorbed. Let filling cool.

Place 1 1/2 tablespoons of cooled filling onto each half-circle of dough. Close them up, using remaining butter to seal edges. Fry in hot vegetable oil.

Helen Harmes, Aldergrove, British Columbia

◆ DAIRY & VEGETARIAN ◆

Verenike

A number of churches are involved in the making of verenike for the Relief Sale in Kelowna, British Columbia. The dough is mixed in a commercial mixer. Thousands of verenike are assembled, then frozen on cookie sheets and stored in plastic bags until sale day. The ingredient amounts below make about 350 verenike, depending on size.

Dough:
12 cups milk
12 whole eggs
12 egg whites
2 tablespoons baking
    powder
2 tablespoons salt
1 pound margarine, melted
15 cups flour

Filling:
22 pounds cottage cheese
12 egg yolks
2 tablespoons salt
1 tablespoon pepper

Gravy:
1 pound margarine
1 scant cup flour
1 teaspoon pepper
2 teaspoons salt
6 cups water
5 cans evaporated milk
1/3 pail (ice cream size) sour
    cream

To make the gravy, melt the margarine. Add salt, pepper, and flour and then water. Bring to a boil. Then add evaporated milk, bring to a boil, remove from heat, and add sour cream. Keep hot, but *do not boil again* or the gravy will curdle.

Louise Ens and Agnes Tschetter

Verenike

At the Bethesda Mennonite Church kitchen, about 22 volunteers make more than 4,000 verenike for the Nebraska Relief Sale, in Aurora. They are frozen and stored at meat processors. At the sale, verenike are sold as meals, as well as offered frozen to take home.

Dough:
21 cups flour
12 eggs
2 tablespoons salt
2 cups cream
4 cups milk

Filling:
8 cups well-drained cottage
   cheese
2 eggs
2 teaspoons salt
1/2 teaspoon pepper

Prepare a soft dough from the ingredients listed. Roll out thin and cut in circles using a 4-inch-diameter tin can. Put one dip, from a No. 40 dipper, of cottage cheese filling on each circle. Fold and seal edges well. Cook in boiling water until they float, or fry in deep fat until golden brown. Top with cream gravy.

SERVES ABOUT 190

Verenika (Cheese Pockets)

A group of women from Mountain Lake, Minnesota, make verenika at home for sale at the Minn-Kota Relief Sale in Sioux Falls, South Dakota.

Dough:
10 cups flour
2 tablespoons salt
5 egg whites
1 1/2 cups half-and-half
2 cups milk
1/3 cup sour cream

Filling:
5 pounds dry cottage cheese
8 ounces regular cottage
   cheese
5 egg yolks
1 1/2 teaspoons salt
1 1/2 teaspoons pepper

Gravy:
1/2 cup (1 stick)
   margarine-butter blend
1/2 cup flour
1/4 cup cornstarch
3/4 gallon (12 cups) whole
   milk
1 cup half-and-half
1 teaspoon salt
1/2 teaspoon pepper
1 teaspoon ham base (or ham
   drippings)
4 pounds cubed ham (prefry
   to get juice or drippings
   and add to gravy)

To make dough, mix flour and salt; set aside. Beat together egg whites, half-and-half, milk, and sour cream; stir into flour. Mix to make a soft dough. Let dough rest for several hours so it is more pliable to roll out. Roll. Put filling by heaping teaspoonfuls on dough, fold dough over, and cut to make half-moon pockets. Press edges to seal. Simmer pockets in boiling water about 8 minutes; drain. Dip pockets in melted margarine-butter. Pockets may be served this way or browned on both sides and served with gravy. Pockets freeze well at this point, to be heated and served later.

To make gravy, melt margarine-butter; stir in flour and cornstarch. Add milk and half-and-half slowly, stirring well to prevent lumpiness. Add remaining ingredients; cook to thicken, stirring continually.

Makes about 75 verenika

Veranika

One day is set aside, and approximately 15 women get together to make 1,400 to 1,800 veranika at the Corn Mennonite Brethren Church for the Oklahoma Relief Sale, in Fairview. Irene Penner, of Corn, provides the recipe.

Dough:
6 egg whites, slightly beaten
7 whole eggs, slightly beaten
1 tablespoon salt
1 cup whipping cream
1 pint half-and-half
1/2 cup milk
1 1/2 quarts flour

Filling:
5 to 7 pounds dry cottage cheese
6 egg yolks, slightly beaten
1 whole egg, slightly beaten
Salt and pepper to taste
A little whipping cream

Make a soft dough by mixing all ingredients together. Roll flat and cut with something round. (We use a 1-pound coffee can.) Then stretch dough some and place a full tablespoon of cottage cheese filling a little off center; fold dough over, pinching edges together with fingers. Stand veranika up on cookie sheets with waxed paper squares between them and freeze, or cook fresh in boiling water or hot oil. Serve with onion cream gravy, made by sauteing onion pieces in a little butter and then adding sour cream, salt, and pepper. If gravy is too thick, thin with a little half-and-half or milk.

MAKES ABOUT 60 VERANIKA

Vereneki

This recipe is used to prepare vereneki for the Saskatchewan Relief Sale, at Saskatoon.

Dough:
About 3 cups flour
1 teaspoon baking powder
1 teaspoon salt
2 eggs
1/4 cup oil
1 cup milk

Filling:
1 pound dry cottage cheese
3 egg yolks
Salt and pepper to taste

To make dough, mix together dry ingredients; add eggs, oil, and milk. Mix until smooth, to form a soft dough. Roll out quite thin; cut into squares. Fill with cottage cheese filling.

♥ Spaghetti with Zucchini Sauce

1 large onion, chopped
1 tablespoon vegetable oil
6 cups sliced zucchini
3 cups fresh tomatoes or 1
    jar tomato sauce or
    whole canned tomatoes
1/2 teaspoon salt
1 bay leaf
1/4 teaspoon pepper
1/4 teaspoon basil
1/4 teaspoon oregano

Saute onion in oil. Add zucchini, tomatoes, and seasonings. Simmer, covered, for 15 minutes. Uncover; simmer 10 minutes. Discard bay leaf. Serve sauce over cooked spaghetti; sprinkle grated Parmesan cheese over sauce.

MCC Quilt Auction and Relief Sale, Johnstown

♥ Zucchini Quiche

3 cups grated zucchini
1 onion, chopped
1 cup Bisquick baking mix
4 eggs, beaten
1/2 cup vegetable oil
1/2 cup grated Parmesan
    cheese
1 teaspoon parsley
1/4 teaspoon salt

Mix all ingredients well. Pour into greased 9-inch pie pan. Bake for 30 minutes, or until brown.

Grace Cable, Hollsopple, Pennsylvania
MCC Quilt Auction and Relief Sale, Johnstown

♥ Zucchini Crescent Pie

4 cups unpeeled, thinly
    sliced zucchini
1 cup diced onion
1/2 cup margarine
2 tablespoons dried parsley
1/2 teaspoon salt
1/2 teaspoon pepper
1/4 teaspoon garlic powder
1/4 teaspoon basil leaves
1/4 teaspoon oregano leaves
2 eggs, well beaten
2 cups shredded mozzarella
    cheese
1 can (8 oz) refrigerator
    crescent dinner rolls
2 teaspoons mustard

Saute zucchini and onion in margarine 10 minutes. Stir in spices. Combine eggs and cheese; stir in zucchini mixture. Line a pie plate with the crescent roll dough (or use your own pie dough). Bake crust at 375°F for about 10 minutes. Remove from oven; spread mustard over crust. Pour in zucchini-egg mixture. Return to oven and bake 18 to 20 minutes. If crust begins to brown too quickly, cover pie with foil the last few minutes. Let stand 10 minutes before slicing.

Serves 4 to 6

Barb Yoder, Freeman, South Dakota
Minn-Kota MCC Relief Sale, Sioux Falls, S. Dakota

♥ Easy Garden Vegetable Pie

Susana Siemens, of Winnipeg, Manitoba, shares this easy recipe for a quick lunch that doesn't need a crust.

2 cups sliced fresh broccoli
    or cauliflower
1/2 cup chopped onion
1/2 cup chopped green
    pepper
1 cup (about 4 oz) shredded
    Cheddar cheese
1 1/2 cups milk
3 eggs
3/4 cup Bisquick baking mix
1 teaspoon salt
1/4 teaspoon pepper

Heat oven to 400°F. Lightly grease a 1-1/2 inch-deep 10-inch pie pan. Heat 1 inch salted water to a boil. Add broccoli, cover, and heat to boiling. Cook until almost tender (about 5 minutes). Drain thoroughly. Mix broccoli, onion, green pepper, and cheese in pie pan. Place milk, eggs, baking mix, and salt and pepper in blender container. Blend for 15 seconds; pour over vegetables. Bake 35 to 40 minutes, or until golden brown. Test for doneness by inserting knife in center of quiche; it's done when knife comes out clean. Let stand for a few minutes before cutting.

Note: One package (10 oz) frozen chopped broccoli or cauliflower, thawed and drained, can be substituted for the fresh vegetable. Do not cook frozen vegetable.

Kielka

3 cups flour
2 tablespoons salt
3 eggs
1/2 cup milk

Onion Gravy:
Chopped or sliced onions
Lard or oil
1/2 cup cream
1 cup milk (less or more for
a thicker or thinner
gravy)
Salt and pepper to taste

Mix first four ingredients together to make a dough. With scissors, snip into small pieces. Put into boiling water and cook for a few minutes. Serve hot with onion gravy.

To make gravy, brown onion in a little grease. Add cream and milk; season with salt and pepper. Bring to a boil. Pour over the hot kielka.

Irene Penner, Corn, Oklahoma
Olkahoma MCC Relief Sale, Fairview

Make-Ahead Potatoes

5 pounds potatoes
8 ounces cream cheese,
    softened
8 ounces sour cream
1 teaspoon onion flakes
Milk
1/4 cup melted margarine

Peel potatoes; boil in salted water; drain. Add cream cheese, sour cream, and onion flakes. Mash or whip, adding enough milk for the desired consistency. Spread in a buttered 9x13-inch pan; refrigerate or freeze until needed. When ready to use, drizzle melted margarine over top. Bake at 350°F for 1 hour.

Nancy Steele
Missouri MCC Relief Sale, Harrisonville

Mashed Potatoes

15 pounds potatoes
1 1/2 quarts scalded milk
1/4 cup salt
1/4 cup butter or margarine

Pare potatoes; wash and boil until tender. Mash until smooth. Add milk, salt, and butter. Beat until light and fluffy.

SERVES 50

Martha Tschetter, Freeman, South Dakota
Minn-Kota MCC Relief Sale, Sioux Falls, S. Dakota

Hash Brown Potatoes

2 pounds frozen hash brown
    potatoes
1 pint half-and-half
1 cup shredded Cheddar
    cheese
1/2 pound Velveeta pro-
    cessed cheese, shredded
1/4 cup (half a stick) butter
    or margarine

Spread hash browns in a large casserole. In a saucepan, heat half-and-half and cheeses until cheeses melt. Pour mixture over hash browns. Let set 1 hour. Dot with butter and bake for 1 hour at 350°F.

Iris Frank
East Peoria Mennonite Church
Illinois MCC Relief Sale, Peoria

Hashed Brown Potato Casserole

This recipe has been served at the Minn-Kota Relief Sale board meeting. Its contributor notes that any leftovers are delicious reheated.

2 pounds chunky frozen
    hashed brown potatoes,
    thawed
2 cups shredded Cheddar
    cheese
1 stick (1/2 cup) butter,
    melted
1 pint sour cream
1 can (10 3/4 oz) cream of
    chicken soup
2/3 cup chopped onion
Salt and pepper

Topping:
3 cups cornflakes
1/4 cup melted butter

Thoroughly mix all casserole ingredients in a large bowl. Season as desired with salt and pepper. Spread in a 9x13-inch buttered baking pan. Bake at 350°F for 30 minutes. Mix cornflakes and melted butter for topping; spread over casserole. Return to oven and continue baking, uncovered, about 30 minutes more.

Super Duper Potatoes

This recipe is prepared for the Relief Sale board meeting.

9 medium potatoes
1/4 cup grated or finely
  diced onion (use less or
  more to taste)
8 ounces shredded Cheddar
  cheese
2 cups half-and-half
1/2 cup butter
1 teaspoon salt

Scrub potatoes and cook until tender; cool. Peel and then grate potatoes. Spread in buttered 9x13-inch baking pan, mixing in grated onion. Top with cheese. Heat half-and-half, butter, and salt until butter melts. Pour over potatoes. Bake at 350°F for 1 hour. This dish reheats very well in the microwave.

Amy Hofer, Carpenter, South Dakota
Minn-Kota MCC Relief Sale, Sioux Falls,
South Dakota

New Idea in Scalloped Potatoes

6 medium potatoes
1 cup grated cheese
1 cup diced ham
2 tablespoons flour
1 1/2 teaspoons salt
1 tablespoon dried onion
  soup mix
2 cups hot milk
2 tablespoons catsup
1/2 teaspoon Worcestershire
  sauce
2 tablespoons butter

Pare potatoes and cut into thin slices. Place half the potatoes in a buttered 2-quart casserole. Sprinkle with a third of the cheese, ham, and combined flour, salt, and onion soup mix. Top with remaining potatoes, and then remaining cheese, ham, and seasoning mix.

Combine milk, catsup, and Worcestershire sauce; pour over potatoes. Dot with butter. Cover and bake 1 hour at 350°F, uncovering during last 15 minutes of baking to brown top.

SERVES 6 TO 8

Ardith Epp, Henderson, Nebraska
Nebraska MCC Relief Sale, Aurora

Scalloped Potatoes

This recipe was served for a few years at the annual kickoff dinner preceding the Minn-Kota Relief Sale.

1 cup butter
3/4 cup flour
3 quarts milk
2 cans mushroom soup
20 pounds potatoes
1 onion, minced

Melt butter, add flour, and stir in milk to make a white sauce. Stir in soup, and cook until heated through.

Meanwhile, slice potatoes and onion. Layer in greased roaster. Pour hot sauce over potatoes. Bake at 350°F for 1 hour; then reduce temperature to 250°F to finish.

S*erves* 50

Martha Tschetter, Freeman, South Dakota
Minn-Kota MCC Relief Sale, Sioux Falls, S. Dakota

Amish Potatoes

3 tablespoons butter
8 potatoes, cooked and
**   sliced**
1 1/2 cups half-and-half
Salt and pepper

Melt butter in skillet; add sliced potatoes and brown slightly. Add half-and-half and simmer until potatoes absorb the cream. Add salt and pepper to taste.

Note: You can also cook the potatoes and half-and-half in a crock pot.

Norma Thomas, Hollsopple, Pennsylvania
MCC Quilt Auction and Relief Sale, Johnstown

Potato Patties

10 large potatoes
2 eggs, well beaten
1 heaping tablespoon flour
1/2 teaspoon salt
Vegetable oil or shortening
    for frying
Sour cream

Peel and grind potatoes. Stir in eggs, flour, and salt. Place by tablespoonful into a heated skillet (to which a small amount of oil has been added), flattening each one with the spoon as you add it to the skillet. Cook until brown on both sides. Serve with sour cream.

Vesta Schmidt, Mountain Lake, Minnesota
Minn-Kota MCC Relief Sale, Sioux Falls, S. Dakota

French Fried Mashed Potato Balls

1 cup mashed potatoes
1/2 cup flour
1 teaspoon salt
1 teaspoon baking powder
2 eggs, well beaten
1/2 cup freshly grated
    Parmesan cheese

Mix all ingredients together. Drop by tablespoon into a deep fryer. Fry until golden brown. Drain on absorbent paper.

Sally Ann Reddecliff, Johnstown, Pennsylvania
MCC Quilt Auction and Relief Sale, Johnstown

Baked Potatoes with Choice of Topping

About 400 of these potatoes--200 a day--are sold at the Minn-Kota Relief Sale each year. A choice of two toppings is offered.

The evening before the sale, about a dozen volunteers gather at the church to wash and wrap the potatoes and put them in bags of 50 so volunteers can take them home to bake. The ladies also dice the ham (keeping it chilled overnight), and grind and fry the bacon ends. In addition, they prepare 1-gallon batches of the white sauce, cool it, and store it, chilled, in ice cream pails overnight. At the sale, volunteers cook the frozen vegetables and finish assembling the broccoli-cheese sauce.

400 russet baking potatoes (about 175 pounds)

Cheese-Broccoli and Ham Topping (for 200 potatoes):
22 pounds diced ham
2 gallons white sauce, made in 1-gallon batches from:
    1 gallon milk
    1 pound butter
    2 cups cornstarch
    3 tablespoons salt
    1/2 teaspoon white pepper
2 gallons mild cheese sauce
4 pounds frozen California blend vegetables
6 pounds frozen chopped broccoli

Sour Cream and Bacon Topping (for 200 potatoes):
20 pounds bacon ends (or substitute commercial bacon bits)
4 cartons (16 oz each) sour cream

To Prepare Potatoes:
Wash potatoes, but do not prick. Wrap each one in aluminum foil. Bake 50 potatoes at a time in oven at 350°F for 2 hours. (Or bake about 35 potatoes at a time in a roaster for 4 hours at 350°F; rotate potatoes and make sure there is water at the bottom of the roaster.)

To Prepare Cheese-Broccoli and Ham Topping:
Heat ham in roaster for 2 hours.

In separate large double boilers, cook ingredients for two 1-gallon batches of white sauce. Divide chopped frozen vegetables evenly between two roasters; cook, covered, in a little water until tender. Add 1 gallon prepared white sauce and 1 gallon cheese sauce to each roaster. Stir well to mix. Keep hot in roasters.

To serve, place 1 heaping tablespoon ham on each split potato. Cover with 1/2 cup cheese-broccoli sauce. Sprinkle with paprika.

To Prepare Sour Cream-Bacon Topping
Grind the bacon ends and fry until crisp. Drain. (As an alternative, you can use purchased bacon bits.)

To serve, spoon sour cream over split potatoes and top with about 1 tablespoon crisp bacon bits.

Alma Wollman, Freeman, South Dakota
Minn-Kota MCC Relief Sale, Sioux Falls, S. Dakota

Apricot-Glazed Sweet Potatoes

3 pounds sweet potatoes, cooked, peeled, and cut up
1 cup firmly packed brown sugar
5 teaspoons cornstarch
1/4 teaspoon salt
1/8 teaspoon ground cinnamon
1 cup apricot nectar
1/2 cup hot water
2 teaspoons grated orange peel
2 teaspoons butter or margarine
1/2 cup chopped pecans

Place sweet potatoes in a 13x9x3-inch baking dish and set aside. In a saucepan, combine sugar, cornstarch, and cinnamon. Stir in apricot nectar, water, and orange peel. Bring to a boil, stirring constantly. Cook and stir 2 minutes more. Remove from heat. Stir in butter and nuts. Pour over sweet potatoes. Bake, uncovered at 350°F for 20 to 25 minutes, or until heated through.

Serves 8 to 10

*Virginia Gindlesperger, Johnstown, Pennsylvania
MCC Quilt Auction and Relief Sale, Johnstown*

Apricot Sweet Potatoes

1 cup brown sugar
1 1/2 tablespoons cornstarch
1 teaspoon grated orange peel
1/4 teaspoon salt
1/8 teaspoon cinnamon
1 can (5 1/2 oz) apricot nectar
1/3 cup water
2 tablespoons butter
1 can (18 oz) sweet potatoes, drained
12 frozen (or 1 can) apricots
1/2 cup pecans (optional)

Mix sugar, cornstarch, orange peel, salt, and cinnamon in a heavy 1-quart saucepan. Stir in apricot nectar and the water. Cook, stirring, on high heat until mixture comes to a full rolling boil. Stir in butter.

Layer sweet potatoes and apricots in a greased casserole. Pour hot sauce over. Sprinkle with pecans if desired. Bake uncovered at 375°F for 25 minutes or until hot and bubbly.

Serves 8

*Elizabeth M. Loewen, Mountain Lake, Minnesota
Minn-Kota MCC Relief Sale, Sioux Falls,
South Dakota*

Crispy Onion Rings

3 large onions, cut into 1- to
    2-inch-thick rounds
1 cup all-purpose flour
1/2 cup cornstarch
1 teaspoon baking soda
1/2 teaspoon salt
1 1/2 cups ice water

Separate onions into rings; soak in a bowl of ice water for 2 hours. Make batter by combining flour, cornstarch, baking soda, and salt in a large bowl. Add the 1 1/2 cups ice water to the dry ingredients all at once; whisk until batter is smooth. Refrigerate for at least 1 hour before using.

Heat oil in fryer to 375°F. Place drained onion rings in batter; toss to coat each one well. Drop rings one by one into fryer. Fry, turning once, until golden brown (3 to 4 minutes). Drain well on paper towels. Sprinkle with a little salt or lemon pepper seasoning and serve hot. Serve as is, or accompany with your favorite mustard, tomato ketchup, or salsa.

Sally Ann Reddecliff, Johnstown, Pennsylvania
MCC Quilt Auction and Relief Sale, Johnstown

Baked Beans

1 large can (2 1/2 lbs) lima
    beans
1 medium onion, chopped
Half a medium green
    pepper, chopped
1/2 cup brown sugar
About 1/3 bottle catsup
8 strips bacon

Place beans, onion, and green pepper in a casserole dish, mixing well. Blend brown sugar and catsup; stir into bean mixture. Fry bacon; break into pieces and stir into beans. Bake at 300°F for 1 1/2 to 2 hours.

Ruth Beckley Felix
MCC Quilt Auction and Relief Sale, Johnstown,
Pennsylvania

Baked Beans

About 20 gallons of this recipe are made and sold at the Minn-Kota Relief Sale in Sioux Falls, South Dakota, according to Martha Tschetter, of Freeman.

5 gallons canned pork and
   beans, drained
1/2 gallon catsup
1 1/2 pounds brown sugar
1/2 can dry mustard
1 1/2 pounds diced bacon,
   fried until crisp

Mix all ingredients in a roaster. Bake at medium temperature until heated through (about 1 to 2 hours).

MAKES 150 HALF-CUP SERVINGS

Baked Beans

As part of the annual chicken barbecue dinner prepared on the Oscoda County Fairgrounds at Fairview, where the Northern Michigan Relief Sale is held the first Saturday in August, volunteers make six batches of these beans--enough for about 700 dinners. Sherry Troyer, who has served on the Chicken Dinner Committee, shares this recipe.

4 cans (No. 10 size) great
   northern beans (drained)
5 cups brown sugar
Half a can (No. 10 size)
   ketchup
Half a can (46 oz) tomato
   soup
1 1/2 cups dried onion
2 1/2 pounds bacon, fried
   and crumbled (or diced
   ham)

In a large pan or roaster (we use a steam-table pan), combine all ingredients, mixing well. Refrigerate overnight.

Bake at 350°F for 3 to 4 hours. (For an 11:30 AM dinner, begin baking at about 7:30 AM.)

MAKES 100 TO 120 SERVINGS

♥ *Glazed Carrots*

This recipe from Adella (Stutzman) Gingrich, of Albany, Oregon, was served at an Oregon MCC Fall Festival Workers' Appreciation dinner, where it was given high marks.

**1 pound carrots (scraped and
   sliced on the diagonal)
1/4 cup butter
1/2 cup brown sugar**

Cook carrots in a small amount of water until tender-crisp; drain. Meanwhile, in a separate kettle, melt butter; stir in sugar until well blended. Add carrots. Cook, stirring frequently, until syrup comes to a boil (about 10 minutes) and carrots are evenly coated/glazed.

Alternate method: Carrots may also be put in a baking dish and baked at 300°F for 30 to 45 minutes, stirring every 10 minutes to coat evenly.

Carrot Casserole

**1 pound carrots
1/2 cup chopped onion
1 cup diced celery
2 tablespoons margarine
8 cups cubed bread
1 teaspoon parsley flakes
1 1/2 teaspoons salt
3/4 cup melted margarine
2 eggs, well beaten**

Peel and dice carrots; cook in water until very soft. Drain; mash very fine. Saute onion and celery in the 2 tablespoons margarine. Place bread cubes in a large bowl; mix in sauteed onion-celery mixture, parsley, salt, and melted margarine. Stir in eggs and mashed carrots. Turn into 1 1/2-quart casserole. Bake at 350°F for 30 minutes or more.

*Amy Cable, Hollsopple, Pennsylvania
MCC Quilt Auction and Relief Sale,
Johnstown, Pennsylvania*

Barbecued Green Beans

2 strips bacon, diced
2 tablespoons chopped
   onion
1 can (14 1/2 oz) green beans,
   drained
1/4 cup catsup
2 tablespoons brown sugar
1 1/2 teaspoons
   Worcestershire sauce

Brown bacon and onion in small skillet. Combine with beans in a casserole dish. Mix remaining ingredients; simmer 2 minutes. Pour over bean mixture. Bake at 350°F for 20 to 30 minutes.

Betty Albrecht, Marion, South Dakota
Minn-Kota MCC Relief Sale, Sioux Falls,
South Dakota

Green Beans Au Gratin

4 cups green beans
1 can (10 3/4 oz) Cheddar
   cheese soup
1 small can (2.8 oz)
   French-fried onions

In a buttered casserole dish, layer beans and soup (do *not* dilute). Arrange onions on top. Bake at 300°F for about 20 minutes.

Sally Ann Reddecliff, Johnstown, Pennsylvania
MCC Quilt Auction and Relief Sale, Johnstown

♥ Vegetable Casserole

2 cups chopped celery
2 cups chopped green beans
1 1/2 cups chopped carrots
2 cups chopped tomatoes
1/2 cup diced onion
1/4 cup butter
2 tablespoons (scant) sugar
3 tablespoons Minute
   tapioca

Mix all ingredients thoroughly. Place in 2-quart casserole. Bake at 350°F for 1 1/2 hours.

Mianna Geissinger, Mountain Lake, Minnesota
Minn-Kota MCC Relief Sale, Sioux Falls, South
Dakota

Broccoli Hot Dish

1 package frozen broccoli
1 can water chestnuts, sliced
  thin
1 large container (16 oz) sour
  cream
1 package dried onion soup
  mix
3/4 cup butter
Crushed soda crackers

Cook broccoli in a little water just until thawed; drain. Place in 9x9-inch baking dish; add water chestnuts, mixing well. Combine sour cream and onion soup mix; mix well with vegetables. Melt butter in small skillet; add crushed crackers and saute until heated through. Spread over broccoli casserole. Bake at 350°F for 30 minutes.

Serves 6 to 8

Mrs. Kathy Graber, Freeman, South Dakota
Minn-Kota MCC Relief Sale, Sioux Falls,
South Dakota

♥ Sweet-Sour Cabbage (Gadaemftes Kraut)

1 large onion, chopped
3 tablespoons shortening
1/3 cup sugar
1/3 cup white vinegar
1 to 2 teaspoons salt
1/3 cup water
8 cups shredded cabbage

In a large frying pan, saute onion in shortening until slightly golden. Add sugar, vinegar, salt, and water. Blend well. Slowly add cabbage. Cover and cook over medium heat until cabbage is tender (about 20 to 25 minutes).

Serves 8 to 12

Lahae Waltner, Freeman, South Dakota
Minn-Kota MCC Relief Sale, Sioux Falls,
South Dakota

♥ *Quick 'n Easy Sweet-Sour Cabbage*

2 tablespoons shortening
    (lard)
1 large onion, chopped
2 tablespoons vinegar
2 tablespoons water
1 head cabbage, finely cut (3
    to 4 cups)
1 teaspoon salt
1/2 teaspoon sugar
Large dash pepper

Heat shortening; add onion and saute until clear. Add vinegar and water. Let cook 2 to 3 minutes. Add cabbage, stirring well to blend with onion mixture. Mix in salt, sugar, and pepper. Cook about 5 minutes, stirring constantly, until cabbage is hot but still crunchy. (Add more salt if desired.)

Serves 3 or 4

Bernice Stucky, Freeman, South Dakota
Minn-Kota MCC Relief Sale, Sioux Falls,
South Dakota

♥ *Sauce for Broccoli*

1 cup water
1 teaspoon cornstarch
1 lump butter
1 tablespoon lemon juice
1 tablespoon onion juice

Combine some of the water with the cornstarch to make a smooth paste. Place remainder of the water in a saucepan; add butter and lemon and onion juices. Bring to a boil, stir in cornstarch paste gradually, and simmer until moderately thickened (10 to 15 minutes). Serve over cooked broccoli.

Makes 1 cup

Sally Ann Reddecliff, Johnstown, Pennsylvania
MCC Quilt Auction and Relief Sale, Johnstown

Corn on the Cob

Here's a hint for serving corn on the cob to a large group. It's quick, simple, and there's no waste. Melt butter in a microwave-safe dish large enough to roll an ear of corn in. Everyone butters their own ears.

Erma Kauffman, Cochranville, Pennsylvania
Gap Relief Sale, Pennsylvania

Corn Casserole

1 can cream-style corn
1 can whole-kernel corn
1 stick (1/2 cup) margarine,
    melted
1 cup sour cream
1 box Jiffy cornbread muffin
    mix
2 eggs, beaten

Thoroughly mix all ingredients. Pour into a 9x13-inch baking pan. Bake at 350°F for 30 minutes.

Winifred Saner, Freeman, South Dakota
Minn-Kota MCC Relief Sale, Sioux Falls,
South Dakota

Chicken/Turkey Salad

3 cups chopped cooked
   chicken or turkey
2 cups ring macaroni, cooked
2 cups frozen peas, cooked
   and cooled
1/4 cup sliced almonds
1/4 cup sliced stuffed olives
1/4 cup chopped sweet pickles
1 cup finely chopped celery
1/4 cup ground onion
2 hard-cooked eggs, chopped
1/2 to 3/4 teaspoon salt
1/4 teaspoon pepper
2 cups canned shoestring
   potatoes

Dressing:
2 to 3 cups salad dressing
1/2 cup sour cream

Combine all ingredients except shoestring potatoes and dressing; mix well. (You can do this up to a day ahead.)

To serve, mix salad dressing and sour cream; combine with salad ingredients. Stir in shoestring potatoes immediately before serving.

SERVES 12 TO 16

Rita Ann Graber, Freeman, South Dakota
Minn-Kota MCC Relief Sale, Sioux Falls,
South Dakota

Taco Salad

20 pounds ground beef
1 gallon tomato sauce
4 cups taco seasoning
1 case taco chips
6 heads lettuce, shredded
6 quarts sliced tomatoes
5 pounds shredded cheese

Cook meat until all traces of pink are gone; drain well. Add tomato sauce and taco seasoning; mix well. Cook until thoroughly heated; then remove from heat and cool.

To serve: Layer 1 cup crushed chips, 3/4 cup shredded lettuce, several slices tomato, 4 ounces taco-flavored meat, and 1 ounce cheese.

MAKES 80 SERVINGS

Bertha Stark, Freeman, South Dakota
Bethany Mennonite Church
Minn-Kota MCC Relief Sale, Sioux Falls, S. Dakota

Taco Salad

1 head lettuce, broken into
little pieces
1/2 pound ground beef, fried
and drained
1 small can red beans,
washed
Tomatoes
Corn chips
Grated cheese
French dressing

Toss all ingredients together. Serve.

Alpha Mae Mumaw
Yellow Creek Mennonite Church, Goshen, Indiana

Fruit Salad with Sweet Dressing

1 1/2 pounds pink grapes
1 large can pineapple rings
3 oranges
3 apples

Dressing:
1 tablespoon flour
1/2 cup sugar
1 cup scalded milk
1 egg, well beaten
1 tablespoon butter
1/2 pint whipping cream,
whipped

Halve and seed grapes. Dice pineapple. Peel
and dice oranges and apples. Combine fruits;
set aside.

To make dressing: In a heavy saucepan,
combine flour and sugar. Add scalded milk
and bring to a slow boil. Stir in beaten egg
and butter; cool. Fold in whipped cream.

Just before serving, pour dressing over
drained fruit mixture. Toss gently to mix.

Ruth Beckley Felix
MCC Quilt Auction and Relief Sale, Johnstown,
Pennsylvania

Creamy Waldorf Salad

2 packages (3 oz each)
    lemon-flavored gelatin
2 cups boiling water
1 cup cold water
1 package (3 1/2 oz) instant
    vanilla pudding mix
2 cups milk
1 cup diced apples
1/2 cup chopped celery
1/2 cup chopped nuts

Prepare lemon-flavored gelatin, using the boiling and cold water. Let set until partly set. Also prepare pudding mix, using the milk; cool.

Mix gelatin and pudding together. Add apples, celery, and nuts. Chill well before serving.

Amy Cable, Hollsopple, Pennsylvania
MCC Quilt Auction and Relief Sale, Johnstown

Coconut Fruit Bowl

2 1/2 cups drained pineapple
    tidbits
1 1/3 cups drained mandarin
    oranges
1 cup seedless grapes
1 cup miniature marshmal-
    lows
1 can (3 1/2 oz) flaked
    coconut
2 cups sour cream
1/4 teaspoon salt

Combine pineapple, oranges, grapes, marshmallows, and coconut. Gently stir in sour cream and salt. Chill overnight.

Serves 8

Mrs. Charles Kreider, Sterling, Illinois
Science Ridge Mennonite Church
Illinois Mennonite Relief Sale, Peoria

Apple Overnight Salad

This dish was featured at the salad bar booth of the Minn-Kota Relief Sale in Sioux Falls, South Dakota.

1/2 cup lemon juice
1 cup sugar
4 eggs, well beaten
6 unpeeled apples, diced
1 can (20 oz) crushed pine-
    apple, drained
2 cups ring macaroni,
    cooked
1 large container nondairy
    whipped topping,
    thawed

In top of double boiler, combine lemon juice, sugar, and beaten eggs; cook over boiling water until thick. Cool. Stir in fruit and macaroni. Refrigerate 12 to 24 hours. When ready to serve, fold in whipped topping.

Ruby Waltner and Janelle Ortman, Marion,
South Dakota

 Cranberry Fruit Medley

This is a traditional holiday favorite!

2 cups fresh cranberries
2 medium to large apples
    (cored but not peeled)
2 medium to large bananas
3/4 cup granulated sugar

Coarsely chop cranberries and apples. Dice bananas; add to cranberry-apple mixture along with sugar. Stir well. Place in refrigerator, covered tightly, for at least 3 hours or overnight to blend flavors.

Makes 6 servings

Variation: Add 2 cups miniature marshmallows with the fruit; Just before serving, stir in 1 cup whipped topping.

Faye Claassen, Albany
Oregon MCC Fall Festival, Albany

♥ Tasty Apple Salad

2 cups diced apples
Orange or pineapple juice
   (enough to cover apples)
2 cups diced celery
2 cups diced carrots
2 cups raisins
1 cup unsalted, dry-roasted
   peanuts (broken into
   halves)
1 cup unsalted sunflower
   seeds
Yogurt (plain or
   vanilla-flavored)

Dice apples directly into enough fruit juice to cover them, to prevent browning. Let sit while dicing, measuring, and preparing remaining salad ingredients.

Drain juice from apples. Combine with remaining ingredients, using enough yogurt to form a dressing.

Mianna Geissinger, Mountain Lake, Minnesota
Minn-Kota MCC Relief Sale, Sioux Falls,
South Dakota

Hot Slaw

1 cup finely diced celery
1 medium head cabbage,
   shredded
3 tablespoons solid veg-
   etable shortening or
   margarine
Dash salt
2 teaspoons flour
1 tablespoon sugar
1 tablespoon vinegar
2 tablespoons sour cream

In a small saucepan, cook celery in a little water. Place cabbage in a large skillet; pour celery and water over top. Add shortening and salt. Cover and steam 10 minutes. Sprinkle flour over top; stir to mix well with cabbage. Also stir in sugar and vinegar. If sauce is too thin, add a bit more flour. Stir in sour cream. Cook 2 minutes.

Mary Kaufman, Johnstown, Pennsylvania
MCC Quilt Auction and Relief Sale, Johnstown

♥ Cole Slaw

Ten batches of this slaw are made for about 700 dinners during the annual chicken barbecue dinner on the Oscoda County Fairgrounds for the Northern Michigan Relief Sale, held in August in Fairview.

2 gallons shredded cabbage
1 quart shredded carrots
1 cup diced green pepper

Relief Sale Salad Dressing:
2 1/2 cups sugar
1 1/2 cups vinegar
4 teaspoons dry mustard
4 teaspoons salt
1 cup salad oil
4 teaspoons grated onion
1 tablespoon celery seed

Combine the vegetables in a large bowl; mix well. To prepare dressing, dissolve sugar in vinegar; add remaining ingredients. Mix well by hand or in a blender. Pour dressing over vegetables; toss to mix thoroughly. Refrigerate until ready to serve.

MAKES 70 SERVINGS (4 CUPS DRESSING)

Sherry Troyer, Mio, Michigan
(Chicken Dinner Committee)

♥ Cole Slaw

40 cups shredded cabbage
6 carrots, grated fine
6 stalks celery, cut fine
1 onion, minced
1 green pepper, chopped
4 cups salad oil

Dressing:
6 cups sugar
4 cups vinegar
4 envelopes (1 oz each) Knox
    unflavored gelatine
4 teaspoons salt
4 teaspoons celery salt
1 cup water

Combine vegetables; pour salad oil over and toss to mix. Combine dressing ingredients; boil briefly. Let cool. Pour over vegetables and toss to mix everything well.

SERVES 100

Martha Tschetter, Freeman, South Dakota
Minn-Kota MCC Relief Sale, Sioux Falls,
South Dakota

♥ Tangy Slaw

This salad is passed around the table during Minn-Kota Relief Sale board meeting dinners. It keeps well.

10 cups shredded cabbage
1 1/2 cups chopped green
　　pepper
1 1/2 cups shredded carrot
1/4 cup chopped onion

Dressing:
1 cup salad oil
1/4 cup vinegar
1/2 cup sugar
1/2 teaspoon salt
1/4 teaspoon pepper

Combine vegetables in a bowl; toss to mix well. Mix dressing ingredients in a small bowl. Add to cabbage about half an hour before serving; toss to mix.

Pam Hofer, Carpenter, South Dakota

Napa Cabbage Salad

1 cup slivered almonds
1 small box sesame seeds
1 package (3 oz) flavored
　　Ramen noodles, broken
　　into pieces
1 head Napa cabbage
1 bunch green onions
1 green pepper

Dressing:
3/4 cup salad oil
1/4 cup sugar
6 tablespoons vinegar
1/2 teaspoon pepper

In dry frying pan over medium heat, toast almonds, sesame seeds, and broken-up noodles until golden. Meanwhile, chop cabbage, onions, and green pepper; toss to combine. Mix dressing ingredients and pour over vegetables, tossing to coat. To serve, spoon dry toasted ingredients over cabbage mixture.

Yvonne Schmidt, Freeman, South Dakota
Minn-Kota MCC Relief Sale, Sioux Falls,
South Dakota

Oriental Salad

1 to 2 heads Napa cabbage
2 to 3 bunches green onions
2 packages (3 oz each)
    Ramen noodles
Butter
1 package (2.25 oz) sliced
    almonds
1/3 jar sesame seeds
1/2 cup sugar
3/4 cup oil
3/4 cup vinegar
2 tablespoons soy sauce

Chop cabbage and onions. Crumble 1 package of the Ramen noodles and mix with cabbage and onions. Set aside.

In a frying pan, melt some butter. Add almonds, sesame seeds, and remaining package noodles; brown.

In a small saucepan, mix sugar, oil, vinegar, and soy sauce; add browned almond mixture. Heat to boiling; pour over cabbage mixture. Toss well to mix.

Variation: Chop a few stalks celery and add to cabbage-green onion mixture.

Sharon Dirst
East Peoria Mennonite Church
Illinois Mennonite Relief Sale, Peoria

Potato Salad

Women prepare this recipe in their homes and serve about 20 gallons of it at the Minn-Kota Relief Sale in Sioux Falls, South Dakota.

10 pounds potatoes, boiled
    and sliced
2 dozen hard-cooked eggs,
    chopped
Finely cut celery (optional)
1 1/2 quarts salad dressing
1/2 cup sandwich spread
1/2 cup milk
1/4 cup minced onion
1/4 cup yellow prepared
    mustard
1/4 cup sugar
2 teaspoons salt

Mix all ingredients together. Let stand *at least* 3 hours (longer is better). If salad seems dry, add equal parts extra milk and salad dressing.

SERVES 50

Martha Tschetter, Freeman, South Dakota
Minn-Kota MCC Relief Sale, Sioux Falls,
South Dakota

Potato Salad

This recipe, originally by Clara Driver, of Waynesboro, is prepared in quantity for sale at the Virginia Relief Sale in Fisherville.

2 quarts potatoes, boiled, peeled, and shredded
4 hard-boiled eggs, diced or shredded
1/2 cup chopped onion
1/2 cup chopped celery
1/2 cup finely chopped pickles (or pickle relish)

Dressing:
3/4 cup mayonnaise
3/4 cup sugar
1/3 cup cider vinegar
1/2 cup evaporated milk
2 teaspoons prepared mustard
2 teaspoons salt

Mix all salad ingredients. Combine dressing ingredients; add to potato mixture.

Note: To make the quantity of salad sold at the Virginia Relief Sale, volunteers use: 8 bushels of potatoes, 30 dozen eggs, 12 pounds onions, 20 bunches celery, 3 gallons pickle relish, 6 gallons mayonnaise, 30 pounds sugar, 2 gallons cider vinegar, 32 cans evaporated milk, 1/2 gallon mustard, and 2 boxes salt.

Cornbread Salad

This salad is just as tasty the next day as it is the day it's made.

1 large onion, diced
4 tomatoes, diced
1 green pepper, diced
4 to 5 stalks celery, diced
2 cups cauliflower (broken into small pieces)
1 cup mayonnaise
1 tablespoon sugar
1 tablespoon sweet pickle relish
1 box Jiffy cornbread mix (bake the day before)

In a large bowl, toss vegetables to mix well. Combine mayonnaise, sugar, and relish; stir into vegetables. Just before serving, add cornbread, cut into bite-size pieces.

Joan Belsley, Morton, Illinois
Bethel Mennonite Church, Pekin
Illinois Mennonite Relief Sale, Peoria

Hot Mushroom Salad

1 tablespoon melted butter
1 pound fresh mushrooms,
    sliced
1 small onion, thinly sliced
1 green pepper, cut in thin
    strips
1 to 1 1/2 tablespoons soy
    sauce
1 to 1 1/2 tablespoons
    teriyaki sauce
Lettuce
3 slices bacon, cooked and
    crumbled

Combine all ingredients (except lettuce and bacon) in skillet or wok. Cook, stirring frequently, until mushrooms and onions are tender. Spoon onto lettuce; garnish with bacon. Serve immediately.

SERVES 4

Bev Kennell, Roanoke, Illinois
Cazenovia Mennonite Church

♥ Emma's Bean Salad

1/2 to 1 cup sugar
1/2 cup lemon juice
1 small can kidney beans,
    drained
1 small can lima beans,
    drained
1 small can yellow beans,
    drained
1 small can green beans,
    drained
1 1/2 cups chopped onion
1/2 cup chopped celery
1/2 cup chopped green
    pepper

Bring sugar and lemon juice to a boil. Remove from heat and cool slightly. Mix together remaining ingredients; pour dressing over. Toss well to coat all ingredients with dressing. Refrigerate overnight or longer.

Sally Ann Reddecliff, Johnstown
MCC Quilt Auction and Relief Sale, Johnstown

Broccoli Delight Salad

1 large bunch fresh broccoli,
    cut in pieces (4 to 5 cups)
1 cup raisins
1/4 cup diced red onion
    (optional)
10 strips bacon, fried and
    crumbled
1 cup sunflower seeds

Dressing:
3 or 4 tablespoons sugar
1/2 cup lite mayonnaise
1 tablespoon vinegar

Put washed, drained broccoli in large glass bowl. Add raisins, onion (if desired), bacon, and sunflower seeds. Mix dressing ingredients. Pour over salad. Chill before serving if desired.

SERVES 6

*Tillie Janzen, Mountain Lake, Minnesota
Minn-Kota MCC Relief Sale, Sioux Falls,
South Dakota*

♥ Raw Cauliflower and Broccoli Salad

About 3 gallons of this salad were sold each day as part of the salad bar booth offerings at the Minn-Kota Relief Sale, in Sioux Falls, South Dakota.

2 cups broccoli, broken into
    small pieces
2 cups cauliflower, broken
    into small pieces
1 cup frozen peas, thawed
1/2 cup chopped onion

Dressing:
3 tablespoons lemon juice
3 tablespoons vinegar
1 teaspoon salt
1/2 teaspoon sugar
1/4 teaspoon pepper

Combine salad ingredients; combine dressing ingredients. Pour dressing over salad. Let marinate in refrigerator at least 1 hour (preferably overnight). Stir well before serving.

*Mrs. Silas (Verlyn) Waltner, Marion,
South Dakota*

Salad Dressing

1/2 to 1 cup sugar (to taste)
1/2 to 1 cup vinegar (start
   with 1/2 cup; add more
   to taste if desired)
1 cup salad oil
1 can (10 3/4 oz) tomato soup
   (undiluted)
1 teaspoon dry mustard
1 teaspoon salt
1/2 teaspoon garlic powder
1 teaspoon celery seed
1 teaspoon pepper
1 clove (optional)

Combine all ingredients in a quart jar; shake well to combine. Store covered in the refrigerator.

Susana Siemens, Winnipeg, Manitoba
MCC Manitoba Relief Sale

Creamy Cole Slaw Dressing

This dressing, which has been served at the Oregon MCC Fall Festival workers' dinners, can be used with vegetables other than cabbage. It is especially tasty with a cabbage-apple salad. The recipe makes enough dressing for 1 medium head cabbage.

1 cup mayonnaise
1 cup cream (sweet or sour)
1/2 cup sugar
1/2 cup vinegar
Salt (to taste)

Mix all ingredients together well.

Adella (Stutzman) Gingrich, Albany, Oregon

Homemade French Dressing

A batch of this recipe dresses salads at the board meeting dinners for the Minn-Kota Relief Sale, held in Sioux Falls, South Dakota. The dressing keeps well in the refrigerator.

1/2 cup sugar
3/4 cup ketchup
1/4 cup vinegar
1 cup salad oil
1/4 cup water
1/2 teaspoon onion salt
1/2 teaspoon salt
1 teaspoon celery seed

Put all ingredients in a quart jar; shake very well. Or use a blender to mix all ingredients.

Pam Hofer, Carpenter, South Dakota

Salad Dressing

3/4 cup sugar
1/4 cup vinegar
1/2 cup salad oil
1 small onion, roughly
    chopped
1 teaspoon prepared mus-
    tard
1 teaspoon celery seed
1 teaspoon salt

Mix all ingredients in blender. Dressing keeps well in refrigerator.

Katie Wagler
Daviess County Relief Sale, Montgomery, Indiana

❖ *Snacks* ❖

Children were kept busy at the 1992 Michiana sale in Goshen, Ind. Some decorated and sold big cookies, others used a rope-making contraption to craft brightly colored rainbow rope belts. Children circulated through the auction crowds carrying cardboard boxes full of popcorn while others sold sodas.

-- Love in Action News, MCC.

Little Twister Flavored Pretzels

Trella Harshberger, of Johnstown, Pennsylvania, recommends these pretzels for snacking.

2 bags (1 lb, 2 oz each)
   pretzels
1 cup salad oil
1 package Hidden Valley
   Ranch salad dressing
   mix

Spread pretzels on cookie sheets. Combine oil and dressing mix. Pour over pretzels, mixing well to coat. Bake at 200°F for 1 hour, stirring and lifting pretzels every 15 minutes with a spatula so that oil is well distributed over entire batch.

MCC Quilt Auction and Relief Sale, Johnstown

Carmel Corn

This corn was sold at the children's booth at the Minn-Kota Relief Sale in Sioux Falls, South Dakota.

2 cups brown sugar
1 cup margarine
1/2 cup white corn syrup
2 teaspoons molasses
1 teaspoon salt
1/2 teaspoon baking soda
8 quarts popped corn

In a heavy saucepan, combine sugar, margarine, corn syrup, molasses, and salt. Bring to a boil; cook 5 minutes. Remove from heat and carefully stir in baking soda (mixture may foam up). Pour syrup over corn. Stir well to mix. Bake on cookie sheets in a 250°F oven for 1 hour, stirring every 15 minutes. Store in airtight container.

Ila Joette Waltner, Hurley, South Dakota

At the first Minn-Kota MCC Relief Sale in Sioux Falls, S.D., the concessionaire's sign had not been covered. As two young girls came from the popcorn booth and began hawking popcorn during the auction, Delsie Bartel noticed the sign "Nelson's Concessions" and asked, "For whom are you selling?" Somewhat unsure how to answer, the girls looked at each other and answered hesitantly, "For the Lord." Delsie bought some popcorn!
   — Submitted by Don Klassen, chairman of the Minn-Kota MCC Relief Sale

Carmel Popcorn

S. M. Miller, a teen from Pekin, Illinois, shares this recipe, which is a favorite at youth meetings and for linger-longer munching on Sunday evenings.

2 sticks (1 cup) butter or
　　margarine
2 cups brown sugar
1/2 cup white corn syrup
1 teaspoon salt
1 teaspoon baking soda
1/4 teaspoon cream of tartar
6 quarts popped corn

Mix together butter, sugar, and syrup. Bring to a rolling boil, reduce heat to low, and cook 5 minutes. Remove from heat. Add salt, soda, and cream of tartar; stir until foamy. Spread corn on cookie sheets; pour syrup evenly over. Bake at 200°F for 1 hour and 10 minutes, stirring three times during baking.

Illinois MCC Relief Sale, Peoria

Munch Mix

6 cups Cheerios
1/2 cup sugar
1/4 cup margarine
2 tablespoons corn syrup
1/4 teaspoon baking soda
8 ounces M&Ms

Place Cheerios in a 2-quart glass casserole; set aside. In a 1-quart glass bowl, combine sugar, margarine, and syrup. Microwave on full power 2 minutes, stirring once. Then microwave on low (30%) 3 minutes. Stir in soda. Pour syrup over cereal; toss to coat. Microwave on half-power (50%) 4 minutes. Spread on waxed paper to cool; add M&Ms.

Nila Kauffman
Pleasant View Mennonite Church,
Goshen, Indiana

Rhubarb Jam

4 cups finely chopped
    rhubarb
4 cups sugar
1 cup strawberries
1 package
    strawberry-flavored
    gelatin

In a heavy pan, stir rhubarb, sugar, and strawberries until thoroughly mixed. Place on heat, bring to a boil, and boil 15 minutes. Remove from heat; add gelatin, stirring until dissolved. Seal in sterilized jars.

Variations: For the strawberries and strawberry-flavored gelatin, substitute 1 cup crushed pineapple and 1 package pineapple-flavored gelatin. Or increase the rhubarb to 5 cups, and use 1 package of any flavor gelatin.

Marie Harder, Mountain Lake, Minnesota
Minn-Kota MCC Relief Sale, Sioux Falls,
South Dakota

Blueberry Rhubarb Jam

5 cups diced rhubarb
1 cup water
5 cups sugar
1 can blueberry pie filling
1 package (6 oz)
    raspberry-flavored
    gelatin
Half a package unflavored
    gelatine (Knox)

Cook rhubarb in the water until tender (10 minutes). Add sugar and cook 3 minutes longer, stirring constantly. Add pie filling and cook 8 minutes. Remove from heat and add flavored gelatin and unflavored gelatin (which has been softened in a bit of cold water). Stir until gelatin is completely dissolved. Pour into jars and seal.

Mrs. Helen Schmidt, Marion, South Dakota
Minn-Kota MCC Relief Sale, Sioux Falls,
South Dakota

Zucchini Jam

This recipe, shared by Mrs. Silas (Verlyn) Waltner, of Marion, South Dakota, is a big seller at the Minn-Kota Relief Sale in Sioux Falls.

**6 cups peeled, chopped
    zucchini**
6 cups sugar
1/4 cup lemon juice
1 cup crushed pineapple
**1 package (6 oz) flavored
    gelatin (orange, apricot,
    strawberry, or flavor of
    choice)**

In a large, heavy saucepan, mix together zucchini and sugar. Boil 15 minutes. Add lemon juice and pineapple; boil 8 minutes. Remove from heat and mix in flavored gelatin; stir well. Put into jars. Seal with wax, process, or freeze.

MAKES ABOUT 3 PINTS

Turtle Brand Dandelion Jelly

J. Wayne Beachy, of Midlothian, Virginia, has been making this jelly for more than 20 years. He sells it at First Mennonite Church of Richmond yard sales. Those who dare to try this different sort of jelly always return for more, and they encouraged Beachy to make some for the Virginia Relief Sale in Fisherville.

*   "Turtle Brand" is the Beachy family's trademark for anything they make in their kitchen and give to friends. It's Mr. Beachy's wife's nickname.*

To Prepare Jelly:

Pick 1 quart dandelion flowers. (Morning is the best time.) Rinse in cold water and remove stems.

Bring flowers to a boil in 2 quarts water; boil 3 minutes. Cool and strain, pressing petals with the fingers to extract all the juice. You may have to strain the juice several times to remove all small specks, etc. (I do.)

Measure the liquid. To 3 cups of dandelion liquid, add 2 tablespoons lemon juice and 1 package (1 3/4 oz) powdered fruit pectin. Bring to a boil. Add 5 1/2 cups sugar. Continue stirring. Bring to a boil, and boil hard for 2 1/2 minutes. Pour into jars and seal. Enjoy!

Jerry Yoder and Robert Fisher watch as Martha Troyer checks the apple butter. Mrs. Troyer has been in charge of the apple butter making at every Iowa MCC sale. She says it's important to have just the right amount of apples and sugar and oh, yes, the heat is very important. If it gets too hot it tastes burned.

(Photo by Frank and Ada Yoder)

Cider Apple Butter

Wash 4 gallons (about 20 lbs) Jonathan apples well; core but do not peel. Slice into eighths. Add 1 pound sugar per gallon of apples. Let sit overnight (8-12 hours) until juice forms.

Put apples and juice into a pressure cooker; cook 30 minutes at 10 pounds pressure. Put mixture through a food mill. Stir in 2 cans (12 oz each) frozen apple juice and 1 teaspoon cinnamon per gallon. Put on stove and cook over low heat. Can in pints or quarts.

Mary Wenger
Missouri MCC Relief Sale, Harrisonville

Pickles, Relishes & Sauces

Refrigerator Pickles

16 cups thinly sliced cucumbers
2 cups sliced onions
3 tablespoons salt
2 cups vinegar
4 cups sugar
1 teaspoon tumeric
1 teaspoon celery seed
1/2 teaspoon powdered alum

Mix together cucumbers, onions, and salt. Let stand 3 hours. Drain liquid from vegetables, squeezing to remove as much as possible.

Mix together remaining ingredients; pour over cucumbers. Mix well. Spoon pickles into jars. Keep in refrigerator.

Amy Cable, Hollsopple, Pennsylvania
MCC Quilt Auction and Relief Sale, Johnstown,
Pennsylvania

Grandma Hannah's Ready-to-Eat Pickles

7 cups thinly sliced cucumbers
1 tablespoon celery seed
1 tablespoon salt
1 cup sliced onions
1 cup sliced red or green
pepper (optional)
2 cups sugar
1 cup vinegar

Sprinkle cucumber slices with celery seed and salt. Let set 1/2 hour; drain. Add onions and, if desired, peppers. Mix together sugar and vinegar, stirring until sugar is dissolved (do not heat). Pour over drained vegetables. Pickles can be eaten immediately or stored in the refrigerator.

Carole Giagnocavo, Lancaster, Pennsylvania

"Heinz" Pickles

Bernice Schroll's pickle recipe is considered a family treasure. It was provided by her daughter N. Elizabeth Graber, of Wayland, Iowa.

7 pounds cucumbers
Alum (size of a walnut)

Soak cucumbers 3 days in salt brine strong enough to bear an egg. Then soak 3 days in clear water, changing the water each of the 3 mornings. Then take the alum, and pour boiling water over alum and cucumbers. Simmer 3 hours. Do not boil. (Note: May cut simmering time to 1 1/2 hours instead of 3.)

Pour simmering liquid right off. Have ready the following liquid, which has been brought to a boil:

2 1/2 pints vinegar
2 1/2 pounds sugar
1 ounce cassia buds
1 ounce celery seed
1 ounce whole allspice

Pour boiling liquid over cucumbers, which have been split. Leave in open jar for at least 5 weeks or until used. Or you may put up in quart jars.

Iowa MCC Relief Sale, Iowa City

Lime Pickles

7 pounds cucumbers
2 cups hydrated lime
2 gallons water
9 cups sugar
1 teaspoon celery seed
1 teaspoon mixed pickling
  spices
1 tablespoon or less pickling
  salt
2 quarts vinegar

Wash cucumbers well; slice 1/4 inch thick. Mix lime and water; pour over slices. Let stand 24 hours; stir occasionally very carefully with hands. Drain. Then wash cucumbers to remove lime residue, and soak in clear water for 3 to 6 hours.

Mix together sugar, celery seed, pickling spice, pickling salt, and vinegar. Drain cucumber slices; pour cold vinegar mixture over them. Let stand 12 hours. Then boil cucumbers in the vinegar mixture for 35 minutes, or until cucumbers begin to appear clear. Put in jars and seal.

Red Cinnamon Pickles

For this recipe, use large cucumbers that are beginning to turn "yellowish." Their flesh is lighter in color, which gives the pickles a better red color. Pare the cucumbers, remove seeds and pulp, and cut flesh into 1- to 1 1/2-inch chunks.

2 gallons cucumber chunks
2 cups lime
2 gallons water

Cooking brine:
1 cup vinegar
1 small bottle red food coloring
1 tablespoon alum
Water to cover

Pickling syrup:
4 cups vinegar
15 cups sugar
2 packages Red Hot cinna-
  mon candies
8 sticks cinnamon
4 cups water

Cover cucumber chunks with a solution of the lime and 2 gallons water. Soak for 24 hours. Drain and *rinse well.* Soak in cold water for 3 hours; drain.

Place cucumbers in a large kettle; add brine ingredients. Simmer 2 hours. Drain and *rinse thoroughly.*

Mix together syrup ingredients; bring to a boil (be sure candy is dissolved). Pour syrup over drained cucumbers. Let stand overnight. Drain and heat 3 mornings. On the third morning, pack in jars and seal. Put one cinnamon stick in each jar.

Nina Stutzman, Milford, Nebraska
Nebraska MCC Relief Sale, Aurora

Sweet=Sour Dill Pickles

These pickles are simple, but very good.

Medium-sized cucumbers
12 to 16 onion slices
2 stalks celery, quartered
8 heads fresh dill
4 cups sugar
1/2 cup pickling salt
1 quart vinegar
2 cups water

Wash freshly picked cucumbers; cut into chunks or 1/4-inch-thick slices (enough to fill 4 clean quart jars). To each jar, add 3 or 4 onion slices, 2 pieces celery, and 2 heads dill.

Dissolve sugar and salt in vinegar and water. Bring to a boil. Pour boiling liquid over cucumbers in jars; seal at once. Do not use for 30 days.

Anna Mae Roth, Milford, Nebraska
Nebraska MCC Relief Sale, Aurora

Crisp Pickle Slices

1 gallon medium cucumbers,
sliced quite thin
3/4 cup pickling salt dis-
solved in boiling water

Cooking brine:
6 cups water
2 cups vinegar
1 tablespoon alum
1 tablespoon tumeric

Pickling syrup:
1 1/2 cups vinegar
1 1/2 cups water
6 cups sugar
1 1/2 teaspoons dill seed
1 tablespoon pickling spice
1 tablespoon mustard seed

Cover cucumbers with the boiling water-salt solution. Let stand overnight. The next morning, drain and wash.

Combine ingredients for cooking brine. Add cucumbers and simmer 30 minutes. Drain and rinse.

Bring pickling syrup ingredients to a boil. Meanwhile, pack cucumber slices in jars. Pour boiling syrup over slices and seal immediately.

Mildred Hauder, Milford, Nebraska
Nebraska MCC Relief Sale, Aurora

Favorite Sweet Pickles

7 pounds medium-sized
    cucumbers
Boiling water to cover
1 quart vinegar
8 cups sugar
2 tablespoons pickling salt
2 tablespoons mixed pick-
    ling spice

Day 1: In the morning, wash cucumbers. Cover them with boiling water. Let stand 8 to 12 hours. Drain. *In the evening,* drain. Then cover with fresh boiling water.

Day 2: Repeat Day 1 procedures.

Day 3: Cut cucumbers in 14-inch-thick rings. Combine vinegar, sugar, salt, and spices. Bring to a boil. Pour over sliced cucumbers. Let stand 24 hours.

Day 4: Drain syrup; bring to a boil. Pour over cucumbers.

Day 5: Repeat Day 4 procedure.

Day 6: Drain syrup; bring to a boil. Add cucumber slices; bring to the boiling point. Pack into hot sterilized jars. Seal.

Dill Pickle Spears

4 to 5 quarts cucumbers, cut
    into spears
Ice water
Onion slices
Fresh dill heads *or* dried dill
    seed

Pickling syrup:
3 cups sugar
3 cups water
1 1/2 cups vinegar
1 tablespoon salt

Soak cucumber spears in ice water for 2 hours; drain. Pack spears into jars. To each jar, add a few onion slices and 1 head fresh dill or 1 to 1 1/2 teaspoons dill seed.

Bring syrup ingredients to a boil. Pour boiling syrup over cucumbers in jars; seal. Process in boiling-water bath for 10 minutes.

Stella Roth, Milford, Nebraska
Nebraska MCC Relief Sale, Aurora

Sweet Gherkins

5 quarts (about 7 lbs) small
(1 1/2 to 3 in. long)
cucumbers
1/2 cup salt
8 cups sugar
6 cups vinegar
3/4 teaspoon tumeric
2 teaspoons celery seed
2 teaspoons whole mixed
pickling spice
8 1-inch pieces stick cinnamon
1/2 teaspoon fennel (if
desired)
2 teaspoons vanilla (if
desired)

Wash cucumbers thoroughly. Stem end may be left on if desired.

First day: Morning—Cover cucumbers with boiling water. Let sit for 6 to 8 hours. *After-noon*—Drain cucumbers; cover with fresh boiling water.

Second day: Morning—Drain cucumbers; cover with fresh boiling water. *Afternoon*—Drain cucumbers; add salt. Cover with fresh boiling water.

Third day: Morning—Drain cucumbers; prick each cucumber in several places with a table fork. (You may want to slice thicker ones in half.) Make a syrup of 3 cups of the sugar and 3 cups of the vinegar; add tumeric and spices (but not vanilla). Heat to boiling; pour over cucumbers. (Syrup will only partially cover cucumbers.) *Afternoon*—Drain syrup into pan. Add 2 cups sugar and 2 cups vinegar; heat. Pour over pickles.

Fourth day: Morning—Drain syrup into pan. Add 2 cups sugar and 1 cup vinegar; heat. Pour over pickles. *Afternoon*—Drain syrup into pan. Add remaining 1 cup sugar and the vanilla. Heat-pack pickles into pint jars; cover with syrup. Adjust lids. Process for 5 minutes in boiling water bath. Start to count process-ing time as soon as water returns to boiling.

Makes 7 to 8 pints

Ann Roth, Milford, Nebraska
Nebraska MCC Relief Sale, Aurora

Bread-and-Butter Pickles

30 medium-sized cucumbers
   (1 gallon sliced)
8 medium-sized onions
1/2 cup pickling salt

Pickling syrup:
5 cups sugar
5 cups vinegar
2 tablespoons mustard seed
1 teaspoon tumeric
1 teaspoon celery seed

Slice cucumbers and onions into thin rings. Dissolve salt in ice water; pour over sliced vegetables. Let stand 3 hours. Drain.

Combine syrup ingredients; bring to a boil. Add *well-drained* vegetables; heat to boiling point but *do not boil*. Pack into hot sterilized jars. Seal.

Lime Stick Pickles

4 pounds large green cucumbers
1 gallon water
1 cup hydrated lime

Pickling syrup:
1 quart vinegar
5 cups sugar
1 tablespoon pickling salt
1 tablespoon celery seed
1 tablespoon mixed pickling
   spice

Peel cucumbers; remove seeds; cut into sticks. Soak overnight in a solution of the water and lime. The next morning, drain cucumbers and wash well. Cover with fresh water and soak for 3 hours.

Combine syrup ingredients (do not heat). Drain cucumbers and pour cold syrup over them. Let stand overnight. The next day, simmer pickles in syrup for 30 minutes. Put in jars and seal.

Marcia Roth, Wayland, Iowa

♥ Pickled Beets

The contributor likes to put up very small beets, which she leaves whole, in this pickling syrup. In that case, she notes, you'll need more than 15 beets.

10 to 15 beets (depending on size)
2 cups sugar
2 cups vinegar
2 cups water
1 teaspoon ground cloves
1 teaspoon ground cinnamon

Trim beet tops down to 1 inch. (Do not cut into beets or color will bleed during cooking.) Wash beets well. Cook in boiling water to cover until tender. Drain; cover with cold water. Slip skins off, and trim off tops and roots. Depending on size, cut beets into quarters or eighths, or slice them.

Combine remaining ingredients; bring to a boil. Add beets to syrup; boil 10 minutes. Pack into sterilized jars; seal.

Anna Mae Roth, Milford, Nebraska
Nebraska MCC Relief Sale, Aurora

♥ Country-Style Hot Dog Relish

This relish is delicious on hot dogs and hamburgers.

4 cups sliced cucumbers (do not pare; remove seeds)
3 cups roughly chopped onions
3 cups roughly chopped cabbage
2 cups roughly chopped green tomatoes
3 red peppers, cut in chunks
3 green peppers, cut in chunks
1/2 cup pickling salt
2 tablespoons mustard seed
1 tablespoon celery seed
1 tablespoon tumeric
5 cups sugar
4 cups vinegar
2 cups cold water

Grind all vegetables using a coarse blade. Drain. Sprinkle with salt and let stand overnight. Drain and rinse well.

Combine remaining ingredients; pour over vegetables. Heat to a full boil; boil 7 to 10 minutes. Place in hot jars and seal.

Berniece Beckler, Milford, Nebraska
Nebraska MCC Relief Sale, Aurora

Sandwich Spread

N. Elizabeth Graber's mother, Bernice Schroll, included a layer of this sandwich spread in the peanut butter sandwiches she made for her daughter's school lunches. Elizabeth, of Wayland, Iowa, says the combination was her favorite sandwich!

Green tomatoes
2 red peppers
2 green peppers
1 teaspoon salt
1/2 cup water
6 sweet pickles, ground
1 cup sugar
1/2 cup vinegar
2 rounded tablespoons flour
1 cup sour cream
2 tablespoons prepared
  mustard
3 well-beaten eggs

Grind enough green tomatoes to measure 1 pint after juice is squeezed out. Grind red and green peppers, add to green tomatoes, and sprinkle salt over all. Let stand 1 hour. Drain. Add the 1/2 cup water to the ground vegetables and cook until tender. Mix in the ground sweet pickles.

Combine remaining ingredients and cook until consistency of dressing. Stir in ground vegetables. Put up in sterilized jars while hot.

Iowa MCC Relief Sale, Iowa City

♥ Chili Sauce

7 to 8 quarts ripe tomatoes
2 green peppers, chopped
2 red peppers, chopped
2 stalks celery, diced
3 medium onions, diced
1 cup sugar
1 cup vinegar
2 tablespoons salt
2 tablespoons paprika
1 1/2 teaspoons *each:* ground
  cloves, allspice, black
  pepper, cinnamon
1/2 teaspoon dry mustard

Cover tomatoes with boiling water to make it easy to slip off skins. Quarter or chop tomatoes; place in a large pot. Add remaining ingredients and cook until thick, stirring occasionally. Pour into hot sterilized jars and seal.

Makes 8 pints

Anna Mae Roth, Milford, Nebraska
Nebraska MCC Relief Sale, Aurora

♥ *Ikra*

This vegetable appetizer or relish is served at Faspa, a light Sunday supper of breads, buns, salads, cold cuts, and cheeses. It's also wonderful anytime with fresh white bread or crusty rolls or as an accompaniment to a light lunch of cold cuts, cheese, and bread. From the Russian Mennonite experience, this traditional recipe has been passed down over several generations and is similar to some Mediterranean appetizers made with eggplant. The proportions may be varied a bit depending on what vegetables are available.

4 to 6 sweet green peppers (enough to make 2 cups chopped)
10 cups grated carrots
6 cups stewed tomatoes (or peeled chopped fresh tomatoes in season)
2 tablespoons chopped fresh parsley
4 teaspoons salt
6 cups chopped onion (about 4 large)
1/3 cup vegetable oil (half olive oil)
Sugar to taste

Quarter green peppers, removing seeds and stems. Place in a saucepan, pour boiling water over, and parboil for about 5 minutes. When cool enough to handle, chop to make 2 cups.

Place raw grated carrot, tomatoes, parsley, and salt in a large, heavy pot. In a large frying pan, saute chopped onions and then chopped peppers in oil in batches until onion is transparent, using part of the oil for each batch. Add each sauteed batch to the large pot as it is completed. Simmer slowly for 1 hour or more until vegetables are tender but not mushy. Add sugar to taste.

If you wish to store the relish on the shelf, put it in preserving jars, adjust lids, and process in a canner in a boiling water bath for 15 minutes, to seal jars. Refrigerated, this relish will also keep well without processing for several weeks: pour very hot relish into hot sterilized jars; cap jars firmly, using new rubber rings.

Marlene Neustaedter, Winnipeg, Manitoba
MCC Manitoba Relief Sale

♥ Salsa

10 cups cut-up skinned
   tomatoes
4 cups chopped onions
4 cups chopped green Bell
   peppers
1 cup chopped yellow
   banana peppers
Half a jar jalapeno peppers
   (or use fresh)
10 whole garlic cloves,
   pierced
3 1/2 teaspoons pickling salt
1/3 cup vinegar
2 cans (12 oz each) tomato
   paste

Combine all ingredients except tomato paste. Cook until vegetables are tender. Stir in tomato paste. Cook 15 minutes. Remove garlic cloves. Pack salsa in hot sterilized jars. Process in boiling-water bath for 15 minutes.

Vada Roth, Milford, Nebraska
Nebraska MCC Relief Sale, Aurora

♥ Hot Sauce

Over the years, the Orange Cove Mennonite Brethren Church, El Buen Pastor (The Good Shepherd), of about 40 members, has worked hard and served thousands of hot meals from its booth at the West Coast Mennonite Sale and Auction for World Relief. The Mexican combination plate, which includes rice, beans, and tacos, is very popular among attendees. Amalia Martinez, who makes the hot sauce for the combination plate, is pleased to share this old family recipe. She notes that the sauce can also be used in enchiladas.

1 pound fresh tomatoes,
   peeled (or use peeled
   canned tomatoes)
1/4 to 1/2 pound serrano
   chiles
10 cloves garlic
Salt to taste

Boil tomatoes and chiles together until the chiles turn light green. Put mixture in blender with garlic and salt; blend until smooth.

♥ Sauce for Making Chili

With jars of this sauce in the pantry, it's quick and easy to put together a tasty batch of chili for a family meal.

1 1/2 cups chopped onions
1 cup chopped green pep-
  pers
1 1/2 cups chopped celery *or*
  1 1/2 teaspoons celery
  seed
6 quarts chopped tomatoes
1/3 cup vinegar
1/3 cup sugar or honey
1 tablespoon salt
1 quart water
1 tablespoon whole allspice
1 tablespoon whole cloves
A 2-inch piece cinnamon
  stick
2 bay leaves
1 teaspoon ginger
1 teaspoon chili powder
1 clove garlic, chopped

Combine onions, green peppers, celery, tomatoes, vinegar, sugar, salt, and water in a large kettle. Tie spices in a cheesecloth bag; add to kettle. Bring vegetables to a boil; reduce heat and simmer slowly for about 1 1/2 hours. Remove spice bag. Ladle into hot sterilized pint jars; seal. Makes about 6 pints.

To make chili, you'll need the following:

1 1/2 to 2 pounds ground beef
Salt (to taste)
1 can kidney beans
1 can tomato soup
2 cups water
1 pint home-made chili sauce (above)
Chili powder (to taste)

Brown ground beef, adding salt to taste. Add beans, soup, water, chili sauce, and chili powder. Simmer 20 minutes. Serve with crackers. Serves 10.

Vivian Gering, Freeman, South Dakota
Minn-Kota MCC Relief Sale, Sioux Falls,
South Dakota

Spicy Beverage

The contributor recommends this as a very delightful drink to serve at a youth group get-together.

2 quarts hot milk
1 cup Spiced Syrup (see
    ingredients below)
1/8 teaspoon salt

Spiced Syrup:
2 cups water
1 1/2 tablespoons cloves
1/2 cup red cinnamon
    candies
1/2 cup sugar

To Prepare the Spiced Syrup:
Combine ingredients in saucepan. Simmer 15 minutes, stirring occasionally; strain, discarding cloves. Use 2 tablespoons syrup to flavor 1 cup milk.

To Prepare the Spicy Beverage:
Mix hot milk, Spiced Syrup, and salt. Serve in mugs, topped with marshmallows or whipped cream.

MAKES 8 SERVINGS

Mrs. Helen Schmidt, Marion, South Dakota
Minn-Kota MCC Relief Sale, Sioux Falls, South
Dakota

Rhubarb Juice

10 cups chopped rhubarb
10 cups water
2 cups sugar

Boil rhubarb in the water until very soft; strain. Stir sugar into strained juice and bring to a boil. Pour into hot, sterilized jars and seal; or cool and freeze.

To Make Punch from Rhubarb Juice:
Add 2 large bottles 7-Up, Sprite, or ginger ale and 1 large can (12 oz) frozen orange juice, thawed.

Mrs. Helen Schmidt, Marion, South Dakota
Minn-Kota MCC Relief Sale, Sioux Falls, South
Dakota

Golden Punch

1 can (46 oz) pineapple juice
1 can (12 oz) frozen orange
   juice, thawed (don't use
   Awake)
1 can (12 oz) frozen lemonade, thawed
1 to 1 1/2 quarts water
1 bottle (28 oz) ginger ale

Mix together all ingredients except ginger ale. If desired, freeze part of this liquid in a ring mold to place in the punch bowl for chilling. Just before serving, place fruit-juice mixture in punch bowl and add ginger ale.

SERVES 50

Martha Tschetter, Freeman, South Dakota
Minn-Kota MCC Relief Sale, Sioux Falls,
South Dakota

Lemonade

This is the only drink, other than carbonated soft drinks and coffee, that is made and sold at the Minn-Kota Relief Sale in Sioux Falls, South Dakota. And it sells as fast as the water flows!

1 container (20 oz) Country
   Time or Kool-Aid
   powdered lemonade mix
1 can (6 oz) frozen orange
   juice, thawed
2 gallons cold water

Mix ingredients well; chill thoroughly.

MAKES 2 GALLONS

Silverlake Mennonite Brethren Church, Freeman,
South Dakota

Swiss Tea

The recipe for this drink, sent from the Ohio Relief Sale, is popular in the Swiss-German community of Kidron.

1/2 cup green Tenderleaf tea
2 sticks cinnamon, broken in
   pieces
1/2 teaspoon (or big pinch)
   saffron
1 1/2 cups sugar (more or
   less to taste)

Add tea, cinnamon, and saffron to 1 quart boiling water; simmer 15 to 20 minutes; strain. Add enough hot water to make 1 gallon tea. Stir in the sugar until dissolved.

Hot Spiced Apple Cider

Apples and apple cider are big feature items at the Oregon MCC Fall Festival in Albany. Apples, which are sold by the bag, are donated by a local Mennonite orchardist, Beryl Forrester. Cider is sold cold or hot by the cup and cold by the gallon. For the 1994 Fall Festival, 500 gallons of cider were made. The apples for the cider are picked by volunteers in late September and pressed and bottled for cider the day before the sale. Ken Snyder, of Salem, shares his recipe.

4 teaspoons whole cloves
**4 teaspoons whole allspice
seeds**
4 cinnamon sticks
2 gallons apple cider

Tie spices together in cheesecloth (this makes it easier to serve spiced cider). Add spice bag to cider and heat to desired temperature--*but do not boil.* Serve hot.

Note: If cider is too tart, add 1/2 to 1 cup brown sugar. For more information about the cider-making process and the equipment used, contact Ken Snyder at (503) 362-5535.

A group of shoppers browses through the SELFHELP crafts at the 1994 Michiana Mennonite Relief Sale in Goshen, Ind. (Photo by Marion Troyer, Goshen)

Pineapple Punch

1 can (12 oz) frozen orange
   juice
1 can (6 oz) frozen lemonade
1 quart water
1 quart 7-Up (half a 2-liter
   bottle)
2 quarts pineapple sherbet
1 quart vanilla ice cream

Mix juices and water. Just before serving, add 7-Up. Stir in sherbet and ice cream.

Lisa Kauffman
Pleasant View Mennonite Church,
Goshen, Indiana

Yeast Breads & Rolls

No-Knead Bread

2 packages yeast
1/2 cup warm water
2/3 cup sugar
2/3 cup dry milk
2/3 cup vegetable oil
2 eggs
1 teaspoon salt (less if
　　desired)
2 cups hot water
4 cups whole-wheat flour
3 1/2 cups white flour

In a small bowl, dissolve yeast in the warm water; set aside. In a large bowl, mix sugar, dry milk, oil, eggs, and salt. Add the hot water; mix well. Then stir in yeast mixture. Mix in the flours. Cover and let rise until double (about 1 hour). Stir down and let rise until double twice more for finer texture.

Grease two 9x5-inch loaf pans. Divide dough between the pans. Let rise for 15 minutes. Bake at 350°F for 30 minutes.

Makes 2 loaves

Variations: To make dough into rolls, grease hands and cookie sheets. Roll dough into 2-inch-diameter balls. Place 2 inches apart on sheets. Bake at 350°F for 13 minutes, or until brown. To make buns, roll into 3- to 4-inch-diameter balls. Bake 15 to 20 minutes.

Jane Roth
Pleasant View Mennonite Church
Michiana MCC Relief Sale, Goshen

French Bread

Loaves of this crusty bread are featured at the Minn-Kota MCC Relief Sale in Sioux Falls, South Dakota. The recipe's contributor is the chef at the Swan Lake Christian Camp.

4 tablespoons dry yeast
1 cup warm water
1 teaspoon sugar
4 tablespoons sugar
4 tablespoons shortening
4 teaspoons salt
4 cups hot water
14 cups flour
1 egg
2 tablespoons milk
Sesame seeds or poppy
   seeds (optional)

Dissolve yeast in the warm water with the 1 teaspoon sugar; set aside. Combine the 4 tablespoons sugar with the shortening, salt, and hot water. Cool to lukewarm; add yeast mixture. Stir in flour. Let rise until doubled.

Divide dough into 4 parts; roll each to fit on a 20x24-inch cookie sheet. Slash each loaf four or five times diagonally across the top. Mix egg and milk; brush over top of each loaf. Sprinkle with sesame or poppy seed if desired. Let rise until double. Bake at 375°F for 20 minutes.

MAKES 4 LOAVES

Alvin W. Goerzen, Newton, Kansas

Honey-Whole Wheat Bread

Judy Buller, of Beatrice, Nebraska, donates loaves of this bread to the Nebraska Mennonite Relief Sale in Aurora.

2 packages active dry yeast
1/2 cup warm (105° to 115°F)
   water
1/3 cup honey
1/4 cup shortening
1 tablespoon salt
1 3/4 cups warm water
3 cups whole-wheat flour
3 to 4 cups white flour

In a large mixing bowl, dissolve yeast in the 1/2 cup warm water. Stir in honey, shortening, salt, the 1 3/4 cups warm water, and the whole-wheat flour. Beat until smooth. Mix in enough white flour to make a dough that's easy to handle.

Turn dough onto lightly floured surface. Knead about 10 minutes. Place in greased bowl. Cover and let rise in warm place until double (about 1 hour). Punch down; divide dough in half. Form into 2 loaves and place in greased baking pans. Let rise until double (about 1 hour). Bake at 375°F for 40 to 45 minutes, or until loaves are golden brown and sound hollow when tapped. Remove from pans and cool.

MAKES 2 LOAVES

Sesame Multigrain Bread

6 cups warm water
1 cup honey
3 heaping tablespoons yeast
2 cups rye flour
1 cup oatmeal
1 cup milk powder
3 to 4 cups whole-wheat flour
3 tablespoons salt
1 cup (shy) vegetable oil
1 cup sesame seeds
1/2 to 3/4 cup sunflower seeds
1/2 cup millet
        (optional--could be bitter)
Unbleached white flour

In a large mixing bowl, combine warm water, honey, and yeast; let set. When frothy, add rye flour, oatmeal, milk powder, and enough of the whole-wheat flour to make a batter. Cover with plastic wrap; let rise until it reaches top of bowl (about 20 to 30 minutes).

Stir down. Add salt, oil, sesame and sunflower seeds, and millet (if desired). Then stir or work in enough unbleached white flour to make a dough. Knead for 5 to 10 minutes, or until dough is of a good texture. Let dough rise; punch down. Let it rise again; punch down.

Inclement weather didn't keep people away from the 1990 Rocky Mountain Mennonite Relief Sale. Although rain and snow was falling until after noon, a new record was established that day.
(Photo by Stan Oswald)

Form into loaves to fit: four large (9 1/2 x 5-inch) pans *plus* four tiny (6x3-inch) pans. Bake at 350° to 375°F: mini-loaves for 25 to 30 minutes; large loaves for 30 to 35 minutes.

MAKES 4 LARGE AND 4 SMALL LOAVES

Lola Hershberger, Denver, Colorado
Rocky Mountain Mennonite Relief Sale

Pilgrims' Bread

Alvin W. Goerzen, of Newton, Kansas, submitted this recipe for a bread that can be found at the Minn-Kota Sale in Sioux Falls, South Dakota.

1/2 cup yellow cornmeal
1/2 cup brown sugar
1 tablespoon salt
2 cups boiling water
1/4 cup vegetable oil
2 packages dry yeast
1/2 cup warm water
3/4 cup whole-wheat flour
1/2 cup rye flour
4 1/4 to 4 1/2 cups un-
    bleached white flour

In a small bowl, combine cornmeal, sugar, and salt. Gradually stir cornmeal mixture into the boiling water. Add oil. Cool to lukewarm. Dissolve yeast in the warm water. Add to cornmeal mixture. Beat in whole-wheat and rye flours. By hand, stir in white flour.

Turn dough onto lightly floured surface. Knead until smooth and elastic. Place in a lightly greased bowl, turning once to grease surface. Cover and let rise in a warm place until double. Punch dough down; turn onto lightly floured surface. Divide in half and knead a second time for 3 minutes. Shape dough into 2 loaves; place in greased pans. Cover and let rise again in warm place until double in bulk. Bake at 350°F for 35 to 40 minutes.

MAKES 2 LOAVES

Farm Bread

This bread is a good seller at the baked-goods booth at the Minn-Kota Relief Sale in Sioux Falls, South Dakota.

4 cups scalded milk, cooled
2 cups uncooked rolled oats
2 1/2 tablespoons soft
    shortening
2 packages yeast
1 teaspoon sugar
1/4 teaspoon ginger
1/2 cup warm water
2/3 cup molasses
1 tablespoon salt
2 cups whole-wheat flour
7 1/2 cups white flour
1 egg white

Place milk, oats, and shortening in a bowl; mix and let stand 1 hour at room temperature. Dissolve yeast, sugar, and ginger in the warm water. Let stand 8 minutes, or until bubbly. Stir yeast mixture, molasses, and salt into oat mixture. Stir in whole-wheat flour and enough of the white flour to make a dough that is easy to handle.

Knead dough 8 minutes. Let rise in greased bowl 1 1/2 hours; punch down. Knead 10 minutes more. Return to bowl; let rise 45 minutes or until double; punch down. Divide into thirds and shape into loaves. Let rise 45 minutes on greased baking sheet or in loaf pans. Brush tops of loaves with egg white and sprinkle with rolled oats. Bake at 325°F for 45 minutes.

MAKES 3 LARGE LOAVES

White Bread

1 tablespoon yeast
2 cups warm water
1 1/2 cups bread mix
1/4 cup sugar
1/8 cup vegetable oil
4 cups flour

Mix yeast in the warm water until dissolved. Then add bread mix and remaining ingredients.

Katie Wagler
Daviess County Relief Sale, Montgomery, Indiana

Raisin Bread

2 packages yeast
1 cup water
2 teaspoons sugar
1 cup milk
1/2 cup butter
1/2 cup sugar
2 teaspoons salt
3 eggs
6 1/2 cups flour
2 1/2 cups raisins

Dissolve yeast in the water with the 2 teaspoons sugar. Scald milk; add butter, sugar, salt, eggs, flour, and raisins. Let rise until double in bulk (at least 1 hour). Divide dough in fourths; place in four loaf pans. Let loaves rise until double in bulk. Bake at 375°F for 30 to 40 minutes.

MAKES 4 LOAVES

Alice Klassen, Coaldale
Alberta MCC Relief Sale, Coaldale

Cinnamon Bread

The people of Morton, Illinois, are familiar with the cinnamon bread made by Frances E. Bumgardner. She has made the bread for a variety of community benefit sales, and her church, First Mennonite Church of Morton, turned out 200 loaves for the 1991 Illinois Mennonite Relief Sale.

2 or 3 packages yeast
1 tablespoon sugar
1 cup warm water
1 stick (1/2 cup) margarine
2/3 cup sugar
1 1/3 cup powdered milk
2 teaspoons salt
4 cups hot water
12 cups flour
1 cup sugar
4 teaspoons cinnamon

Dissolve yeast and the 1 tablespoon sugar in the warm water; stir and set aside.

Measure into a Tupperware Fix-n-Mix bowl the margarine, the 2/3 cup sugar, powdered milk, and salt. Add the hot water, stirring until margarine is melted. Stir in 6 cups of the flour. Add the yeast mixture. Gradually add at least 6 cups more flour, to make a dough that is easy to knead.

Turn dough onto floured board; knead at least 100 times. Put into bowl and seal. Set aside in warm place for about 1 1/2 hours, until doubled in bulk. Punch down and divide into four parts. Let rest 10 minutes. Mix the 1 cup sugar with the cinnamon.

Roll each portion of dough into a 7x15-inch rectangle. Brush lightly with water. Sprinkle 1/4 cup of the cinnamon-sugar mixture over the dough. Roll up as for a jelly roll. Moisten edge and seal. Place in a well-greased pan. Repeat with the other three portions. Let rise in a warm place until loaves reach just above top of pans. Bake at 350°F for 35 to 40 minutes.

MAKES 4 LOAVES

Christmas Braid

5 1/2 cups plus 2 tablespoons
flour
1 package yeast
2 cups milk
1/2 cup sugar
6 tablespoons butter or
margarine
1 teaspoon salt (optional)
1 egg
1 cup raisins
1 cup finely chopped mixed
candied fruit
1/2 cup chopped nuts
1 egg yolk
1 tablespoon water

In a large bowl, combine 3 cups of the flour with the yeast. In a saucepan, heat milk, sugar, butter, and salt (if desired) to 120° to 130°F. Add to flour mixture. Add egg. Beat on low speed with an electric mixer for 30 seconds; increase speed to medium and continue beating for 3 minutes. Stir in raisins, candied fruit, nuts, and enough of the remaining flour to form a stiff dough.

Turn out onto a floured surface and knead until smooth and elastic (8 to 10 minutes). Place in a greased bowl, turning once to grease top. Cover and let rise until doubled (about 1 1/2 hours). Divide dough into thirds; then divide into thirds again. Roll each piece into a 15-inch rope. Place 3 ropes 1 inch apart on a greased baking sheet. Begin braiding loosely in the middle and work toward the ends. Pinch ends together and tuck under. Repeat with remaining ropes to make two more loaves. Cover and let rise until doubled (30 to 40 minutes). Combine egg yolk and water; brush over braids. Bake at 350°F for 20 to 25 minutes, or until browned.

MAKES 3 LOAVES

Mrs. Paul (Mary Helen) Wade, Sterling, Illinois
Science Ridge Mennonite Church
Illinois MCC Relief Sale, Peoria

Kringel

2 cups milk
1 1/2 packages dry yeast or
    1-inch square fresh yeast
1/3 cup warm water
1/2 teaspoon sugar
1/2 cup shortening
2 teaspoons salt
5 to 6 cups flour (enough to
    make a soft dough)
3/4 pound butter (or part
    butter; part margarine),
    softened
2 cups raisins (washed and
    drained)

Scald milk; let cool. Dissolve yeast in the warm water with the sugar. When milk is lukewarm, mix in mixing bowl with shortening, salt, and 2 cups of the flour. Beat. Add yeast mixture and enough of the remaining flour to make a soft dough. Beat. (I use my electric mixer.) Let rise.

Roll out on a floured surface into a 1/2- to 3/4-inch-thick rectangle. Spread the butter over two-thirds of the dough. Fold dough into thirds, unbuttered third first. Then fold into thirds again in the opposite direction. Roll again. Cut into 4 strips.

Place raisins (or almond paste filling) in center of each strip. Press edges of each strip together to make a long roll; then twist each roll. Place on cookie sheets and let rise. Mix some sugar with a little milk and brush on top of each Kringel. Bake at 400°F for 25 to 30 minutes or until browned.

Note: You can refrigerate the dough overnight after spreading it with the butter and folding it up. The dough is easier to work with when it's cold. Roll the dough for the second time and make the Kringel the next day.

Makes 4 Kringel

Hildegard Jantzen, Beatrice, Nebraska
Nebraska MCC Relief Sale, Aurora

Sour Cream Twists

3 1/2 cups flour
1 cup shortening
1 package yeast
1/2 cup warm water
2 teaspoons sugar
1 cup sour cream
1 egg plus 1 egg yolk
1 teaspoon vanilla
3/4 teaspoons salt
1 cup white sugar

Mix flour and shortening as for pastry. Dissolve yeast in the warm water with the 2 teaspoons sugar. Add to flour-shortening mixture along with sour cream, egg and yolk, vanilla, and salt. Mix well; dough will be quite soft. Put in refrigerator for 1 hour to rise.

Pat out half the dough to 1/4-inch thick, using sugar if dough sticks to board. Spread dough with 1/2 cup of the white sugar, working it in with a finger. Fold dough into thirds; flatten again to 1/4-inch thick. Cut into 1x3-inch strips. Twist into desired shapes and bake at once at 375°F for about 20 to 25 minutes. Repeat same procedure with remaining half of dough.

Herta Janzen, Coaldale
Alberta MCC Relief Sale, Coaldale

Mak Kuchen (Poppy Seed Rolls)

1 1/4 cups milk, scalded
1/4 cup lard or shortening
1/4 cup sugar
1 teaspoon salt
1 package yeast
3 1/2 to 4 cups flour

Filling:
2 1/4 cups poppy seeds,
   ground
2 1/4 cups sugar
3/4 to 1 cup water

Combine scalded milk, lard, sugar, and salt. Cool to lukewarm. Add yeast and flour. Knead well. Cover. Let rise and punch down two or three times.

To make filling, mix poppy seeds and sugar. Bring the water to a boil; add poppy seed mixture. Bring back to a boil, stirring constantly. Add more water if needed. Cool.

After last rising, divide dough into 3 equal parts; let rise 10 minutes. Roll each ball of dough into a rectangle. Spread with one-third of the poppy seed filling. Roll up like a jelly roll and seal edges. Place in pans and let rise 10 to 15 minutes. Brush tops with beaten egg. Bake at 350°F for 35 minutes.

Mid-Kansas MCC Relief Sale, Hutchinson

Orange Butter Rolls

1 package yeast
1/4 cup warm water
1/4 cup sugar
1 teaspoon salt
2 eggs
1/2 cup sour cream
6 tablespoons softened
    margarine
2 3/4 to 3 cups flour

Filling:
3/4 cup sugar
3/4 cup coconut
2 tablespoons orange rind

Glaze/Topping:
3/4 cup sugar
2 tablespoons orange rind
1/2 cup sour cream
1/4 cup margarine
1/4 cup coconut

Soften yeast in the warm water. In a large bowl, combine yeast mixture with sugar, salt, eggs, sour cream, and softened margarine. Stir until blended. Gradually add flour, mixing well. Let dough rise in a greased bowl in a warm area. While dough rises, prepare filling by mixing the sugar, coconut, and orange rind well; set aside.

Divide dough in half. Roll each half into a circle about 12 inches in diameter. Spread each circle first with some softened margarine and then with half the filling mixture. Cut in pie-shaped wedges and roll up crescent-style (wide end first). Place point-end down in a well-greased 13x9-inch pan. Let rolls rise again. Bake in a 325°F oven for 20 to 25 minutes or until brown.

Meanwhile, prepare glaze by combining sugar, orange rind, sour cream, and margarine in a heavy saucepan. Bring to a boil, stirring constantly, and boil for 3 minutes. Spread on rolls while warm. Then sprinkle the 1/4 cup coconut over the glaze.

Brenda Oyer, Gridley, Illinois
Salem Evangelical Mennonite Church, Gridley
Illinois MCC Relief Sale, Peoria

Although twice as many peppernuts were made than ever before for the Ritzville, Wash., sale, the baked goods booth sold them out just as quickly. Those attending the sale watched demonstrations of wheat weaving, cider pressing, flour ground with an antique mill and apple butter made in a huge copper kettle over an open fire. According to "Mennonite Weekly Review" six poppy seed rolls made by Lorene Stucky of McPherson, Kansas, brought up to $110 each!

— Love in Action News, MCC

Hot Cross Buns

5 cups flour
1/2 cup sugar
1 1/4 teaspoons salt
1 tablespoon grated lemon
   rind
2 packages dry yeast
1/2 cup milk
1/2 cup potato water
1/2 cup butter
2 eggs
3/4 cup lukewarm mashed
   potatoes
3/4 cup raisins
1 egg yolk beaten with 2
   tablespoons water

In a large bowl stir together 1 1/2 cups of the flour with the sugar, salt, lemon rind, and yeast. In a small saucepan, combine milk, potato water, and butter; heat. Gradually add warm liquid to dry ingredients; beat 2 minutes at medium speed. Add eggs, mashed potatoes, and 1/2 cup more flour. Beat at high speed for 2 minutes. Add enough of the remaining flour to make a stiff dough.

Turn out onto a floured board and knead 8 to 10 minutes. Place in a greased bowl. Cover and let rise until doubled in bulk (about 1 hour). Punch down. Knead in raisins. Shape into balls. Brush tops with the egg yolk-water mixture. Let rise 1 hour. Bake at 375°F for 25 minutes. While warm, frost with a mixture of egg white and powdered sugar.

Makes 24 buns

Lynette Preheim, Marion, South Dakota
Minn-Kota MCC Relief Sale, Sioux Falls,
South Dakota

Semmel (German Crusty Rolls)

This recipe was contributed by Elizabeth Reimer, of Beatrice, Nebraska, who notes that these rolls are a real favorite in her community. They were served on Sunday for breakfast when she was growing up, but they're good any time with jam, cheese, honey or with eggs.

1 package yeast
1/4 cup water
2 cups warm water
4 cups flour
1/2 teaspoon salt (or to taste)

Dissolve yeast in the 1/4 cup water to which a little sugar has been added. Measure the warm water into a mixing bowl; beat in 2 1/2 cups of the flour. After yeast starts action, beat it into the flour mixture; then add salt and remaining flour. Cover tightly, and let rise until double. Stir down and refrigerate for a few hours or overnight. (The dough is sticky; cooling it makes it easier to handle.)

Dipping a tablespoon into water for easier handling, drop dough by the spoonful onto well-greased baking sheets. Do not place too close together. Bake at 450° to 500°F until brown.

Makes about 14 to 16 semmel (depending on size of spoonful)

Dampfnoodles

Bread dough
1 cup water
1/4 cup butter
1 teaspoon salt

Use bread dough that has been raised, punched down, and raised again. Form bread dough into little balls (about 1 1/2 inches in diameter). Place balls in an electric frying pan containing the water, butter, and salt. Let rise until double. Cover pan and cook at 240° to 250°F for 40 minutes. Do not peek while dampfnoodles are cooking, or they will flop. Let steam escape slowly before uncovering. Serve with stew.

Selma Waltner, Freeman, South Dakota
Minn-Kota MCC Relief Sale, Sioux Falls, S. Dakota

Refrigerator Rolls

1 1/2 cups milk
1 cup butter or margarine
1/2 cup sugar
1 teaspoon salt
3 eggs
1 package dry yeast
2 teaspoons sugar
1/8 cup lukewarm water
5 to 5 1/2 cups flour
Softened butter

Scald milk; stir in the 1 cup butter, the 1/2 cup sugar, and the salt. Cool; then add eggs one at a time to milk mixture. Dissolve yeast and the 2 teaspoons sugar in the lukewarm water. Add yeast mixture and then flour to milk mixture. Beat well. Let rise until double. Punch down and place in refrigerator overnight.

The next day, divide dough into three parts. Roll each part into a round, as for pie crust. Spread with a little softened butter. Cut each round into 16 wedges. Roll up each wedge from wide end to pointed end. Let rolls rise on a greased pan until light (1 1/2 hours). Bake at 375°F for 10 to 15 minutes.

MAKES 48 ROLLS

Missouri MCC Relief Sale, Harrisonville

No-Knead Refrigerator Rolls

2 packages dry yeast
2 1/2 cups lukewarm water
3/4 cup sugar
3/4 cup margarine
2 eggs
2 teaspoons salt
7 1/2 cups flour
Cinnamon-sugar mixture

Dissolve yeast in the lukewarm water. Add sugar, margarine, eggs, salt, and then flour. Beat with electric mixer until well mixed. Then put dough in a large bowl in refrigerator and let rise. Punch down; divide dough in half. Roll out; sprinkle with cinnamon-sugar mixture. Roll up and cut into rolls. Place rolls in pans (5 to a pan) and let rise again. Bake at 350°F until brown.

MAKES 40 ROLLS (8 PANS)

Dorothy Bean, Chenoa, Illinois
Meadows Mennonite Church
Illinois MCC Relief Sale, Peoria

Zwiebach

2 cups milk
1 tablespoon sugar
2 tablespoons yeast
1 tablespoon salt
1/2 cup vegetable oil
Flour

Combine milk and sugar; warm slightly. Add yeast; let set a short while until yeast is dissolved. Add remaining ingredients, plus a small amount of flour; mix. Add a little more flour and mix. Continue adding flour and mixing until dough is smooth and soft. Knead well (or use a dough mixer). Cover with a towel and let rise until double in bulk; punch down. Form into zwiebach (see instructions below). Let rise again until double. Bake at 350°F for 15 to 20 minutes.

How to Form Zwiebach:
Take a good-sized lump of dough with well-greased hands. While holding dough in your left hand, between the forefinger and the thumb, pinch off little pieces of dough the size of an egg. Set on a greased baking sheet. Then, for each egg-sized piece, pinch off a smaller piece and set firmly on top of larger piece.

Irene Penner, Corn, Oklahoma
Oklahoma MCC Relief Sale, Fairview

Jake Dick, a retired insurance man, has donated a dining room table to the Minn-Kota MCC Country Auction and Fair in Sioux Falls, S.D., every year since his retirement in 1987. One year, the table brought $1,625 to MCC in auction. This hobby, which he picked up only after retirement, has worked well for him. "It's a way I can use what talent I have to pay something back to my faith," he was quoted in the Observer/Advocate newspaper.

Zwiebach

2 packages dry yeast
1 cup warm water
3 cups scalded milk
1/3 cup sugar
4 to 5 teaspoons salt
1/2 cup lard or shortening,
   melted
1/2 cup margarine, melted
9 to 10 cups flour

Dissolve yeast in the warm water. Add cooled milk, sugar, salt, and melted fat. Add half the flour; beat well. Add remaining flour gradually; mix. Let dough rise until double; punch down.

Shape zwiebach by pinching off dough to make 1 1/2-inch balls. Place balls on cookie sheets 3 inches apart. Pinch off another ball a little smaller and place on top of the first one. The top ball will fall off unless you punch it down in the middle with your index finger. Let rise until light. Bake at 400°F for about 20 minutes.

MAKES 72 ROLLS

Alvin W. Goerzen, Newton, Kansas
Minn-Kota MCC Relief Sale, Sioux Falls,
South Dakota

Kleine Zwieback

Many plastic bags full of these golden rolls are sold at the Nebraska Relief Sale, in Aurora.

1 package dry yeast
1/4 cup water
2 cups milk
1 stick (1/2 cup) margarine
1 teaspoon salt
1 tablespoon sugar
1 1/2 pounds flour
3/4 pound (1 1/2 cups) butter

Dissolve yeast in the water. Scald milk; pour over margarine, salt, and sugar. When lukewarm, add the yeast mixture. Add flour to make a stiff dough. Mix well. Let rise.

Bring the 3/4 pound butter to room temperature. Knead it into the dough. Refrigerate dough overnight. Divide dough into four parts; roll out very thin, and cut into rounds with a 1 3/4-inch cutter. Place rounds one on top of another, two deep, on an ungreased cookie sheet. Let rise until doubled. Bake at 375°F until slightly brown. Break apart and toast at 250° to 275°F until toasty brown. (If they are very thick, toast longer.)

Edna Ensz, Beatrice, Nebraska

Zwieback

These rolls are sold at the priced baked goods booth at the Minn-Kota Relief Sale, in Sioux Falls, South Dakota.

4 cups milk
4 teaspoons sugar
4 teaspoons salt
1 3/4 cup lard *or* 2 sticks (1 cup) butter or margarine plus 3/4 cup lard (at room temperature)
3 tablespoons yeast (dissolved in water)
11 to 14 cups flour

Scald milk; add sugar, salt, and lard. Add dissolved yeast. Stir in enough flour to make a soft dough. Knead; let rise. Knead the dough down again, and let it rise again. Form into zwieback. Bake at 400°F for 15 to 20 minutes.

MAKES 3 TO 4 DOZEN ROLLS

Marjorie Baerg, Butterfield, Minnesota

 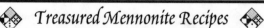

Mom's Zwieback

This recipe is used for rolls sold at the priced baked goods booth at the Minn-Kota Relief Sale, in Sioux Falls, South Dakota, and served at the annual kick-off dinner for the sale.

2 cups milk
1 cup half-and-half
1 stick (1/2 cup) butter
3/4 cup shortening or lard
1 1/2 tablespoons yeast
1 to 1 1/2 cups warm water
1/2 cup sugar (optional)
1 1/2 tablespoons salt
About 10 cups flour

Heat milk and half-and-half until hot but not boiling. Add butter and shortening; stir to melt. Cool almost completely. Put yeast into the warm water with the sugar (if desired). Let yeast dissolve. Then add to milk mixture along with salt and just enough flour to make a pasty mixture. Work in the rest of the flour to make a soft dough. Let rise 1 hour or so. Shape into zwieback (waiting 15 minutes between pans so later pans won't rise too big while waiting to be baked). Let rise until double. Bake at 350°F until light brown.

MAKES 4 OR 5 DOZEN ROLLS

Mrs. Dennis (Shirley) Ries, Freeman,
South Dakota

Zucchini Orange Coconut Bread

1 cup vegetable oil
1 3/4 cups sugar
3 eggs
2 teaspoons almond extract
3 cups flour
1 teaspoon baking soda
1 teaspoon baking powder
1 teaspoon salt
3/4 cup orange juice
1 1/2 cups coconut
2 cups grated zucchini

Mix together all ingredients. Divide batter evenly between two bread pans. Bake at 350°F for 50 to 55 minutes.

MAKES 2 LOAVES

Lena Sala, Hollsopple, Pennsylvania
MCC Quilt Auction and Relief Sale, Johnstown

Rhubarb Bread

1 1/2 cups white sugar
2/3 cup vegetable oil
1 egg
1 cup buttermilk
1 teaspoon vanilla
2 1/2 cups flour
1 teaspoon baking soda
1 teaspoon salt
1 1/2 cups diced rhubarb
1/2 cup chopped nuts *or* 1
    cup washed, drained
    raisins
1/2 cup sugar mixed with a
    dash of cinnamon
1 tablespoon butter, melted

Combine the 1 1/2 cups sugar, oil, egg, buttermilk, and vanilla in a mixing bowl. Mix well. Sift together flour, soda, and salt. Add to liquid mixture. Stir in rhubarb and nuts or raisins. Pour batter into two greased loaf pans. Sprinkle with the sugar-cinnamon mixture; drizzle with melted butter. Bake at 325°F for 1 hour. Remove loaves from pans and brush with butter. Sprinkle with a mixture of sugar and cinnamon.

MAKES 2 LOAVES

Tillie Janzen, Mountain Lake, Minnesota
Minn-Kota MCC Relief Sale, Sioux Falls,
South Dakota

Beginning with the fourth Minn-Kota sale, California fruit growers donated half a semi load of fresh peaches and nectarines to the sale. The other half went to the Arthur, Ill., sale. In 1992, a craftsman delivered a round oak table with leaves and storage cabinet to the California sale as an expression of appreciation for the fruit they have donated.

Pumpkin Bread

This recipe from the Arnaud Christian Fellowship *cookbook, published in 1988, was contributed to that volume by Elly Kathler.*

3 1/2 cups flour
1/2 teaspoon baking soda
2 teaspoons baking powder
1 1/2 teaspoons salt
1 teaspoon cinnamon
1/2 teaspoon cloves
4 eggs, beaten
2 2/3 cups sugar
2 cups cooked pumpkin
2/3 cup water
1/2 cup vegetable oil
2/3 cup raisins
2/3 cup chopped walnuts or
    other nuts (optional)

Sift together first six (dry) ingredients. To beaten eggs, add sugar, pumpkin, water, and oil; mix well. Add liquid ingredients to dry ingredients, mixing until dry ingredients are well moistened. Then fold in raisins and nuts (if used). Pour batter into two greased 9x5-inch loaf pans. Bake at 350°F for 1 hour or until tester inserted in loaves comes out clean. Wrap and store loaves for 24 hours before serving.

MAKES 2 LOAVES

Ben Sawatzky, Winnipeg, Manitoba
MCC Manitoba Relief Sale

Dale High Nut Bread

The contributor encourages you to use your imagination when making this bread: add bananas, oranges, dates, applesauce, or whatever suits your tastes.

3 cups flour (sifted *before*
    measuring)
1 cup sugar
1/4 teaspoon salt
3 1/2 teaspoons baking
    powder
1 egg
1 cup milk
1 teaspoon vanilla (optional)
1 cup chopped nuts
1 tablespoon solid vegetable
    shortening (Crisco)

Combine flour, sugar, salt, and baking powder; set aside. Beat egg; add milk and vanilla (if desired) to it. Add liquid ingredients to dry ingredients, combining well. Stir in nuts. Then melt shortening and add to batter last. Divide batter between two bread pans. Bake at 350°F for 45 minutes.

MAKES 2 LOAVES

E.A.F.
MCC Quilt Auction and Relief Sale,
Johnstown, Pennsylvania

Morning Glory Muffins

2 cups flour
1 1/4 cups white sugar
2 teaspoons baking soda
2 teaspoons cinnamon
1/2 teaspoon salt
3 eggs, beaten
1 cup vegetable oil
2 teaspoons vanilla
2 cups grated carrots
1/2 cup raisins
1/2 cup coconut
1/2 cup chopped nuts
1 apple, shredded

Combine flour, sugar, baking soda, cinnamon, and salt; mix thoroughly. Beat together eggs, oil, and vanilla. Blend into flour mixture. Then fold in carrots, raisins, coconut, nuts, and shredded apple. Bake at 350°F for 20 minutes, or until tester comes out clean.

MAKES 14 LARGE MUFFINS

Susana Siemens, Winnipeg, Manitoba
MCC Manitoba Relief Sale

Pumpkin 'n' Spice Muffins

2 eggs
1/2 cup sugar
3/4 cup canned pumpkin
1/4 cup vegetable oil
1 1/2 cups flour
1 teaspoon baking powder
1/2 teaspoon baking soda
1/2 teaspoon salt
1/4 teaspoon cinnamon
1/4 teaspoon cloves
1/4 teaspoon nutmeg
3/4 cup raisins
1/2 cup chopped nuts
    (optional)

Preheat oven to 400°F. Beat together eggs, sugar, pumpkin, and oil. Stir in remaining ingredients, mixing until blended. Spoon batter into muffin tins, filling cups two-thirds full. Bake 18 to 20 minutes.

Phyllis Garber, Goshen, Indiana
Yellow Creek Mennonite Church
Indiana MCC Relief Sale, Goshen

Heather's Corn Muffins

In 1988, a little girl wanted to do something to help the Southern Tier Menno-nite Relief Sale, in Bath, New York. With the encouragement of her mother, the 10-year-old baked corn muffins. Her mother bought a pretty little wicker basket and lined it with a cloth napkin, and they put the muffins in it. When the girl came to the platform with the basket of muffins, the vigorous bidding began.

The sight of the young girl standing with her baked goods may have prompted bidders to be generous. The muffins brought $100 the first year--after being bought and sold several times. Heather has continued the tradition, and in 1994 her muffins contributed $750 to relief efforts.

2 cups corn meal
1/2 cup all-purpose flour
2 teaspoons baking powder
1/2 teaspoon baking soda
1/2 teaspoon salt
1 tablespoon sugar
1/4 cup vegetable oil
1 1/2 cups buttermilk
2 eggs

Preheat oven to 350°F. Mix all ingredients together; beat vigorously. Pour into greased muffin pan. Bake for 20 minutes.

MAKES 12 MUFFINS

Rhubarb Muffins

1 1/2 cups flour
2 teaspoons baking powder
1/2 teaspoon salt
1/2 teaspoon cinnamon
1/2 cup sugar
1/4 cup oil
1/2 cup milk
1 egg
1 cup chopped rhubarb

Combine all ingredients except rhubarb; mix well. Then blend in the rhubarb. Pour into greased muffins tins or paper cups. Bake at 400°F for 20 to 25 minutes.

MAKES 12 MUFFINS

Barb Schrag, Freeman, South Dakota
Minn-Kota MCC Relief Sale, Sioux Falls,
South Dakota

Mincemeat Muffins

This recipe's contributor notes that the batter for these muffins may be stored in the refrigerator and baked when desired.

2 cups flour
1 cup whole-bran cereal
1 cup granulated sugar
2 teaspoons baking powder
1 teaspoon baking soda
1 teaspoon salt
2 eggs, beaten
3/4 cup vegetable oil
1 cup milk
1 cup mincemeat

Mix together dry ingredients. Then mix wet ingredients and fold into dry ingredients. Spoon into 24 large greased or paper-lined muffin cups. Bake at 350°F for 20 to 25 minutes or until done.

MAKES 24 LARGE MUFFINS

Susana Siemens, Winnipeg, Manitoba
MCC Manitoba Relief Sale

Cheese Biscuits

2 cups flour
4 teaspoons baking powder
2 tablespoons white sugar
3/4 teaspoon salt
1 cup grated sharp cheese
1/4 cup chopped green tops
    of onions (chives)
1/3 cup vegetable oil
3/4 cup milk

Measure flour, baking powder, sugar, and salt together. Add cheese and onions; stir. Add oil and milk. Stir to form a soft ball of dough (adding more milk if needed). Turn dough out onto lightly floured board and knead 8 to 10 times. Roll or pat to a thickness of 3/4 to 1 inch. Cut with biscuit cutter. Place biscuits close together on a greased pan for moist sides. Bake at 425°F for 15 minutes.

Anne Neufeld, Coaldale
Alberta MCC Relief Sale, Coaldale

Sour Cream Coffee Cake

3/4 cup butter or margarine
1 cup sugar
3 eggs
1 cup sour cream
3 cups flour
1 teaspoon baking soda
1 teaspoon baking powder
1 teaspoon salt

Nut Topping:
1/2 cup chopped pecans
1/2 cup brown sugar
1 teaspoon cinnamon

Cream butter and sugar until light. Beat in eggs, one at a time. Add sour cream. Mix together dry ingredients; gradually stir into creamed mixture. In a separate small bowl, combine topping ingredients. Pour half the batter into a buttered (or use a vegetable-oil spray) 9-inch tube pan. Sprinkle half the topping mixture over the batter. Add remaining batter and then remaining topping. Bake at 350°F for 1 hour.

Sally Ann Reddecliff, Johnstown, Pennsylvania
MCC Quilt Auction and Relief Sale, Johnstown

Fruity Coffee Cake

4 cups sliced fresh fruit
1 cup water
2 tablespoons lemon juice
1/2 to 1 cup sugar (to taste)
6 tablespoons cornstarch
1 cup butter or margarine
1 1/2 cups sugar
4 eggs
1 teaspoon vanilla
3 cups flour
1 1/2 teaspoons baking
    powder

Glaze:
1 cup powdered sugar
1/2 teaspoon vanilla
2 tablespoons melted butter
    or margarine
Warm milk

Cook fruit in the water until tender. Stir in lemon juice. Mix together the 1/2 to 1 cup sugar and the cornstarch (adding cinnamon to taste if desired). Stir into hot fruit. Cook, stirring, until thick. Cool.

Mix butter, the 1 1/2 cups sugar, eggs, and vanilla until smooth. Add flour and baking powder; mix until smooth. Spread two-thirds of the batter in a greased jelly roll pan. Spread cooked fruit over. Spoon remaining batter over fruit. Bake at 375°F for 30 minutes.

While cake is baking, mix together glaze ingredients with enough warm milk to make pourable. Pour glaze over cake while still warm. Serve warm or cold.

MAKES 18 OR MORE SERVINGS

Donna Wharton, Marion, South Dakota
Minn-Kota MCC Relief Sale, Sioux Falls, S. Dakota

Quick Coffee Cake

1 cup sugar
1 tablespoon oil
1 egg
1 teaspoon vanilla
1 cup milk
2 cups flour
1 tablespoon baking powder
1/2 teaspoon salt

Combine all cake ingredients. Beat by hand until smooth. Pour into a greased 9x13-inch pan. Mix together topping ingredients. Sprinkle over batter. Bake at 350°F for 35 minutes.

Debby Ross
Missouri MCC Relief Sale, Harrisonville

Topping:
1 cup brown sugar
1 teaspoon cinnamon
1/4 cup melted margarine
1 cup chopped pecans

Lazy Daisy Duff

This is a not-too-sweet companion for fresh berries--especially blueberries--served at breakfast.

1/4 cup butter
1 cup flour
1/2 cup sugar
1 tablespoon baking powder
Pinch salt
2/3 cup milk
2 cups berries or chopped
    fruit

Melt butter in an 8-inch ovenproof frying pan or casserole dish; set aside. In a small bowl, mix flour, sugar, baking powder, and salt. Quickly stir in the milk, to form a batter. Spoon batter over melted butter in pan. Top with the fruit. *Do not stir.* Bake at 350°F for about 35 minutes.

Susana Siemens, Winnipeg, Manitoba
MCC Manitoba Relief Sale

Rull Kuchen

3 eggs
3/4 cup sweet cream
1/4 cup sweet milk
1 teaspoon salt
1/2 teaspoon baking powder
About 4 cups flour (enough
    to make a soft dough)

Put all ingredients except flour into a large bowl. Stir in enough flour to form a soft dough. Knead on a lightly floured surface. Roll out dough. (If you like crisp crullers, roll very thin; if you like puffy ones, roll about 1/4 inch thick.) Cut dough into squares or oblong pieces. Fry in hot (375°F) oil until brown.

Nebraska MCC Relief Sale, Aurora

Roll Kuchen

The women at the Kelowna, British Columbia, Relief Sale make about 45 batches of this recipe--and usually run out of dough before they've satisfied every request! It was submitted by Susan Federau.

4 eggs
3 cups whipping cream
1/4 cup melted margarine
2 teaspoons salt
3 teaspoons baking powder
6 to 7 cups flour

Mix ingredients in order given.

MAKES ABOUT 4 DOZEN

Rull Kuchen

2 eggs
1 cup milk
1 teaspoon baking powder
1/4 teaspoon salt
About 3 cups flour (enough
    to make a soft dough)

Combine all ingredients, mixing well. Roll the soft dough out very thin, cut it into 2x4-inch strips, and fry in deep fat.

Nebraska MCC Relief Sale, Aurora

Rollkuchen

Many women work at the Saskatoon Relief Auction making and frying the dough to serve between 4,000 and 5,000 of these treats. The contributor, Hilda Patkau, of Clavet, Saskatchewan, suggests serving these with watermelon, or with syrup. She also notes that they can be frozen and reheated.

7 eggs
2 cups creamilk
1 cup whipping cream
2 1/2 tablespoons salt
About 8 cups flour
2 teaspoons baking powder

Mix all ingredients together, adding more flour if necessary to make a soft dough. On a floured surface, roll dough very thin (about 1/8 inch thick). Cut in strips or rectangular pieces. Fry quickly in hot fat or oil until golden brown, turning once. Drain on paper towels.

Note: You may use thick farm cream and milk instead of creamilk and whipping cream.

Kuchli (Nothings)

This recipe's contributor recommends using natural sour cream and "soft" flour.

1 dozen large eggs
1 tablespoon salt
1 scant teaspoon baking
    soda
1 pint slightly sour cream
Flour

Beat eggs and salt in a large bowl. Dissolve baking soda in cream. Add enough flour to make a rather heavy dough. Knead dough on floured board until it no longer sticks to board. Then take a sharp knife and make slits through the lump. If dough is sticky, add more flour and keep kneading, about 30 minutes.

Make dough into balls the size of walnuts; put between plastic to keep from getting crusty. Roll as thin as possible; then stretch and fry in hot oil. Sugar the nothings as soon as they are fried.

MAKES 85 TO 90

Mrs. Metta Nussbaum
Ohio Mennonite Relief Sale, Kidron

Knie Blatza (Nothings)

1 dozen eggs
1 teaspoon salt
1 1/2 cups sweet or sour
    cream
1 teaspoon cream of tartar
    (or 1/2 teaspoon baking
    soda if sour cream is
    used)
8 to 12 cups flour

Mix first four ingredients with beater; beat in some of the flour. When dough gets too thick to beat, knead in rest of flour. Shape into balls the size of walnuts. Cover with waxed paper and damp towel; let rest 20 minutes. Roll flat and round. Place over knee and stretch thin. Fry in deep fat. Sprinkle with sugar.

MAKES 85 TO 90 "KNEE-PATCHES"

Mrs. Amos Amstutz
Ohio Mennonite Relief Sale, Kidron

Nothings

4 eggs
1 teaspoon salt
2 tablespoons oil
1/2 cup rich milk
3 cups flour

Mix as to roll. Let rise in a warm place. Take dough by tablespoons; roll thin and stretch. Fry in hot fat. Sprinkle with sugar.

Mrs. Ira Amstutz
Ohio Mennonite Relief Sale, Kidron

Froese-Fritz Apple Fritters

8 cups flour
1/4 cup baking powder
4 teaspoons salt
1 1/3 cups dry milk powder
1 1/4 cups sugar
8 eggs
8 cups water
Apple rings

Mix all ingredients (except apples) with a whisk. Dip apple rings in batter. Drop into hot oil (375°F) to fry.

Ann Froese Fritz
Rocky Mountain Mennonite Relief Sale, Rocky
Ford

Sam Fretz, 5, of Denver, Colo., helps his father, Joe, remove an apple from a hand-powered peeler and corer at the Rocky Mountain Mennonite Relief Sale.

(Photo by J.R. Thompson)

Oppel Kuchen (Apple Fritters)

1 egg
1/2 cup milk
1/2 teaspoon baking powder
1/4 teaspoon salt
1 cup flour
Apples, cut into small
    chunks

Mix all ingredients (except apples) together. Then add as many cut apples as the batter will hold. Drop by spoonfuls into deep fat; fry on both sides. Drain on absorbent paper. Sprinkle with sugar and eat.

Variation: Fresh cherries may be used in place of the apples.

Nebraska MCC Relief Sale, Aurora

Raisin Fritters (New Year's Cookies)

Recipes for New Year's Cookies--the raisin fritters known traditionally by such names as Portzelky, Poertzelki, and Portzilka--appear in the section titled "Cookies, Squares & Bars."

Funnel Cakes

4 eggs
3 cups milk
1/4 cup sugar
4 cups flour
4 teaspoons baking powder
2 teaspoons salt
Vegetable oil for frying
Confectioner's sugar

Beat eggs; add milk and sugar. Sift dry ingredients together; add to egg-milk mixture. Beat with a wire whisk until smooth.

Heat oil to 375°F. Pour 1/2 cup batter through funnel into heated oil. Fry a couple of minutes on each side. Drain on paper towels and sprinkle with confectioner's sugar before serving.

Ardith Epp
Nebraska MCC Relief Sale, Aurora

Ruth Ellen Doughnuts

Ruth Ellen's homemade doughnuts are an annual feature at the Southern Tier Mennonite Relief Sale in Bath, New York. The Riehl family started making these doughnuts at the third sale. In 1994, they made 375 dozen of this recipe, which was provided by Mildred Weaver, of Bath. People love to watch the doughnut-making; it always draws a crowd.

2 cups milk
1 cup sugar
3/4 cup shortening (or vegetable oil)
2 teaspoons salt
1 package yeast
1 cup warm water
2 eggs
10 to 11 cups bread flour (or enough to make a soft dough)

Scald milk. Stir in sugar, shortening, and salt; set aside to cool. Dissolve yeast in the warm water; set aside. Beat eggs. When milk mixture is cool, mix in eggs and yeast; stir in enough flour to make a soft dough.

Let dough rise until double in size. Roll out and cut into doughnuts. Let rise again until light. Fry in hot (365°F) lard. Sugar or glaze according to your taste.

MAKES ABOUT 65 AVERAGE-SIZE DOUGHNUTS

Berliner Pfannkuchen (Prune-Filled Doughnuts)

This is a favorite ethnic recipe of the Jantzen family in the Beatrice, Nebraska, community. Mrs. Gerald (Rogena Friesen) Jantzen, of Plymouth, has donated these doughnuts to the priced foods booth at the Nebraska MCC Relief Sale in Aurora. They sell quickly! She notes that they also freeze well.

1 pint milk
3/4 pound soft butter
1/2 cup sugar
2 packages dry yeast
8 egg yolks
4 whole eggs
About 8 cups flour
2 large packages
    medium-sized pitted
    prunes (cooked about 5
    minutes to soften)

Scald milk; add butter and sugar. Let cool slightly. Dissolve yeast in 1/2 cup hot (105° to 115°F) water. Add 1 to 2 cups flour to the milk mixture; beat well. Then add dissolved yeast and beat well. Beat in egg yolks and then whole eggs one at a time, beating well after each egg. Add remaining flour; beat until smooth and shiny. Let rise until double.

Have ready enough cold water to dip your teaspoon into so the dough will not stick to it and a small bowl of flour to drop your dough into so you can work with it (the dough is soft and sticky). Take a teaspoon of dough with the wet spoon and drop it into the flour. Then work the dough around a prune, being sure the dough covers the prune well. By the time you've made all the berliners, the first ones will be ready to fry. Fry in hot (375°F) oil or fat until brown. Roll in sugar before serving.

MAKES ABOUT 125

The children have hearty appetites at the 1992 pancake and sausage breakfast that begins at 6 a.m. at the Michiana Mennonite Relief Sale in Goshen, Ind.

(Photo by Marion Troyer)

Buckwheat Pancakes

These yeast-raised pancakes were one of the contributor's favorite foods when she was young. The recipe--never committed to paper until recently—was passed down from Mrs. Diller's grandmother, who was from southern Ohio. Mrs. Diller's mother always made the pancakes from memory. Not until a few years ago, at her daughter's urging, did she work out the recipe and write it down. Today, Mrs. Diller's family likes these pancakes for supper with real maple syrup.

1 cup white flour
1/2 cup whole wheat flour
1 cup buckwheat flour
5 heaping tablespoons sugar
2 teaspoons salt
1 package dry yeast
2 cups warm water
1/3 cup baking soda dissolved
    in a bit of warm water

Mix flours, sugar, and salt in a large bowl. Mix the yeast with the warm water; then mix it into the dry ingredients. Let batter rise, covered, for 2 hours. Just before frying, mix the soda water into the batter.

Corinne Hanna Diller, Houston, Texas
Houston Mennonite Church
Texas MCC Relief Sale, Houston

Russian Pancakes

The Dutch called them Flensjes. The low Germans in Prussia and Russia asked for Phlinzen. Whatever they are called, though, these pancakes are the soul food of the Germans from Russia who settled in Kansas. Made from ingredients readily available on early farms, they are a quick bread that is easy to make and serve.

Russian pancakes are usually served individually. Traditionally, filling is added, the pancake is rolled, and then it's eaten with a fork. Pancakes can also be eaten as a finger food. Another serving possibility is to layer pancakes with a filling and then cut the stack into wedges.

Russian pancakes are usually sprinkled with sugar or cinnamon-sugar. They are often served with watermelon. They can also be served with chopped boiled eggs, bacon, or cream gravy. However they're served, they are a substantial and very versatile food.

5 eggs
1 tablespoon sugar
2 teaspoons salt
1 stick (1/2 cup) margarine, melted
6 cups milk
4 cups flour

Beat eggs; add sugar, salt, and margarine; mix. Add two-thirds of the milk and half the flour; mix well. Add remaining milk and flour; mix again. Pour batter into hot, greased pan; lift and tilt pan so that batter covers bottom. Brown pancake lightly on first side; flip to other side and brown.

Vernon Wiebe, Hillsboro, Kansas
Mid-Kansas Relief Sale, Hutchinson

Pflinzen

1 cup flour
1/2 teaspoon salt
3/4 cup milk
3/4 cup water
1 egg

Place flour and salt in a bowl; gradually add liquids and egg. Beat until batter is smooth (batter will be thin). Pour about 1/4 cup batter into a hot greased frying pan. Allow it to run over entire surface, forming a thin layer. When edges begin to brown, turn pancake and fry on other side.

MAKES 6 OR 8 PANCAKES

Frances Von Riesen, Beatrice, Nebraska
Nebraska MCC Relief Sale, Aurora

Pancakes All Over the Pan (Russian Pancakes or Crepes)

The contributor suggests making a white sauce of sugar, cornstarch, milk, and vanilla, boiled until slightly thickened, to pour over these pancakes before serving.

3 eggs
2 cups rich milk
1 teaspoon salt
2 cups flour
1 teaspoon baking powder
1/8 teaspoon sugar

Place all ingredients in a bowl; beat well. At one edge of hot, slightly greased skillet, pour about 3 tablespoons of batter. Quickly tilt pan to cover bottom completely. When edges begin to brown, turn over to brown on other side. Sprinkle with sugar and cinnamon and roll up.

Irene Penner, Corn, Oklahoma
Oklahoma MCC Relief Sale, Fairview

Kirschen Pflinzen

This very old German Mennonite dish has been handed down through the Claassen family. Faye (Birky) Claassen, of Albany, Oregon, says her family often takes it to reunions and picnics and serves it cold. The trick, she shares, is to have the batter for the pancakes thin enough but not too thin! Mrs. Claassen won a Grand Champion in International Foods competition with this recipe at the 1974 Oregon State Fair.

Pflinzen:
1 1/2 cups flour
1 tablespoon granulated
  sugar
1/2 teaspoon salt
2 cups (approximately) milk
3 eggs, slightly beaten

Kirschen:
2 to 3 cups canned or frozen
  (and thawed) red sour
  cherries and their juice
3/4 cup granulated sugar (or
  to taste)
2 heaping tablespoons
  cornstarch
2 tablespoons cool water
Red food coloring

Make Pflinzen batter by combining flour, sugar, and salt; gradually add milk and eggs. Beat well until batter is very smooth. Batter should be very thin.

Prepare Kirschen by adding enough water to the cherries and their juice to make 4 to 4 1/2 cups cherries and liquid. Heat to boiling. Make a smooth paste of the sugar, cornstarch, and cool water. Add paste to hot cherries; cook, stirring, until clear. Stir in several drops red food coloring. Keep cherries hot (but not boiling) while frying the Pflinzen.

Heat and lightly grease an 8-inch frying pan. Pour in just enough batter to cover bottom of pan, tilting pan so batter runs over entire surface. Fry (over medium heat) until edges are golden brown; turn and fry other side.

As Pflinzen are fried, stack immediately in a clear glass bowl with Kirschen: Start with two Pflinzen, then a layer of Kirschen, then two more Pflinzen, and so on, ending with cherries. To serve, cut completely through stack into pie-shaped wedges. Serve warm or cool.

Oregon MCC Fall Festival, Albany

Noni Snicki or Nolles Nicki (Crepe Suzettes)

Filling:
2 cups cottage cheese
2 teaspoons sugar
2 tablespoons flour
2 eggs
1 teaspoon cinnamon

Pancakes:
1 cup flour
1 1/2 to 2 cups milk
2 or 3 eggs, beaten
1 to 2 tablespoons vegetable
    oil
1/2 teaspoon salt

Mix all filling ingredients well; set aside while making pancakes.

Prepare pancake batter by mixing flour and milk until smooth. Add remaining ingredients; mix until smooth. Pour enough batter over bottom of large skillet to make a big but very thin pancake. When brown on first side, flip to brown other side. After making all the pancakes (or as you make each one), spread some filling on the brownest side and roll up pancake. Place in cake pan and bake in a 350°F oven for about 30 minutes.

Variations: These pancakes can also be filled with cooked rhubarb or with applesauce. Or, sprinkle them with sugar and serve with sour cream.

Gertie Graber, Freeman, South Dakota
Minn-Kota MCC Relief Sale, Sioux Falls,
South Dakota

The Ontario Relief Sale is famous for the 6,000 fruit pies which volunteers prepare. During the sale, 1,500 additional fresh strawberry pies are prepared and sold. Sitting in the bleachers high above the pie operation, volunteers carefully stem strawberries. Is this pie making in the sky? In the first 25 years, more than 125,000 pies were sold at the sale.

— Love in Action News, MCC

Brownie Pie

Bertha Stark, of Freeman, South Dakota, says that although this pie is special, it's very easy to make. Because of that, she suggests preparing at least two pies at a time. The ingredients given here make one crust, but enough filling for two pies.

Crust:
3 egg whites
Pinch of salt
3/4 cup sugar
3/4 cup chocolate wafers or graham crackers, coarsely crushed
1/2 cup chopped walnuts
1/2 teaspoon vanilla
1/2 teaspoon almond extract

Filling:
1 package lemon pie filling, prepared
1 cup whipping cream, whipped

To make the crust: Beat egg whites and salt until frothy; gradually add sugar, beating until whites form very stiff peaks. Fold in crumbs and walnuts, then vanilla and almond extracts. Turn into a well-greased pie tin, spreading evenly. Bake at 325°F for 35 minutes. Remove from oven and cool completely.

To make the filling: Prepare lemon pie filling according to package directions. Fold whipped cream into cooled filling. Fill pie crusts (makes enough to fill two pies).

SERVES 8

Minn-Kota MCC Relief Sale, Sioux Falls, South Dakota

Ground Cherry Pie

Two of these very tasty pies are auctioned each year at the Minn-Kota Relief Sale in Sioux Falls, South Dakota, and sell for $150 apiece. This recipe has raised more than $1,200 for world relief through auctions and church functions.

1 1/2 cups cooked ground
   cherries
3/4 cup sugar
3 tablespoons Minute
   tapioca
Pastry for double-crust pie

Mix filling ingredients. Pour into a pastry-lined pie pan, add upper crust, and bake 45 minutes.

Mrs. Helen Schmidt, Marion, South Dakota

Tart Apple Pie

1/3 cup white sugar
1/3 cup brown sugar
1/2 teaspoon cinnamon
1 cup applesauce
2 cups sliced apples
One unbaked 9-inch pie
   shell

Topping:
3/4 cup flour
1/3 cup brown sugar
6 tablespoons butter

Combine sugars, cinnamon, applesauce, and apples. Place in pie shell. For topping, combine flour and brown sugar; cut in butter. Spread crumbled mixture over top of pie. Bake until filling is hot and bubbly and crust is browned.

Bernice Lehman, Johnstown, Pennsylvania
MCC Quilt Auction and Relief Sale, Johnstown

People attend relief sales from outside the general vicinity of the event, it's true. But one woman from a small central California town was on her way to Fresno to do some shopping when she heard about the West Coast Sale for World Relief on the car radio and decided to stop there first. She left with a quilt and some other items for $13,000.

Boysenberry Pie

At the West Coast Mennonite Sale and Auction for World Relief in Fresno, California, one year's sale is barely over before the women of Dinuba Mennonite Brethren Church start planning for next April's sale. Throughout the summer, they stock their freezers and pantries with the boysenberries, peaches, nectarines, apricots, and apples from which they'll make the mouth-watering fresh fruit pies sold at the sale.

"It's pie-making time," announces the church bulletin the Sunday before the sale. Four days later, gallons of the frozen and canned fruit arrive at the church kitchen, where 20 women roll dough, mix fillings, and pinch crust edges to make more than 800 pies. "We just bake till the fruit's all gone," says Janet Warkentin, one of the coordinators.

Pies are sold by the piece at the pie and coffee booth. Whole pies are popular purchases at the baked goods booth.

Pie Crust (full recipe)
16 cups flour
3 cups shortening
4 cups milk
2 tablespoons salt

Boysenberry Filling (per pie)
4 cups berries
3/4 cup sugar
2 tablespoons cornstarch
2 tablespoons
  raspberry-flavored
  gelatin

Make pastry; roll into bottom and top crusts and set aside. Mix filling ingredients thoroughly and pour into crust. Top with a second crust; pinch edges to seal. Spray top crust with milk from a spray bottle; sprinkle with sugar.

Kathy Heinrichs Weist, Kingsburg, California

English Walnut Pie

1 rounded tablespoon flour
1/4 cup sugar
1/8 teaspoon salt
3 eggs, well beaten
1/4 cup water
1 cup King syrup (your
   choice)
2 tablespoons butter (don't
   use margarine), melted
1 cup chopped walnut meats
One unbaked 9- or 10-inch
   pie shell

Combine flour, sugar, and salt. Add beaten eggs. Combine water, syrup, and butter; mix well with eggs. Spread walnuts over bottom of pie shell. Pour filling over nuts. Bake at 425°F for 10 minutes; then reduce heat to 350° and bake 35 minutes longer. If crust browns too quickly, cover edges with aluminum foil halfway through baking time.

Erma Kauffman, Cochranville, Pennsylvania
Gap Relief Sale, Gap, Pennsylvania

Poppy Seed Pie

Pieces of this pie disappear at the Minn-Kota Relief Sale board meeting in Sioux Falls, South Dakota.

1 cup poppy seeds
4 egg yolks
3 cups milk
2 cups cream
2 cups sugar
1 teaspoon vanilla
2 tablespoons cornstarch
2 tablespoons flour
3 baked pie shells

Mix together all filling ingredients; cook until thick. Divide evenly among the 3 baked pie shells. Make your favorite egg white meringue to spread over each pie. Brown meringue in hot oven.

Pam Hofer, Carpenter, South Dakota

Diabetic Pumpkin Pie

This pie makes its own crust.

1/2 cup Bisquick
2 beaten eggs (or 1 carton
    egg substitute)
1 can (16 oz) pumpkin
1/2 cup (scant) Sugar Twin
1 can (12 oz) evaporated
    skim milk
1/4 teaspoon nutmeg
1 teaspoon cinnamon
2 1/2 teaspoons vanilla

Combine all ingredients. Pour into a *greased* pie pan. Bake at 350°F (325° for a glass pie plate) for 1 hour.

Rosalie R. Forrester, Bloomington, Illinois
Faith Evangelical Mennonite Church
Illinois MCC Relief Sale, Peoria

Custard Pumpkin Pie

1 cup cooked pumpkin
3 eggs, separated
1/2 cup white sugar
1/2 cup brown sugar
1 tablespoon cornstarch
1/2 teaspoon salt
1/4 teaspoon ginger
1/4 teaspoon cloves
1 teaspoon cinnamon
2 cups milk, scalded
One unbaked 9-inch pie
    shell

To pumpkin, add beaten egg yolks, sugars, cornstarch, salt, and spices. Gradually add scalded milk, mixing thoroughly. Fold in stiffly beaten egg whites. Pour mixture into *unbaked* pie shell. Bake at 425°F for 10 minutes; then reduce heat to 350° and bake for 30 minutes more.

Mrs. Lovell Franks, East Peoria, Illinois
East Peoria Mennonite Church
Illinois MCC Relief Sale, Peoria

Pumpkin Pie

This recipe from the Altona Women's Institute Cookbook, *published in 1959, was contributed to that volume by Mrs. P. L. Dick.*

1 1/2 cups cooked pumpkin
1 teaspoon flour
1 cup sugar
1 teaspoon cinnamon
1 teaspoon ginger
1/8 teaspoon nutmeg
1/2 teaspoon mace
1/4 teaspoon salt
3 eggs, well beaten
1/2 cup milk
Pastry for deep-dish
      single-crust pie

Mix pumpkin, flour, sugar, spices, and salt. Combine beaten eggs and milk; add to pumpkin mixture. Stir it all together. Pour into a deep pie plate lined with a good rich pastry. Bake in a moderate oven (350°F) for about 35 minutes.

Ben Sawatzky, Winnipeg, Manitoba
MCC Manitoba Relief Sale

Pumpkin Pie

The oldest member of Bethel Mennonite Church, Emily L. Miller of Pekin, Illinois, shares this recipe.

3 eggs
1/2 teaspoon salt
1 cup brown sugar
1/4 cup white sugar
1 tablespoon flour
1 1/2 teaspoons cinnamon
1/2 teaspoon ginger
2 cups canned pumpkin
3 cups milk (part
      half-and-half)
One unbaked pie shell

Beat eggs until light; add salt and brown sugar and beat until fluffy. Mix in white sugar, flour, and spices. Stir in pumpkin and milk. Pour into pie shell. Bake at 425°F for 15 minutes; reduce heat to 350° and bake until done.

Illinois MCC Relief Sale, Peoria

Pumpkin Pie

3 eggs
1 1/2 cups cooked pumpkin
1/2 cup powdered milk
1/2 cup brown sugar
1/2 cup white sugar
1/2 teaspoon salt
1 tablespoon cornstarch
1 teaspoon cinnamon
1/2 teaspoon nutmeg
1/2 teaspoon ginger
1/4 teaspoon cloves
1 teaspoon vanilla
1 1/2 cups water
One unbaked pie shell

Place eggs in large bowl; beat well. Add remaining ingredients (except water). Beat together to combine, adding the water 1/2 cup at a time. Pour into a prepared unbaked pie crust. Bake at 425°F for 15 minutes; then lower heat to 350° and bake 30 minutes more or until done.

Mrs. Roger (Lavonne) McGuire, Morton, Illinois
First Mennonite Church, Morton
Illinois MCC Relief Sale, Peoria

Pumpkin or Squash Pie

3 eggs, separated
2 cups cooked pumpkin or
    squash
1 3/4 cups white sugar
2 tablespoons flour
1 teaspoon cinnamon
1/4 teaspoon cloves
1/4 teaspoon ginger
1/4 teaspoon nutmeg
1 pint milk
1 can condensed milk
One unbaked pie shell

In separate bowls, beat egg yolks well; beat egg whites until fluffy. Combine pumpkin, sugar, flour, spices, and beaten yolks. Stir in both types of milk. Add egg whites to pumpkin mixture; mix in with an egg beater. Pour filling into prepared unbaked pie shell. Bake at 425°F for 15 minutes; then reduce heat to 375° and bake 15 minutes more, or until knife inserted into center of pie comes out clean.

MCC Quilt Auction and Relief Sale,
Johnstown, Pennsylvania

Sour Cream Raisin Pie

2 eggs
1 cup sugar
1 cup raisins
1 cup sour cream
1/2 teaspoon cinnamon
1/2 teaspoon cloves
1/4 teaspoon salt
2 tablespoons vinegar
One unbaked pie shell

Beat together eggs and sugar. Mix in remaining ingredients. Pour into unbaked pie shell. Bake at 350°F for 50 minutes.

Bernice Schroll
(Submitted by N. Elizabeth Graber,
Wayland, Iowa)
Iowa MCC Relief Sale, Iowa City

Grandma's Egg Custard Pie

3 large eggs
1/2 cup sugar
1/2 teaspoon salt
2 2/3 cups milk
1 teaspoon vanilla
One unbaked pie shell

Beat eggs slightly. Beat in sugar, salt, milk, and vanilla. Pour into pastry-lined pie pan. Bake at 350°F for 15 minutes; reduce heat to 325° and bake 25 minutes more, or just until silver knife inserted in custard comes out clean. Serve cold.

Ethel P. Thomas, Johnstown, Pennsylvania
MCC Quilt Auction and Relief Sale, Johnstown

Custard Pie

4 eggs
1/2 cup sugar
1/4 teaspoon salt
2 1/2 cups milk
1/2 teaspoon vanilla
Pinch nutmeg
One unbaked pie shell

Beat eggs slightly; mix in sugar, salt, milk, vanilla, and nutmeg. Pour into unbaked pie shell. Bake at 400°F for 25 to 30 minutes.

Bernice Schroll
(Submitted by N. Elizabeth Graber,
Wayland, Iowa)
Iowa MCC Relief Sale, Iowa City

Peanut Butter Pie

2 egg yolks
1 1/2 cups scalded milk
1 cup brown sugar
3 tablespoons peanut butter
1 tablespoon flour or 1 1/2
    teaspoons cornstarch
1/4 teaspoon salt
One baked pie shell

Combine egg yolks, milk, sugar, peanut butter, flour, and salt. Cook until thickened, stirring often. Cool slightly; pour into baked pie shell. Top with your favorite meringue; place in a hot oven just long enough to brown meringue.

Bernice Schroll
(Submitted by N. Elizabeth Graber,
Wayland, Iowa)
Iowa MCC Relief Sale, Iowa City

Leo Greco, left, and Jim Doyne, radio personalities from WMT Radio, sample the fresh strawberry pie during a commercial break at the Iowa MCC Relief Sale in Iowa City.
(Photo by Frank and Ada Yoder)

Mince Meat

15 pints chopped apples
5 pints ground beef, cooked
    and salted
2 pints molasses
3 pints sugar
5 pints raisins
2 pints cider vinegar
2 tablespoons cinnamon
1 tablespoon *each:* black
    pepper, nutmeg, and
    cloves

Combine all ingredients; heat to boiling. Can while hot, or freeze.

Bernice Schroll
(Submitted by N. Elizabeth Graber,
Wayland, Iowa)
Iowa MCC Relief Sale, Iowa City

Creamy Butter Pecan Pie

1 can (14 oz) Eagle Brand
    sweetened condensed
    milk
1 1/2 cups cold water
1 package (3 1/2 oz) instant
    butter pecan pudding mix
6 ounces nondairy whipped
    topping
One baked 9-inch pie shell

Combine milk and water; add pudding mix. Beat until well blended. Chill 5 minutes. Fold in whipped topping. Pour into baked pie shell.

Variation: Substitute your favorite flavor of pudding mix for the butter pecan.

Becky Miller
Pleasant View Mennonite Church, Goshen, Indiana

Strawberry Parfait Pie

1 package (3 oz)
    strawberry-flavored
    gelatin
1 1/4 cups hot water
1 pint vanilla ice cream
1 1/2 cups sliced fresh
    strawberries
One baked 9-inch pie shell

Dissolve gelatin in the hot water. Add ice cream, stirring until melted. Chill until thick, *but not set.* Fold in berries. Turn into baked pie shell. Chill until firm. Serve with whipped cream.

Variation: Substitute peach-flavored gelatin and fresh peaches.

Ester V. Mishler, Johnstown, Pennsylvania
MCC Quilt Auction and Relief Sale, Johnstown

Perischke

Three to four hundred of these small pies--made by the women of the Mountain Lake, Minnesota, area--are sold each year at the Minn-Kota MCC Relief Sale in Sioux Falls, South Dakota. The pies can be prepared ahead, frozen unbaked, and then baked the day before the sale.

9 cups flour
4 1/2 cups shortening (at
    room temperature)
1/2 teaspoon baking powder
1 tablespoon salt
2 tablespoons vinegar
3 eggs
2 cups milk (approximately)

Mix dough ingredients as you would for a pie dough. Roll out. Cut into 5-inch squares. Put several tablespoons of a filling of your choice in the center of each square. (See filling suggestions below.) Fold corners into middle; seal. Bake at 375° to 400°F for about 25 minutes.

Dried Fruit Filling: Cook dried apricots, prunes, raisins, peaches, or any combination of dried fruits with just enough water and sugar to make a jamlike filling.

Fresh Apple Filling: Spread sliced apples in center of dough square; sprinkle with sugar and cinnamon.

Makes enough dough for 40 to 50 pies

Henry Kleiver found that loosening his belt could make a big difference at a relief sale. He bought a belt buckle for 20 cents and donated it to the Nebraska Relief Sale auction. It brought $89 to the total.

Butter Tarts

1 pound butter
1 pound flour (about 4 cups
sifted)
1 egg
Tart filling of choice

Using a knife, cut butter into flour until lumps are the size of peas. Beat egg in 1-cup measure; add enough water to fill cup. Mix egg mixture into butter-flour mixture with a fork. Even if dough is crumbly, start rolling together. Roll out three times; then put in refrigerator and cool for 1 hour. Remove dough, and roll out two more times. Refrigerate until next day.

Roll out dough one more time. Cut into circles large enough to fill muffin tins. Fill with cherry, apricot, or poppy seed filling. Bake at 400°F for 15 minutes.

Margarete Claassen, Beatrice, Nebraska
Nebraska MCC Relief Sale, Aurora

Sour Cream Cocoa Cake

2 1/2 cups flour
2 cups sugar
6 tablespoons cocoa
2 teaspoons baking soda
1/2 teaspoon salt
1/2 teaspoon cinnamon
4 eggs, well beaten
2 cups thick sour cream
1 teaspoon vanilla

Sift dry ingredients together *three* times. Mix eggs, sour cream, and vanilla. Add to dry ingredients; beat well. Bake at 375°F for 35 minutes.

Lanna Waltner, Hurley, South Dakota
Minn-Kota MCC Relief Sale, Sioux Falls,
South Dakota

♥ Down-Side Up Fudge Cake

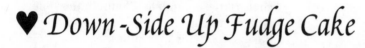

1 tablespoon solid vegetable
   shortening (Crisco)
3/4 cup white sugar
1/2 cup milk
1 teaspoon vanilla
1 cup flour
1 1/2 tablespoons cocoa
1 teaspoon baking powder
1/2 teaspoon salt

Topping:
1/2 cup chopped nuts
1/4 cup cocoa
1/2 cup white sugar
1/2 cup brown sugar
1 1/4 cups *boiling* water

To make the cake batter, cream shortening and sugar; stir in milk and vanilla. Sift together flour, cocoa, baking powder, and salt. Add to creamed mixture, mixing thoroughly. Pour into greased 8-inch-square pan.

Top batter first with nuts. Then combine cocoa and sugars; sprinkle evenly over nuts. Pour the boiling water (be sure it's boiling) over batter and topping.

Bake at 350°F for 35 minutes. Cool 15 minutes; then invert cake onto serving plate. Serve plain or with whipped topping.

Note: You can decrease the amount of cocoa if desired and omit the nuts.

E.A.F.
MCC Quilt Auction and Relief Sale,
Johnstown, Pennsylvania

Wacky Cake

When you want something smaller than a sheet cake, try this recipe.

1 1/2 cups flour
1 teaspoon baking soda
1/4 teaspoon salt
1 cup sugar
2 tablespoons cocoa
3/8 cup vegetable oil
1 1/2 tablespoons vinegar
1 cup cold water
1 teaspoon vanilla

Frosting:
1 1/2 cups white sugar
3 tablespoons milk
3 tablespoons margarine
1/4 cup chocolate chips

Into a mixing bowl, sift together flour, soda, salt, sugar, and cocoa. Make a well in the dry ingredients. Add oil, vinegar, water, and vanilla. Beat *by hand* until thoroughly mixed. Pour into 8-inch-square pan. Bake at 350°F for 30 to 35 minutes.

To make frosting, carefully bring sugar, milk, and margarine to a rolling boil, stirring. Remove from heat; add chips. Stir vigorously until chips melt and frosting is of spreading consistency.

Mrs. Alice (Wilbert) Graber, Parker,
South Dakota
Minn-Kota MCC Relief Sale, Sioux Falls,
South Dakota

Miracle Whip Cake

2 cups flour
1 cup sugar
1/2 cup cocoa
1/4 teaspoon (level) baking
   soda
1/2 teaspoon baking powder
1 cup Miracle Whip
1 cup water
1 teaspoon vanilla

Combine all ingredients. Bake at 350°F for 30 minutes.

Rosalie R. Forrester, Bloomington, Illinois
Faith Evangelical Mennonite Church
Illinois MCC Relief Sale, Peoria

Schichtkuchin (Layer Cake)

This recipe makes enough batter for 8 or 9 thin layers.

1 cup butter
1 1/2 cups sugar
4 eggs
3 cups flour
3 teaspoons baking powder
1 cup milk

Cream butter and sugar. Add eggs; beat well. Mix flour and baking powder; add to creamed mixture alternately with milk. Spreading only a thin layer of batter in each pan, divide batter evenly among nine greased 8-inch or eight greased 9-inch round cake pans. Bake at 350°F for about 10 minutes. Cool. Then fill with chocolate, lemon, almond paste, or fruit filling.

Erna Marie Reimer
Nebraska MCC Relief Sale, Aurora

♥ Angel Food Supreme Cake

This is a favorite recipe of Pam Hofer, of Carpenter, South Dakota, who makes more than one of these cakes for the dessert booth at the Minn-Kota Relief Sale in Sioux Falls, South Dakota. Volunteers slice the cakes and top the slices with whipped cream and strawberries before serving.

1 cup Softasilk cake flour
3/4 cup plus 2 tablespoons sugar
1 1/2 cups egg whites
1 1/2 teaspoons cream of tartar
1/4 teaspoon salt
3/4 cup sugar
1 1/2 teaspoons vanilla
1/2 teaspoon almond extract

Heat oven to 375°F. Have tube pan ready; do not grease.

Sift flour with the 3/4 cup plus 2 tablespoons sugar to blend well. Set aside.

Place egg whites, cream of tartar, and salt in a large mixing bowl. Beat until foamy. Gradually add the 3/4 cup sugar, 2 tablespoons at a time. Continue beating until meringue holds stiff peaks. Fold in flavorings.

Sprinkle about one-third of the flour-sugar mixture over the meringue; fold in gently. Repeat two more times. Carefully push batter into tube pan. Gently cut through batter with a knife to remove air bubbles. Bake in preheated oven for 30 to 35 minutes. Remove from oven and invert pan over funnel or soda bottle. Let hang until cake is cool.

Yvonne Devers remembers the year a young lady created a stuffed bear and donated it to the MCC Quilt Auction and Relief Sale in Johnstown, Pa. It so happened that her young man, one of the auctioneers, decided to buy it. After bidding as high as he could go, the poor fellow decided he'd have to quit. Sale volunteers then literally passed the hat to help him win the bid on the bear. Needless to say, after much fun and laughter, he got the bear. The girl is now his wife! Could it be that he bought an engagement bear?

♥ Angel Food Cake

**2 cups egg whites (1 dozen
  jumbo eggs)**
2 teaspoons cream of tartar
1/2 teaspoon salt
2 cups sugar
**2 cups cake flour (Softasilk)
  sifted with 1/2 cup sugar**
2 teaspoons vanilla

Beat egg whites until foamy. Add cream of tartar; beat just until stiff enough to stand in peaks. Add salt. Slowly add the 2 cups sugar, continuing to beat until stiff peaks form. Then fold in flour-sugar mixture and finally vanilla. Put in tube pan and into cold oven. Turn heat to 350°F for 20 minutes, then to between 350° and 375° for 10 to 15 minutes. Invert cake to cool.

*Ethel P. Thomas, Johnstown, Pennsylvania
MCC Quilt Auction and Relief Sale, Johnstown*

Buttermilk Cake

2 cups flour
1 cup granulated sugar
1/2 cup brown sugar
1/2 teaspoon cinnamon
1 teaspoon salt
1 teaspoon baking soda
1 teaspoon baking powder
1 cup buttermilk
**2/3 cup shortening or
  margarine**
2 eggs
1 teaspoon vanilla

Topping:
1 cup brown sugar
1 teaspoon cinnamon
1/2 teaspoon vanilla

Mix together flour, sugars, cinnamon, salt, baking soda, and baking powder. Add buttermilk, shortening, eggs, and vanilla; beat well. Spread batter in cake pan. Combine topping ingredients; sprinkle over batter. Bake at 350°F for 25 to 30 minutes.

*Mrs. Richard (Marilyn) Oyer, Gridley, Illinois
Salem Evangelical Mennonite Church, Gridley
Illinois MCC Relief Sale, Peoria*

Banana Cake

2 cups all-purpose flour
1/4 teaspoon salt
1 1/3 cups sugar
1/3 cup shortening
2 eggs
1 teaspoon baking soda,
    moistened in vinegar
1 cup milk
2 large (or 3 small) bananas,
    mashed

Mix ingredients in order given. Spread batter in cake pan. Bake at 350°F.

Shirley Shoemaker
MCC Quilt Auction and Relief Sale,
Johnstown, Pennsylvania

Cranberry Cake

2 cups flour
1/2 teaspoon salt
2 teaspoons baking powder
1 1/2 cups sugar
1/4 cup soft butter or marga-
    rine
1 cup milk
3 cups whole raw cranber-
    ries

Butter Sauce:
1/2 cup butter
1 cup sugar
1 tablespoon cornstarch
1/2 cup whipping cream
1 teaspoon vanilla

Mix cake ingredients, adding cranberries last. Pour into greased 13x9-inch pan. Bake at 375°F.

Mix all sauce ingredients except vanilla; bring to a boil. Remove from heat; stir in vanilla. Serve warm over cake.

SERVES 12 TO 15

Arlene Dick, Mountain Lake, Minnesota
Minn-Kota MCC Relief Sale, Sioux Falls,
South Dakota

Anhaltskuchen (Loaf Cake Topped with Almonds)

This cake is sold at the priced baked goods booth at the Nebraska Relief Sale in Aurora.

1 cup butter
2 cups sugar
6 eggs
2 cups enriched flour, sifted
1/4 teaspoon almond extract
1 package (2.25 oz or 1/2 cup) slivered almonds

Cream butter and sugar well. Add eggs; beat until light and fluffy. Add flour and almond extract. Mix well. Spoon into greased 5 1/2x9-inch loaf pan. Smooth batter to sides, leaving the center somewhat hollowed out so that loaf bakes more level. Sprinkle almonds over batter. Bake at 325°F for about 1 hour, or until golden brown. Cool on rack. To serve, cut into 1/2-inch-thick slices.

MAKES ABOUT 16 SLICES

Mrs. Lawrence (Ann) Reimer, Beatrice, Nebraska

Chocolate Applesauce Cake

1/2 cup shortening
2 unbeaten eggs
2 cups applesauce
2 cups flour
1 1/2 cups sugar
1 1/2 teaspoons baking soda
2 tablespoons cocoa
1/2 teaspoon cinnamon
1/2 teaspoon ground allspice
1/2 teaspoon ground cloves
1/2 teaspoon ground nutmeg
1/2 cup chopped nuts
1 package (6 oz) chocolate chips
2 tablespoons sugar

Beat together shortening, eggs, and applesauce. Add flour, the 1 1/2 cups sugar, baking soda, cocoa, and spices. Spread batter in greased and floured 9x13-inch pan. Top batter with nuts, chocolate chips, and the 2 tablespoons sugar. Bake at 350°F for 40 minutes.

Linda King, Roanoke, Illinois
Metamora Mennonite Church
Illinois MCC Relief Sale, Peoria

♥ "Baked-on" Frosting for an Applesauce Cake

This very old recipe came originally from Margarete (Claassen, Goertz) Penner. It was submitted by Faye Claassen, of Albany, Oregon.

1 egg white
1/4 teaspoon baking powder
3/4 cup brown sugar
1/4 cup chopped nuts

Beat egg white until frothy. Add baking powder; beat until stiff. Gradually add brown sugar; beat until creamy. Spread over hot (baked) cake; sprinkle with nuts. Return cake to 350°F oven and bake just until topping bubbles and turns light brown.

Oregon MCC Fall Festival, Albany

Granny Cake

Volunteers make about 30 of these cakes to serve with 700 dinners at the Northern Michigan MCC Relief Sale chicken barbecue dinner, in Fairview.

1 1/2 cups white sugar
2 teaspoons baking soda
2 cups flour
1/2 teaspoon salt
2 eggs, beaten
1 can (20 oz) crushed pine-
apple
1/2 cup brown sugar
1/2 cup chopped nuts

Glaze:
1/2 cup sugar
1 stick (1/2 cup) margarine
1 cup evaporated milk
1 teaspoon vanilla

Stir together the white sugar, baking soda, flour, and salt. Add eggs and pineapple; mix well. Pour into a 13x9-inch pan. Sprinkle brown sugar and nuts over batter. Bake at 350°F for 35 to 40 minutes.

About 20 minutes before cake is finished baking, prepare glaze. Combine sugar, margarine, and milk in a saucepan. Bring to a boil and boil 15 minutes. Remove from heat and stir in vanilla. Pour glaze over hot cake when you take it from oven.

MAKES 24 SERVINGS

Sherry Troyer, Mio, Michigan
Chicken Dinner committee

Poor Man Cake

2 cups sugar
4 cups flour
1 teaspoon baking soda
1 teaspoon salt
1 teaspoon cinnamon
1 teaspoon ground nutmeg
1 teaspoon ground cloves
1 box (16 oz) raisins
2 cups cold water
1/2 cup solid vegetable
    shortening (Crisco)
1 cup cold water

In a large mixing bowl, mix together sugar, flour, baking soda, salt, and spices. Place raisins and the 2 cups cold water in a saucepan; boil 15 minutes. Add shortening and the 1 cup cold water; stir until shortening melts.

Pour raisin mixture into dry ingredients; mix well. Bake at 350°F: 40 to 60 minutes for a 13x9-inch pan or 30 minutes for two 8-inch-square pans. (You can also bake the cake in two bread/loaf pans.) Test with a toothpick for doneness.

MCC Quilt Auction and Relief Sale,
Johnstown, Pennsylvania

Texas Chocolate Cake

2 cups flour
2 cups sugar
2 sticks (1 cup) margarine
3 tablespoons cocoa
1 cup water
1/2 cup buttermilk
2 eggs
1 teaspoon baking soda
1 teaspoon vanilla
1/2 teaspoon cinnamon

Icing:
3 tablespoons cocoa
1 stick (1/2 cup) butter
6 tablespoons milk
1 box powdered sugar
    (approximately)
1 teaspoon vanilla
1 cup chopped nuts (optional)

Sift together flour and sugar. Combine margarine, cocoa, and water; bring to a boil. Pour over flour-sugar mixture; mix well. Add remaining ingredients; mix well. Pour into greased and floured 13x9-inch pan. Bake at 350°F for about 30 minutes. Cool about 15 minutes before icing.

About 5 minutes after taking cake from oven, combine cocoa, butter, and milk in a saucepan. Bring to a boil. *Remove from heat* and beat in powdered sugar in batches until icing is of desired consistency; add vanilla and nuts toward end. Beat well. Spread icing on warm cake.

Missouri MCC Relief Sale, Harrisonville

♥ *Great-Grandmother Troyer's Eggless Wonder Spice Cake*

Old meets new in this very old cake recipe because great-granddaughter Janelle Claassen, of Newberg, Oregon, developed the topping/filling.

1 3/4 cups granulated sugar
1/3 cup margarine (or 1/4 cup lard)
3 cups all-purpose flour
1/2 teaspoon salt
1 1/2 teaspoons cinnamon
1/2 teaspoon ground nutmeg
1/4 teaspoon cloves
2 cups buttermilk
2 teaspoons baking soda

Topping/Filling:
2/3 cup granulated sugar
3 tablespoons cornstarch
1 1/4 cups apple juice
1 cup raisins (plumped)
2 tablespoons margarine or butter

Cream together sugar and margarine. Sift together flour, salt, and spices. Stir together buttermilk and baking soda. Add buttermilk and flour mixtures alternately to the creamed mixture, beating well after each addition. Pour batter into two greased and floured 8-inch round cake pans. Bake at 350°F for 30 to 35 minutes, or until toothpick inserted in center comes out clean.

To make topping/filling, combine sugar and cornstarch. Add juice and raisins. Cook over medium heat, stirring frequently, until thick. Add margarine and remove from heat. Cool slightly. Spread between layers and over top of cake (topping will drizzle down sides of cake).

Variation: For a chocolate version of this cake, reduce flour to 2 1/2 cups, add 1/2 cup cocoa, and omit the spices.

Oregon MCC Fall Festival, Albany

Karovei

This recipe for a yeast-leavened sweet cake makes close to a dozen.

2 cups cream
2 cups sugar
Half a stick (1/4 cup) butter
1/4 cup lard
2 1/2 teaspoons salt
3 large eggs
2 cups flour
3 packages yeast
Additional flour (to make a soft dough)

Mix cream, 1 1/2 cups of the sugar, the butter, lard, and salt. Bring to a boil; then remove from heat and let cool to lukewarm. Beat eggs; mix in remaining 1/2 cup sugar. Let stand.

Make a sponge of the 2 cups flour, the yeast, and enough lukewarm water to make a fairly thick batter. Let sponge rise until cream mixture is lukewarm. Then stir cream and egg mixtures into sponge. Stir in enough additional flour to make a soft dough.

Knead dough twice at 25-minute intervals. Then let rise in a warm place for about 3 hours. Divide dough among 10 to 12 pie pans, spreading to cover bottom of pan. Let rise until double in size (about 3 hours). Bake at 325° to 350°F for 20 minutes. Cool.

Ice with your favorite frosting; decorate with corn or another decorative candy or with colored sugar.

MAKES 10 TO 12 CAKES

Mid-Kansas MCC Relief Sale, Hutchinson

Jelly Roll

6 eggs, separated
1 cup sugar
1 cup white flour
1 teaspoon baking powder
1 teaspoon vanilla
1 can lemon pie filling or jar
  strawberry jam

Beat egg whites until very stiff; add sugar. Then beat egg yolks and mix into beaten whites. Add flour, baking powder, and vanilla; mix well.

Line a rimmed cookie sheet with waxed paper or spray with cooking spray. Spread batter over sheet. Bake at 325° to 350°F for 10 to 15 minutes. Remove from cookie sheet immediately after baking and place on counter, which has been spread with sugar. (This coats the outside of the jelly roll with sugar.). Spread pie filling or jam on cake; roll up.

Mary B. Duerksen, Mountain Lake, Minnesota
Minn-Kota MCC Relief Sale, Sioux Falls,
South Dakota

Pumpkin Roll

3 eggs
2/3 cup cooked pumpkin
1 teaspoon baking powder
3/4 cup flour
1 cup sugar
1 teaspoon salt
1/2 teaspoon cinnamon

Filling:
1 package (8 oz) cream
  cheese, softened
2 tablespoons butter, softened
1 teaspoon vanilla
1 cup powdered sugar

Mix all cake ingredients in a bowl with a spoon. Grease a jelly roll pan and line with waxed paper. Spread batter over bottom of pan. Bake at 375°F for 15 minutes. Sprinkle powdered sugar on a clean tea towel; turn pan over on tea towel to remove cake. Roll up as for jelly roll. Let cool.

While cake is cooling, prepare filling by beating all ingredients until smooth. Unroll cooled cake and spread filling over inside. Roll back up. Refrigerate until serving time.

Note: This roll freezes well.

Grace Cable, Hollsopple, Pennsylvania
MCC Quilt Auction and Relief Sale, Johnstown

Never-Fail "Seven Ones" Cupcakes

Faye (Birky) Claassen, of Albany, Oregon, passes on this very old recipe from her mother, Katie (Troyer) Birky, who made these cupcakes often for the family and for unexpected guests. Mrs. Claassen says her mother used water when milk was in short supply and often topped the cupcakes with a hot vanilla-cornstarch pudding. The name comes from the seven ingredients, all in amounts of one (cup or teaspoon).

1 egg
1 tablespoon lard or butter
1 teaspoon vanilla
Milk or water
1 cup flour
1 cup granulated sugar
1 teaspoon baking powder

Put egg in a 1-cup measuring cup; stir slightly to break yolk. Add lard and vanilla. Then fill cup with milk or water.

Sift together flour, sugar, and baking powder. Put measuring-cup mixture into mixing bowl; add sifted dry ingredients; mix well. Pour or spoon batter into greased muffin cups (or paper liners), filling cups two-thirds full. Bake at 350°F for 25 minutes.

Oregon MCC Fall Festival, Albany

For Silence Bowers, 82, making quilts for the Iowa MCC Sale is a labor of love. She has donated at least one quilt to every sale since 1980. Mrs. Bowers learned her quilt-making skills from her mother.

Because she was one of nine children and her mother sewed all their shirts and dresses, there were always plenty of scraps left for "Crazy Patch" quilts. They were usually done up with colored thread and fancy stitches.

When asked if she had saved any of those old quilts, she replied "Yes — there's one tucked away upstairs, it's a Crazy Patch filled with wool for warmth."

Mrs. Bowers still lives on Clark Street in Iowa City. "Been here since 1946." She takes in roomers and boarders. So far 87 people have rented rooms from her. "The youngest one was 10-days old and the oldest was 87 years old."

— Submitted by Frank Yoder

Peppernuts

Members of the Executive Food Committee for the 1994 Iowa MCC Sale knew that they didn't have to worry about making peppernuts. For years, Helen Spendler and Orpha Kemp from the Iowa City Mennonite Church had taken care of that chore--mixing, seasoning, rolling, cutting, baking, and bagging hundreds to be sold in the Farmers Market. But Helen had fallen and broken her hip, and the job was too big for Orpha alone.

The committee asked area churches and Sunday school classes to consider filling the need. By sale day, enough peppernuts were made for sale in half a dozen booths.

Frank Yoder, who submits the recipe that has been used at the sale, says he sampled a few from each booth. Although they weren't just like those of Helen and Orpha, they were good.

2 cups (4 sticks) margarine
8 cups brown sugar
8 eggs
2 teaspoons anise oil
2 teaspoons baking soda (dissolved in 1/4 cup hot water)
9 cups flour
2 teaspoons cream of tartar
2 teaspoons cinnamon
2 teaspoons nutmeg
2 teaspoons ground cloves

Cream margarine and sugar in a large bowl. Add eggs and anise oil; mix well. Add dissolved soda. Mix together 4 cups of the flour with the cream of tartar, cinnamon, nutmeg, and cloves. Add to the creamed mixture; gradually add remaining flour. Roll into long, thin rolls and freeze. To bake, cut frozen rolls into thin slices. Place on greased cookie sheets. Bake at 350°F for 8 to 10 minutes.

Christmas Peppernuts

The contributor notes that peppernuts freeze well and can be eaten without thawing.

1/2 cup vegetable oil
1 cup brown sugar
2 eggs
1 tablespoon vanilla
2 cups flour
1 teaspoon baking soda
1 teaspoon baking powder
1 cup raisins
1 cup nuts (preferably walnuts)
1 cup coconut

Cream together oil and sugar. Beat in eggs and vanilla. Stir in flour, baking soda, and baking powder; mix well. In a food chopper, grind raisins, nuts, and coconut. (To keep raisins from sticking together, wash them in hot water just before grinding.) Mix into dough. Chill dough for 1 hour. Roll on lightly floured board into rolls about 1/2 inch thick. Cut with floured knife. Bake at 325°F for about 8 minutes.

MAKES ABOUT 2 QUARTS PEPPERNUTS

Mary B. Duerksen, Mountain Lake, Minnesota
Minn-Kota MCC Relief Sale, Sioux Falls,
South Dakota

Peppernuts

1/2 pound (2 sticks) butter
1 1/2 cups white sugar
2 well-beaten eggs
2 tablespoons dark syrup
3 3/4 cups flour
2 teaspoons baking soda
1 teaspoon *each*: cinnamon, ginger, and cloves
1/2 teaspoon anise oil

Cream butter and sugar. Add well-beaten eggs and syrup. Sift together dry ingredients; add to creamed mixture. Stir in anise oil; mix well. (If dough is too dry, add a small amount of cream.) Chill overnight (or longer if desired; dough keeps well in refrigerator). To bake, roll into thin ropes and cut into small pieces. Bake at 350°F for 7 minutes.

Aganetha S. Harder, Mountain Lake, Minnesota
Minn-Kota MCC Relief Sale, Sioux Falls,
South Dakota

Mrs. J. H. Epp's Raisin Peppernuts

1 1/2 cups sugar
1/2 cup butter
2 eggs
1 cup raisins, ground
1 cup coconut, ground
1 cup peanuts, ground
1/2 teaspoon baking soda
2 tablespoons buttermilk
1 teaspoon nutmeg
1 teaspoon baking powder
2 2/3 cups flour

Cream sugar and butter until fluffy. Add eggs, fruit, and nuts. Dissolve baking soda in the buttermilk; add. Sift together dry ingredients; blend into batter. Store dough in tightly covered container in the refrigerator overnight or longer.

To bake, roll dough into thin ropes and slice with sharp knife dipped in flour or cold water. Pieces should be about the size of a hazelnut. Place pieces separately on greased baking sheets. Bake at 375°F for 10 minutes, or until golden brown.

Note: Freezing the ropes makes them easier to slice.

Arlene Dick, Mountain Lake, Minnesota
Minn-Kota MCC Relief Sale, Sioux Falls, S. Dakota

Fruit and Spicy Peppernuts

Between 400 and 450 one-pound bags of a variety of peppernuts are sold at the Oklahoma Mennonite Relief Sale in Fairview. These are one of the favorites.

1/2 cup butter
1 1/2 cups sugar
2 eggs
1/2 cup raisins, ground
4 teaspoons buttermilk
3 cups flour
1 teaspoon baking soda
1/2 teaspoon salt
1 teaspoon nutmeg
1/2 teaspoon cinnamon
1/2 teaspoon cloves
1 cup coconut
1 cup chopped nuts

Cream butter, sugar, and eggs until fluffy. Add raisins and buttermilk. Sift together all dry ingredients and add to creamed mixture. Then add coconut and nuts; mix well. Store in tightly covered container in the refrigerator overnight. (This helps dough to season and flavors to blend.) To bake, roll dough in pencil-like ropes and cut in 1/2-inch pieces with sharp knife or scissor that has been dipped in flour. Place pieces separately on cookie sheet and bake at 375°F for 8 to 10 minutes, or until golden brown.

MAKES 1/2 TO 3/4 GALLON PEPPERNUTS

Erna Sallaska, Balko, Oklahoma

Peppernuts

Irene Penner, of Corn, Oklahoma, offers two slightly different recipes for these traditional cookies.

1 cup margarine
1 cup white sugar
2 cups brown sugar
2 beaten eggs
1 teaspoon salt
1 teaspoon pepper
1/2 teaspoon allspice
1 teaspoon cinnamon
5 1/4 cups flour
1 teaspoon baking soda, dissolved in 1/2 cup coffee

Mix margarine, sugars, and eggs with mixer. Add dry ingredients and mix together; then add coffee-soda mixture. Chill dough. Make rolls of dough (about the size of a nickle) and cut. Place on cookie sheets and bake at 350°F for about 10 minutes.

Peppernuts

1 1/2 cups sugar
1/2 cup butter or margarine
2 eggs
1/2 cup (or more) raisins, grd.
1/2 cup coconut
1/2 cup finely chopped nuts
1 teaspoon nutmeg
1 teaspoon baking soda
4 teaspoons buttermilk
1/2 teaspoon salt
3 cups flour

Mix all ingredients and form into rolls; refrigerate. When cold, cut into small cookies. Bake in a moderate oven.

Variation: Decrease nutmeg to 1/2 teaspoon and substitute 1/2 teaspoon baking powder for half the baking soda. Add dates to the recipe; grind with the raisins.

Oklahoma MCC Relief Sale, Fairview

Pfeffernuesse (Peppernuts)

2/3 cup clear honey
1/2 cup margarine
1 1/8 cups brown sugar
1/4 cup cream
1 1/2 teaspoons baking soda
1/2 teaspoon cinnamon
1/4 teaspoon *each:* allspice, ginger, nutmeg, and cloves
1 teaspoon cardamon
Grated peel of half a lemon
3 cups flour

Combine honey, margarine, sugar, and cream in a saucepan; bring to a boil and then cool. Mix in baking soda, spices, and lemon peel. Stir in flour to form a soft dough. Form into finger-thick rolls. Refrigerate. Cut into 1/4-inch-thick pieces. Bake on cookie sheets at 375°F for 6 to 7 minutes.

Herta Janzen
Alberta MCC Relief Sale, Coaldale

New Year's Cookies (Portzilka)

Portzilka means "tumbling over," which is what these raisin fritters do when they are dropped into the deep hot fat in which they're fried. Traditionally, Portzilka were made especially for New Year's Day—and many people simply call them New Year's Cookies. The following three recipes were contributed from the Nebraska MCC Relief Sale, in Aurora.

2 cakes yeast (dissolved in 1
    cup water with 1 table-
    spoon sugar)
4 eggs
1 tablespoon salt
3 cups raisins (wash first)
3/4 cup sugar
1 cup milk
About 7 to 8 cups flour

To dissolved yeast mixture, add eggs, salt, and raisins (floured before adding). Then add sugar and milk. Stir in enough flour to form a stiff dough. Mix well. Set in a warm place to rise until double in size. Drop by tablespoon into hot fat or cooking oil. Fry to a delicate brown.

New Year's Cookies

1 cup sifted flour
2 teaspoons baking powder
1 tablespoon sugar
1 teaspoon salt
4 eggs, beaten
Milk
Raisins

Sift the dry ingredients together. Then add eggs. Add enough milk to make a soft dough when worked with a spoon. Add raisins. Drop spoonfuls of dough into deep fat. Fry until done.

New Year's Cookies

1 cake yeast (dissolved in 1/4
    cup water)
2 cups milk, scalded and
    cooled
1/4 cup sugar
3 eggs, well beaten
1 1/4 teaspoons salt
1/4 cup butter, melted
3/4 pound raisins
About 4 to 5 cups flour

Add dissolved yeast to the milk. Then add sugar, eggs, salt, and butter. Plump raisins in hot water for a minute or two. Drain and add to milk mixture. Stir in enough flour to make a soft dough. Let rise until doubled. Heat oil in kettle or deep fat fryer to 350° to 375°F. Dip spoon in hot fat, then into dough, drop dough by spoonful into oil. Turn to fry to a golden brown. Drain and roll in granulated or powdered sugar as for doughnuts, or dip in sugar as they are eaten.

New Year's Cookies (Portzelky)

Volunteers at the Kelowna, British Columbia, Relief Sale make about 37 batches of this fritter recipe--and could sell more! They keep four cauldrons frying at once. The contributor, Edith Warkentin, reports that the volunteers recommend mixing the batter by hand.

12 cups raisins
1/3 cup yeast
2 tablespoons sugar
2 cups warm water
10 cups water
3 1/2 cups powdered milk
1 cup soft margarine
4 cups sugar
2 tablespoons (1/8 cup) salt
18 well-beaten eggs
22 cups flour

Pour boiling water over raisins; set aside until other ingredients are mixed; then strain and add.

Dissolve yeast and the 2 tablespoons sugar in the 2 cups warm water. Let set until foamy. Combine the 10 cups water, powdered milk, and margarine; heat to lukewarm. Stir in sugar, salt, eggs, and yeast mixture. Gradually stir in flour. Let batter stand for 1 hour before frying.

Linda Wiest fries the famous raisin fritters at the West Coast Mennonite Sale for World Relief in Fresno.

Raisin Fritters (Poertzelki)

Business is always brisk at the raisin fritter booth at the West Coast Mennonite Sale and Auction for World Relief, in Fresno, California. Volunteer booth managers Delbert and Linda Wiest, along with scores of church workers of all ages, fry 18,000 fritters in two days to bring in about $5,000 for relief efforts. In assembly-line fashion, the workers mix dough, dip scoops into the deep fryer, pluck the fritters from the oil, sugar them in paper bags, and sell them piping hot to eager customers.

The Wiests, who raise Sunmaid raisins in a vineyard that has been in the family since 1945, know their product well. As in the homes of her mother-in-law and her mother before her, Linda Wiest's house is filled with the aroma of frying fritters on New Year's Day, drawing friends and family inside for warm fellowship. Raisin fritters, also known by the names Poertzelki (portz-uh-kyuh) and New Year's cookies, are traditionally a New Year's Day treat.

The fritters can be made with chopped apples, cherries, or other fruit, but Central California Mennonite raisin growers wouldn't think of making them with anything but natural sun-dried raisins.

5 1/2 cups flour
Yeast
1/2 cup sugar
3 cups water
3 cups milk
1 tablespoon butter
1 teaspoon salt
4 eggs, beaten
2 cups raisins, floured

Measure out flour; set aside. Dissolve yeast and 1 teaspoon of the sugar in 1/2 cup very warm (not hot) water. Let set until foamy. Heat remaining 2 1/2 cups water with milk and butter to lukewarm. Stir in remaining sugar, salt, eggs, and yeast mixture. Gradually stir in flour until dough is soft and can be dipped by spoonfuls. Fold in raisins. Let rise until double in bulk (about 1 hour).

Heat vegetable oil in a deep fryer (or at least 3 inches deep in a pan) to 325° to 350°F. Dip metal ice cream scoop in hot oil; then dip a scoopful of fritter dough into oil, dipping scoop in oil each time. Fry fritters until brown on outside. Check inside for doneness and adjust time and temperature as needed.

Arlene Rempel and Erna Peters make New Year's Cookies at the first Nebraska MCC Relief Sale in 1983.

New Year's Cookies

Another contribution from the Nebraska MCC Relief Sale, in Aurora, this recipe for New Year's cookies is used at the sale. According to Carol Janzen, of Henderson, Nebraska, 3,000 to 4,000 cookies are sold each year. The volunteers use a microwave at the sale to warm the water, milk, and margarine. A small heater is placed in the cupboard to make a warm place for the bowls of dough to rise.

2 1/2 teaspoons yeast
1/4 cup warm water
5 eggs
3/4 cup sugar
3 tablespoons margarine,
    melted
2 1/2 cups warm milk
7 cups flour
2 teaspoons baking powder
2 1/2 teaspoons salt
3 cups raisins

Dissolve yeast in the warm water; let set 5 minutes. Beat eggs and sugar in a large Tupperware bowl with a wire whisk. Add margarine, milk, 2 cups of the flour, baking powder, and salt. Stir with a big spoon. Add yeast mixture; then stir in the remaining flour, 1 cup at a time. Stir in raisins. Cover bowl with lid and let rise in a warm place for 1 hour. Drop with medium-size dipper or medium spoon into oil heated to 350°F. Deep fry to golden brown. Drain on paper towels and then roll in sugar.

MAKES 50 COOKIES

New Year's Cookies (Kuchen)

1 cake yeast
2 teaspoons salt
1 cup (or more) raisins or
    chopped apples
2 cups milk
1/2 cup sugar
6 or 7 eggs, beaten
Flour

Glaze:
1 pound powdered sugar
1 tablespoon cornstarch
2 teaspoons vanilla
Hot water

Combine all cookie ingredients except flour. Then mix in enough flour to make a spongy dough. Let rise. Fry in deep hot oil; drain on paper towels. Glaze cookies (mix glaze ingredients with enough hot water to make a heavy glaze) or roll in sugar.

Irene Penner, Corn Oklahoma
Oklahoma MCC Relief Sale, Fairview

Roderkuchen (Bow Ties)

These dry cookies have an
unusual shape.
1 cup egg yolks
1 cup sour cream
1 1/2 cups sugar
Flour

Mix together egg yolks, sour cream, and sugar. Add enough flour to make a stiff dough. Roll out dough about 1/4 inch thick. Using a fluted wheel, cut dough into rectangular pieces. Make a small slit in the center of each piece and then pull one end of the rectangle through the slit to form a "bow tie." Fry in deep fat heated to 350°F.

Erna Marie Reimer, Beatrice, Nebraska
First Mennonite Church
Nebraska MCC Relief Sale, Aurora

Sugar Cookies

3 cups sugar
2 cups oil
4 eggs
2 cups buttermilk
5 1/2 to 6 cups flour
2 tablespoons baking powder
2 teaspoons baking soda
1 tablespoon vanilla

Beat together sugar, oil, and eggs. Add buttermilk, flour, baking powder, baking soda, and vanilla. Drop on cookie sheets. *Do not flatten.* Sprinkle sugar over tops of cookies. Bake at 450°F until light brown.

Erma Swartzendruber
Pleasant View Mennonite Church, Goshen, Indiana

Sugar Cookies

Mary Edna Martin makes a batch of these delicious soft cookies for the Pennsylvania Relief Sale, in Harrisburg, to be sold with the coffee. The recipe came from her grandmother, Mary Kilmer Horning, and her mother, Anna Horning Zimmerman. The family often got together to make these cookies.

2 tablespoons baking soda
1 quart buttermilk
6 cups sugar
1 pound solid vegetable
　　shortening (Crisco),
　　melted
1/2 pint sour, thick cream
1 1/2 tablespoons vanilla
13 1/2 cups all-purpose flour

Dissolve soda in buttermilk. Add sugar, hot melted shortening, cream, and vanilla. Add 7 1/2 cups of the flour; mix well. Then add the remaining 6 cups flour and mix by hand. Bake at 400°F for 8 to 10 minutes. Let cool. Frost.

MAKES ABOUT 135 MEDIUM-SIZED COOKIES

*Submitted by Mrs. Harold (Irene) Zimmerman,
Food Committee Assistant Chairman*

Chuck's Sugar Cookies

3/4 cup butter or margarine
3/4 cup sugar
1 egg, slightly beaten
1 tablespoon vanilla
2 cups all-purpose flour
1/2 teaspoon baking soda
1/2 teaspoon cream of tartar
1/2 teaspoon salt

Cream butter and sugar. Add egg and vanilla. Mix dry ingredients together; add to creamed mixture. Roll dough into small balls, dip in sugar, and press with a fork. Bake at 350°F for 8 to 10 minutes.

MAKES 3 DOZEN COOKIES

*Iris Frank
East Peoria Mennonite Church
Illinois MCC Relief Sale, Peoria*

Auctioneers take bids for a desk during the wood auction at the 1994 Ohio Mennonite Relief Sale.

Relief Sale Sugar Cookies

These large cookies are hand-decorated and sold individually at the Ohio Mennonite Relief Sale, in Kidron. The ingredient amounts given below are for half a recipe (80 cookies). Simply double all the ingredients to make the full 160-cookie recipe. The cookies can be baked ahead and stored in bread bags in the freezer.

4 1/2 cups white sugar
3 cups margarine
4 1/2 teaspoons baking soda
4 1/2 teaspoons salt
7 eggs
1 pint buttermilk
**4 1/2 teaspoons lemon
    extract or other flavoring**
**14 to 15 cups flour (about 3 1/4
    lbs)**
4 1/2 teaspoons baking powder

Cream sugar, margarine, baking soda, and salt. Then add eggs, buttermilk, and lemon (or other) extract. Mix well. Then stir in flour and baking powder. Mix well. Chill (overnight is best). Roll out dough and cut with a *shortening can* to make large cookies. Bake at 375°F until lightly browned (about 10 minutes). Cool and decorate as desired.

Stay-Soft Sugar Cookies

2 cups white sugar
1 cup butter-flavored solid
    vegetable shortening
    (Crisco)
4 eggs
1 cup milk
1/2 teaspoon vanilla
1 teaspoon baking soda
4 tablespoons baking
    powder
4 cups flour

Cream together sugar, shortening, eggs, milk, and vanilla. Add remaining ingredients. Mix well. Drop by teaspoon onto greased cookie sheets. Bake at 350°F for 12 to 15 minutes, or until edges are golden brown.

Note: If you'd rather roll the dough for cut-out cookies, increase the flour to 5 1/2 cups.

MAKES 4 DOZEN COOKIES

*Tillie Janzen, Mountain Lake, Minnesota
Minn-Kota MCC Relief Sale, Sioux Falls,
South Dakota*

Molasses Sugar Cookies

3/4 cup shortening
1 cup sugar
1/4 cup light molasses
1 egg
2 cups flour
2 teaspoons baking soda
1 teaspoon cinnamon
1/2 teaspoon cloves
1/2 teaspoon ginger
1/2 teaspoon salt

Cream shortening and sugar. Add molasses and egg; beat well. Sift in remaining ingredients. Form dough into balls; roll in sugar. Bake at 375°F for 8 to 10 minutes.

*Mel Long, Sterling, Illinois
Science Ridge Mennonite Church
Illinois MCC Relief Sale, Peoria*

Molasses Crinkles

The people of the Swiss/German community of Kidron, Ohio, consider these cookies a favorite treat.

3/4 cup shortening
1 cup brown sugar
1 egg
1/4 cup molasses
2 1/4 cups flour
1/2 teaspoon salt
2 teaspoons baking soda
1 teaspoon cinnamon
1 teaspoon ginger
1/2 teaspoon cloves

Mix together all ingredients. Chill dough in refrigerator. Shape chilled dough into 1-inch-diameter balls. Roll in granulated sugar and place 2 inches apart on greased cookie sheets. Bake at 350°F for 12 to 15 minutes.

MAKES 4 DOZEN COOKIES

Ohio MCC Relief Sale, Kidron

Ginger Snaps

These cookies can be found at the food booth and the concession stands at the Minn-Kota Relief Sale, in Sioux Falls, South Dakota.

3/4 cup melted butter or 1/2
    cup melted margarine
1 cup sugar
1 egg, beaten
3 tablespoons molasses
About 2 cups flour
1 1/2 teaspoons baking soda
1 teaspoon cinnamon
1/2 teaspoon cloves
1/2 teaspoon ginger

Cream butter and sugar. Add egg and molasses. Sift together dry ingredients. Add to creamed mixture. Form into small balls; roll in sugar. Bake at 350°F for 10 to 12 minutes.

MAKES ABOUT 3 DOZEN COOKIES

Lorraine Deckert, Dolton, South Dakota

Ginger Cookies

1 cup butter
1 cup brown sugar
2 eggs
1 cup molasses
About 3 1/2 cups flour
2 teaspoons baking soda
    dissolved in 1/3 cup
    boiling water
2 tablespoons ginger (or
    more, to taste)

Icing:
1 cup sugar
Water
2 egg whites

Mix together all ingredients for cookie dough. Chill. Roll out dough; cut into cookies. Bake at 350° to 375°F for about 10 minutes.

To make icing, mix the sugar with a little water. Bring to a boil, and boil until syrup threads. Let syrup cool a little. Beat egg whites; add cooled syrup to whites, beating until mixture is the consistency of icing. While it's still warm, spread icing on cookies.

Mrs. Rosalie R. Forrester, Bloomington, Illinois
Faith Evangelical Mennonite Church
Illinois MCC Relief Sale, Peoria

Honey Cookies

This is a very old family recipe from the files of Caroline (Birky) Stutzman, submitted by her daughter Adella (Stutzman) Gingrich, of Albany, Oregon. Mrs. Gingrich notes that the recipe contains no salt.

1 cup sugar
1 scant cup butter or lard
2 eggs
1/2 cup sour cream
1 cup honey
2 teaspoons baking soda
Flour (approximately 5 cups)
Lemon or orange flavoring

Mix all ingredients together well. Roll out immediately and cut into squares. Bake on greased baking sheet at 350°F for about 10 minutes, or until lightly browned.

Oregon MCC Fall Festival, Albany

Honey Cookies

Women from the Bethel Mennonite Church, Aldergrove, British Columbia, make about 56 dozen of these cookies to sell at the MCC British Columbia Relief Sale, in Kelowna.

1 cup syrup
1 cup granulated sugar
1 cup brown sugar
1 cup milk
3/4 cup butter
1 teaspoon cinnamon
1/2 teaspoon cloves
1/2 teaspoon nutmeg
1 cup whipping cream
1 egg, beaten
1 well-rounded teaspoon
    baking soda
2 well-rounded teaspoons
    baking ammonia dis-
    solved in 1/2 cup hot
    water
6 1/2 cups flour

Boiled Icing:
2 cups sugar
2 ounces water
3 egg whites

Mix together syrup, sugars, milk, butter, and spices; warm. To warmed mixture, add cream, egg, baking soda, and baking ammonia mixture. Mix well. Then stir in flour. (Dough will be soft.) Chill in refrigerator overnight. The next day, form into balls, flatten slightly, and bake at 375°F for 12 to 13 minutes.

To prepare icing, put ingredients in top of a double boiler. Place over boiling water. Beat exactly 5 minutes. Cover baked cookies with boiled icing; let icing dry. Then pack into containers and freeze.

MAKES 9 TO 10 DOZEN COOKIES (DEPENDING ON SIZE OF BALLS)

Grete Borck and Elsie Dyck

California fruit growers have donated a number of semi-loads of fresh fruit to sell at MCC relief sales in mid to late summer. After sharing a semi-load with the Arthur, Ill., sale in 1990, and again in 1991, the Minn-Kota Relief Sale received a letter from the West Coast MCC office expressing the fruit growers' concerns whether their donations were the best way to help MCC, and soliciting reciprocal donations for the sale in Fresno.

Jake A. Dick, from Mountain Lake, Minn., volunteered to make a round oak table and donate it to the California sale as a way of saying "thank you" for the fruit. The round oak tables and matching storage cabinet for the table leaves have frequently been top-selling items at the Sioux Falls relief sale. Wishing to take part in the gesture, the board voted to help pay some of the construction costs.

Not being able to find a freight line that could guarantee safe arrival of the table, Mr. Dick decided to deliver it in person and had it packed into the trunk of his car several days before leaving for California. In the middle of the night before he left, he was awakened and heard a voice, "Repack the table." Arising early in the morning, he took it all out, re-wrapped it in extra packing and stashed it in the front of the trunk with suitcases in the back.

While driving on an interstate highway 250 miles from Fresno, the Dicks' car was rear ended. The trunk lid was buckled, the suitcases were smashed, the car top was buckled, the hood popped open, and both Mr. and Mrs. Dick suffered whiplash injuries. A wrecker hauled the car into town to a repair shop which pulled the rear fenders away from the rear wheels so they could drive on. The insurance company considered the car a total loss. Upon opening the trunk at the sale and remove the table, there was not a scratch on it and it sold at auction April 4, 1992 for $2,500. The Lord had been looking out for His own.

— Submitted by Don Klassen, chairman of the Minn-Kota MCC Relief Sale

Lemon Poppyseed Cookies

2 cups flour
3/4 teaspoon salt
1/3 cup poppyseeds
1/2 pound (2 sticks) butter or
margarine
1/2 cup sugar
2 tablespoons grated lemon
zest (yellow skin from
about 3 lemons)
1 egg
1/4 teaspoon vanilla

Combine flour, salt, and poppyseeds; set aside. Cream butter, sugar, and lemon zest. Beat in egg and vanilla. Gradually add flour mixture to creamed mixture; beat. Cover and refrigerate at least 30 minutes. Form chilled dough into 2-inch-diameter logs. Refrigerate or freeze for 30 minutes. Heat oven to 350°F. Cut the logs into 1/4-inch-thick slices. Bake on ungreased cookie sheets for 9 to 10 minutes, or until edges are brown.

MAKES ABOUT 40 COOKIES

*Mrs. Dennis (Shirley) Ries, Freeman,
South Dakota
Minn-Kota MCC Relief Sale, Sioux Falls,
South Dakota*

Peppermint Cookies

2 cups cream
1 cup butter
3 cups sugar
5 eggs
Oil of peppermint (to taste)
3 tablespoons baking
ammonia dissolved in
1/4 cup boiling water
5 teaspoons baking powder
8 1/2 cups flour

Mix together cream and butter; then add sugar and eggs. Cream all four ingredients together, adding flavoring when almost creamed. Then stir in baking ammonia mixture, baking powder, and flour. Chill dough overnight. The next day, roll out dough and cut into desired shapes. Bake at 375°F for 10 to 15 minutes (depending on size of cookies).

From the Mennonite Treasury of Recipes
MCC British Columbia Relief Sale, Kelowna

Refrigerator Norwegian Cookies

The contributor relates that when she was growing up, her mother made these cookies for the family only at Christmas. The children ate them with a bowl of ice cream.

1 cup lard
1 cup butter
1 cup white sugar
1 cup brown sugar
3 eggs
4 1/2 cups all-purpose flour
1 teaspoon baking soda
1 teaspoon cinnamon
1 teaspoon salt
1 cup nut meats

Cream shortening and sugar until fluffy. Add stiffly beaten eggs. Sift together flour, baking soda, cinnamon, and salt. Work dry ingredients and then nuts into dough. Knead to form a roll. Chill overnight. Cut into slices and bake at 350°F for 8 to 10 minutes, or until lightly browned.

Iris Frank
East Peoria Mennonite Church
Illinois MCC Relief Sale, Peoria

Mexican Wedding Cakes

1 cup margarine
1/2 cup sugar
1/2 teaspoon salt
2 teaspoons vanilla
2 cups flour
1 cup chopped walnuts

Cream margarine and sugar. Add salt, vanilla, flour, and nuts; mix well. Chill dough. Then shape into balls and flatten with bottom of a design tumbler dipped in flour. Bake at 325°F until lightly brown. Rub tops of cookies in powdered sugar.

Ester V. Mishler, Johnstown, Pennsylvania
MCC Quilt Auction and Relief Sale, Johnstown

In 1990 at the MCC Oregon Fall Festival, as part of the display for the MCC Cash Project Booth to raise funds to supply sheep and ducks in Bolivia, the coordinators brought their daughter's 4-H project, a young sheep. Someone had the idea to auction the sheep without actually selling it to increase interest at the auction. The sheep was auctioned at least 10 times and earned around $615 in addition to what it brought at the booth!
— Submitted by Margery Barkman.

Swedish Creams

1 cup margarine
1/3 cup whipping cream
2 cups flour
Granulated sugar

Filling:
1/4 cup margarine
1 egg yolk
1 teaspoon vanilla
3/4 cup powdered sugar

Mix together the 1 cup margarine, cream, and flour. Chill dough 1 hour. Roll dough 1/8 -inch thick; cut with donut hole. Roll in granulated sugar, place on greased cookie sheets, and prick with a fork. Bake at 375°F for 7 to 9 minutes.

Mix ingredients for filling. When cookies are cool, spread filling on half the cookies; top each with one of the plain cookies to make a "sandwich."

Eunice Chupp, Goshen, Indiana
Pleasant View Mennonite Church
Indiana MCC Relief Sale, Goshen

Butterscotch Curls

This is a very old family recipe contributed by Adella (Stutzman) Gingrich, of Albany, Oregon.

2 cups flour
4 teaspoons baking powder
1/4 cup shortening
2/3 teaspoon salt
2/3 cup milk
3 tablespoons butter
1/2 cup brown sugar

Sift together flour and baking powder. Add shortening and salt; mix with a fork. Add milk to make a fairly soft dough. Knead slightly; roll out to 1/4 inch thick. Cream the 3 tablespoons butter; spread over dough. Sprinkle brown sugar over butter. Roll up dough as for a jelly roll. Slice into 12 large or 22 small rounds. Place cut side down in well-buttered small muffin tins or rings. Bake at 350°F for 30 minutes. When done, center of rolls will curl up, and edges will be glazed.

MAKES 12 LARGE OR 22 SMALL CURLS

Oregon MCC Fall Festival, Albany

Kifli Cookies

1 cup butter (at room temperature)
1 cup (8 oz) cream-style
  cottage cheese
2 cups all-purpose flour

Cinnamon-Nut Filling:
2 unbeaten egg whites
1/2 cup sugar
2 cups finely chopped nuts
2 tablespoons ground
  cinnamon

Beat together butter and cottage cheese until light and fluffy. Add flour, beating until dough forms a ball. Divide dough into three equal portions. Wrap each portion separately and refrigerate until firm (several hours or overnight).

To bake cookies, preheat oven to 375°F. Prepare filling (mix the ingredients together); set aside. On floured surface, roll out dough, one portion at a time, into a 10-inch circle. Spread circle with one-third of the filling, covering dough to within 1/2 inch of the edge. Cut circle into 24 pie-shaped wedges. Beginning at the outer edge, roll up each wedge lightly. Place, point side down, on greased cookie sheet. Bake 13 to 15 minutes (watch carefully). Remove cookies from sheet and cool on rack. Frost with a mixture of powdered sugar, butter, and milk.

MAKES 6 DOZEN COOKIES

Laura Ann Belsley, Morton, Illinois
Bethel Mennonite Church, Pekin
Illinois MCC Relief Sale, Peoria

Oatmeal Cookies

1 cup butter or margarine
1 cup brown sugar
1 cup white sugar
2 eggs
1 teaspoon vanilla
3 cups flour
1 teaspoon baking soda
1 teaspoon baking powder
1/4 teaspoon salt
2 cups quick-cooking rolled
  oats

Cream butter and sugars; add eggs and vanilla. Then mix in dry ingredients, and finally oats. Bake at 375°F for 15 to 20 minutes.

Katie Wagler
Daviess County Relief Sale, Montgomery, Indiana

$250 Cookies

2 cups butter
2 cups granulated sugar
2 cups brown sugar
4 eggs
2 teaspoons vanilla
4 cups flour
5 cups quick-cooking rolled
  oats, blended in blender
1 teaspoon salt
2 teaspoons baking powder
2 teaspoons baking soda
24 ounces chocolate chips
1 Hershey chocolate bar (8
  oz), grated
3 cups chopped nuts

Cream together butter and sugars. Add eggs and vanilla; mix well. Add flour, oats, salt, baking powder, and soda. Stir in chips, grated chocolate, and nuts. Roll dough into balls or drop by spoonful onto greased cookie sheets. Bake at 375°F for 10 minutes.

MAKES ABOUT 112 COOKIES

Helen Klassen
MCC British Columbia Relief Sale, Kelowna

Apple Cookies

1 1/2 cups brown sugar
1/2 cup margarine
1 egg
2 1/2 cups flour
1 teaspoon baking soda
1/2 teaspoon salt
1 teaspoon cinnamon
1/2 teaspoon cloves
1/2 teaspoon nutmeg (op-
  tional)
1/3 cup milk
1 cup finely chopped apples
1 cup raisins
1 cup chopped walnuts
  (optional)

Cream sugar and margarine. Mix in egg, and then flour, baking soda, salt, spices, and milk. Stir in apples, raisins, and walnuts (if desired). Bake at 350°F for 10 to 12 minutes.

Ohio MCC Relief Sale, Kidron

Monster Cookies

The contributor suggests that if you want to make regular-size cookies, simply halve the amounts in this recipe.

6 eggs
1 pound brown sugar
2 cups white sugar
1 1/2 teaspoons vanilla
4 teaspoons baking soda
1/2 pound (2 sticks) margarine
1 1/2 pounds peanut butter
1 1/2 teaspoons corn syrup
  (Karo)
9 cups quick-cooking rolled
  oats
1/2 pound chocolate chips
1 cup coconut

Mix ingredients in order given. Drop on cookie sheets, using *ice cream scoop.* Flatten with a fork. Bake at 325°F for 10 to 12 minutes.

Esther V. Mishler, Johnstown, Pennsylvania
MCC Quilt Auction and Relief Sale, Johnstown

Pride of Iowa Cookies

1 cup shortening (part
  butter)
1 cup white sugar
1 cup brown sugar
2 eggs, beaten
1 cup coconut
1 cup nuts and/or raisins
1 package (12 oz) chocolate
  chips
1 teaspoon vanilla
2 1/4 cups sifted flour
1 teaspoon baking powder
1/2 teaspoon salt
1 teaspoon baking soda
2 cups uncooked rolled oats

Cream shortening and sugars; add beaten eggs. Then add coconut, nuts, chips, and vanilla. Add flour, baking powder, salt, soda, and oatmeal. Roll dough into balls the size of a large walnut. Bake at 350°F for about 9 minutes, or until golden brown.

Mrs. Wilbert (Alice) Graber, Parker,
South Dakota
Minn-Kota MCC Relief Sale, Sioux Falls,
South Dakota

Best Ever Chocolate Chip Cookies

1/2 cup solid vegetable
  shortening (Crisco)
1/2 cup margarine
1 cup brown sugar
1/2 cup white sugar
2 eggs
1 teaspoon vanilla
2 cups flour
1 teaspoon baking soda
1/4 teaspoon salt
2 cups chocolate chips

Cream shortenings and sugars. Beat in eggs, and then vanilla. Add dry ingredients, which have been sifted together. Stir in chips. Drop by teaspoons onto greased cookie sheets. Bake at 350°F for 10 or 11 minutes.

Arlene Preheim, Freeman, South Dakota
Minn-Kota MCC Relief Sale, Sioux Falls,
South Dakota

Chocolate Cookies

These cookies need no baking!

2 cups sugar
1 package (7 oz) chocolate
  chips
1 cup cream or milk
1 teaspoon butter
3 cups rolled graham
  crackers
24 marshmallows
1 cup nut meats

Place sugar, chips, and cream in a heavy-bottomed saucepan. Cook to softball stage. Stir in butter. In a large bowl, mix together crackers, marshmallows, and nut meats. Pour hot chocolate mixture over, and stir until ingredients are well mixed. Drop by spoonful onto waxed paper.

Bernice Bachman, Gridley, Illinois
Illinois MCC Relief Sale

Danish Apple Squares

2 1/2 cups flour
1 cup shortening
1/2 teaspoon salt
1 egg yolk plus enough milk
    to measure 2/3 cup
1 cup crushed corn flakes
6 cups sliced apples
1 cup sugar
1 teaspoon cinnamon
1 egg white, stiffly beaten

Glaze:
1 cup icing sugar
1 to 2 tablespoons water
1 teaspoon vanilla

Mix together flour, shortening, salt, and egg-milk mixture to make a dough. Divide dough in half. Roll out one portion into a 10 1/2x15-inch rectangle to fit a cookie sheet. Spread rectangle on cookie sheet, sprinkle with corn flakes, cover with apples, and then sprinkle with sugar and cinnamon. Roll out other portion of dough, place on top, and seal edges. Brush top crust with beaten egg white. Bake at 400°F for 30 to 40 minutes, or until golden brown. Mix glaze ingredients. Drizzle over hot pastry when you take it from oven. Cut cooled pastry into squares to serve.

Alice Klassen
Alberta MCC Relief Sale, Coaldale

People outside of the Mennonite family are moved to help at relief sales in any way they can.

At the first Nebraska Mennonite Relief Sale in 1980, a station wagon with two woman and three or four children arrived the Friday before the sale.

The women informed the workers that "the Mennonites" had helped them in a time of crisis when a flood ransacked their house in Grand Island. Because of this, they wanted to contribute to the mission of the sale. They brought old purses, old women's hats, lamps, nick knacks and more.

After much deliberation, the volunteers decided that these donations indeed deserved the respect and dignity that other donations received because of the motive behind the gift, according to Hilmer D. Peters. They created a "Grandma's Attic" booth and it was a huge success at the sale and to the overall proceeds.

Rhubarb Squares

1 cup butter
2 cups flour
2 teaspoons sugar
5 cups rhubarb
2 cups sugar
Cinnamon (optional)
1 cup cream
6 eggs, separated
1/4 cup flour
1/4 teaspoon salt
3/4 cup sugar
2 teaspoons vanilla
Coconut (optional)

Mix butter, the 2 cups flour, and the 2 teaspoons sugar to form a dough. Roll out to fit a medium cookie sheet. Bake at 350°F for 10 minutes, or until brown.

Mix rhubarb, the 2 cups sugar, cinnamon (if desired), cream, egg yolks, the 1/4 cup flour, and salt together. Spread evenly over baked crust. Bake about 30 minutes.

Beat egg whites until stiff with the 3/4 cup sugar (adding 2 tablespoons at a time); beat in vanilla. Spread beaten whites over rhubarb layer, sprinkle with coconut (if desired), and brown in oven. Cool and cut into squares to serve.

Ann Goossen, Beatrice, Nebraska
Nebraska MCC Relief Sale, Aurora

Poor Man's Bar Cookies

1 stick (1/2 cup) margarine
1/2 cup shortening
1 1/2 cups sugar
4 eggs
1 teaspoon vanilla or lemon
    extract
2 cups flour
1 can pie filling

Cream margarine, shortening, and sugar. Beat in eggs, one at a time, and then flavoring. Gradually add flour. Pour batter onto an ungreased cookie sheet. Score off 24 squares. In each block, place a spoonful of pie filling. Bake at 350°F for 30 minutes, or until light brown.

Norma Thomas, Hollsopple, Pennsylvania
MCC Quilt Auction and Relief Sale, Johnstown

Mabel's Marble Bars

A packaged Swiss or German chocolate cake mix
12 ounces chocolate chips
1 cup chopped nuts
1 package (8 oz) cream cheese
1 egg
1/4 cup sugar

Prepare cake mix batter as directed on package. Stir in chocolate chips and nuts. Pour batter into greased and floured cookie sheet.

Thoroughly beat together cream cheese, egg, and sugar. Spoon blobs of cream cheese mixture onto cake batter and swirl around through batter. Bake at 325°F for no more than 20 minutes.

Florence Blough, Hollsopple, Pennsylvania
MCC Quilt Auction and Relief Sale, Johnstown

Swirl Chocolate Bars

Pans of chocolate treats are made, cut, and wrapped in single portions to be sold at the dessert booth of the Minn-Kota Country Auction and Relief Sale in Sioux Falls, South Dakota. Amy Hofer, of Carpenter, South Dakota, shares this and the following four recipes from that sale.

A packaged German chocolate cake mix
1/2 cup sugar
1 egg
1 package (8 oz) cream cheese
1/2 cup chocolate chips

Prepare cake batter following package directions. Pour into a greased and floured jelly roll pan.

Mix sugar, egg, and cream cheese well. Stir in chips. Drop by teaspoon all over cake batter. Then take a knife and swirl through batter to swirl filling. Bake at 350°F for 25 to 30 minutes. Cool; cut into bars to serve.

Oh Henry Bars

1 cup sugar
1 cup white corn syrup
1 1/4 cup crunchy peanut butter
6 cups Rice Krispies
1 cup chocolate chips

Bring sugar and syrup to a boil; add peanut butter. Stir well. Combine cereal and chips; pour hot syrup over dry mixture. Mix well. Spread in a buttered 9x13-inch pan, patting out evenly. Let cool; then cut into bars to serve.

Layer Bars

1/4 pound butter
1 cup crushed graham
   crackers
1 cup flaked coconut
1 package (16 oz) chocolate
   chips
1 package (16 oz) butter-
   scotch chips
1 cup chopped nuts
1 can (14 oz) Eagle Brand
   sweetened condensed
   milk

Melt butter in a 9x13-inch pan. Layer remaining ingredients in pan in order given. Bake at 350°F for 30 minutes. Cool; then cut into bars to serve.

Cake Flour Brownies

1/2 cup butter
1 cup sugar
2 eggs
2 squares baking chocolate,
   melted
1 cup cake flour, sifted
1/2 teaspoon baking powder
1/2 teaspoon salt
1/2 cup nutmeats
1/2 teaspoon vanilla

Cream butter with sugar. Add eggs one at a time, beating well after each addition. Add cooled melted chocolate, and then the dry ingredients (which have been sifted together), nutmeats, and vanilla. Bake at 350°F for about 25 to 30 minutes. Cool; cut into bars to serve.

Buttermilk Brownies

2 cups flour
2 cups sugar
1/2 cup (1 stick) margarine
1/3 cup vegetable oil
1/4 cup cocoa
1 cup boiling water
1/2 cup buttermilk
2 eggs
1 teaspoon soda
1 teaspoon vanilla

Frosting:
1/4 cup (1/2 stick) margarine
2 tablespoons cocoa
3 1/2 tablespoons buttermilk
2 cups powdered sugar
1/2 teaspoon vanilla
Chopped nuts (for garnish)

In large bowl, mix together flour and sugar; set aside. In a saucepan, mix together margarine, oil, cocoa, and boiling water. Bring to a boil. Add hot liquid to flour-sugar mixture. Mix well. Then add buttermilk, eggs, baking soda, and vanilla. Mix well. Pour into jelly roll pan. Bake at 400°F for 20 minutes.

To prepare frosting, bring margarine, cocoa, and buttermilk to a boil. Remove from heat; stir in powdered sugar and vanilla. Beat until smooth. Use to frost cooled brownies; garnish with chopped nuts (if desired).

Butterscotch Brownies

1/4 cup butter or
    butter-flavored solid
    vegetable shortening
1 cup packed light brown
    sugar
1 egg
3/4 cup flour
1 teaspoon baking powder
1/2 teaspoon salt
1/2 teaspoon vanilla
1/2 cup chopped nuts

Preheat oven to 350°F. Melt butter over low heat. Remove from heat and blend in sugar. Cool; stir in egg. Blend in flour, baking powder, and salt. Mix in vanilla and nuts. Spread in a well-greased 8-inch square pan. Bake 25 minutes. Cut into bars while still warm.

Sally Ann Reddecliff, Johnstown, Pennsylvania
MCC Quilt Auction and Relief Sale, Johnstown

Steamed Pudding

3/4 cup sugar
1 tablespoon butter
1 egg
1 tablespoon cocoa
1/2 cup milk
1 1/2 cups flour
1 teaspoon baking powder
1 teaspoon vanilla

Mix all ingredients with electric mixer until very well blended. Pour into greased and floured pan that can safely be set in a pan of boiling water. Cover outer pan and steam pudding for about 50 minutes, or until toothpick used as a tester comes out clean. Serve warm, with whipped cream or non-dairy whipped topping.

Bernice Schroll
(Submitted by N. Elizabeth Graber,
Wayland, Iowa)
Iowa MCC Relief Sale, Iowa City

Date-Nut Pudding

1 cup boiling water
1 cup chopped dates
1 teaspoon baking soda
1 egg
1 tablespoon butter
1 cup sugar
1 1/2 cups flour
1/2 teaspoon baking powder
Pinch salt
1 cup chopped nuts
Nondairy whipped topping,
    thawed

Pour boiling water over dates and soda. Let stand until cooled to warm. Mash dates; mix in remaining ingredients (except whipped topping), adding nuts last. Spread in jelly-roll pan. Bake at 375°F for 25 minutes. Cut in small squares; mix with whipped topping.

Marilyn Miller
Yellow Creek Mennonite Church, Goshen, Indiana

Ye Olde Date-Nut Pudding

Pudding:
1 cup cut-up dates
1 cup boiling water
1 teaspoon baking soda
1 tablespoon butter
1 cup sugar
2 eggs
1 teaspoon vanilla
1 1/2 cups flour
1/2 teaspoon salt
1/2 teaspoon baking powder
1 cup chopped nuts

Sauce:
1 cup boiling water
1 cup sugar
1 cup chopped dates
1 tablespoon flour

Mix together dates, boiling water, baking soda, and butter; let cool. Meanwhile, beat together sugar, eggs, and vanilla. Sift together flour, salt, and baking powder; add to sugar-egg mixture. Stir in nuts. Spread over jelly-roll pan or 13x9x2-inch pan. Bake at 350°F until tester inserted in center comes out clean (about 30 minutes).

Combine sauce ingredients; pour over warm pudding-cake. To serve, cut in squares. Top with whipped cream.

Mrs. Lovell Franks, East Peoria, Illinois
East Peoria Mennonite Church
Illinois MCC Relief Sale, Peoria

Apple Dumplings Deluxe

These dumplings were sold at the 1994 Oregon MCC Fall Festival and are another way apples are featured at that sale.

Crust:
1 egg, beaten
1 carton (8 oz) sour cream
2 cups all-purpose flour
2 tablespoons granulated
    sugar
2 teaspoons baking powder
1/4 teaspoon baking soda
1/4 teaspoon salt

Filling:
4 cups cooking apples,
    peeled and thinly sliced
1/4 cup granulated sugar
1/2 teaspoon ground cinna-
    mon
1/4 teaspoon ground nutmeg

Topping:
1 1/2 cups water
1 1/4 cups packed brown
    sugar
1 cup granulated sugar
2 tablespoons cornstarch
2 tablespoons lemon juice
2 tablespoons butter or
    margarine

To make crust, combine egg and sour cream in a medium mixing bowl. In a small bowl, combine dry ingredients; add to sour cream mixture. Mix well. On a lightly floured surface, roll dough to a 12-inch square.

To assemble, spread apple slices evenly over dough. Combine sugar and spices; sprinkle over apples. Carefully roll up dough. Cut into 12 one-inch-thick slices. Place slices, cut side down, into a greased 13x9x2-inch pan.

Make topping by combining water, sugars, cornstarch, and lemon juice. Pour over slices. Dot with butter.

Bake, uncovered, at 350°F for 35 to 40 minutes, or until golden. To serve, spoon warm dumplings and juices into individual dessert dishes. Top with cream or ice cream.

MAKES 12 SERVINGS

Note: For "thicker" dumplings, cut roll into eight 1 1/2-inch-thick slices; bake in an 8- or 9-inch-square pan.

Marolyn (Loy) Brenneman, Albany, Oregon
Oregon MCC Fall Festival, Albany

Apple Crisp

3 3/4 gallons (16 lbs) apples,
  pared and sliced
1/3 cup lemon juice
2 cups water
1 quart rolled wheat *or* 1
  quart plus 3/4 cup rolled
  oats
6 pounds brown sugar
1 1/2 quarts flour
2 2/3 tablespoons cinnamon
2 teaspoons salt
2 1/2 pounds butter or
  margarine

Divide apples evenly among four greased baking pans (each about 20x12x2 inches). Mix lemon juice and water; pour over apples.

Thoroughly combine wheat, sugar, flour, cinnamon, and salt. Mix in butter until crumbly. Cover apples with topping (use about 2 quarts per pan). Bake at 350°F for 40 to 60 minutes, or until apples are soft and top crust is browned and slightly cracked.

Let cool before cutting. Serve while still warm, topped with whipped topping or ice cream.

Serves 100

Martha Tschetter, Freeman, South Dakota
Minn-Kota MCC Relief Sale, Sioux Falls, S. Dakota

Apple Rolls

4 cups pared and diced (1/4
  inch) apples
1 cup coarsely broken nuts
1 cup raisins (optional)
2 cups sugar
3 cups flour
2 teaspoons baking soda
1/4 teaspoon salt
1/4 teaspoon allspice
1/4 teaspoon nutmeg
3/4 teaspoons cinnamon
1 cup melted butter or
  margarine
2 teaspoons vanilla
2 large eggs, slightly beaten

In a medium bowl, stir together apples, nuts, raisins, and sugar. Let stand 1 hour, stirring often so mixture makes its own juice. In a large bowl, stir together flour, baking soda, salt, and spices. Add apple mixture and stir well. Add butter and vanilla. Stir in eggs.

Turn into three greased 13-ounce coffee cans. Bake at 325°F for about 1 hour and 15 minutes, or until cake tester inserted in center comes out clean. Serve warm with whipped cream, or cool and ice. These rolls also freeze well.

Virginia Gindlesperger, Johnstown, Pennsylvania
MCC Quilt Auction and Relief Sale, Johnstown

Bohne Beroggae

Filling:
2 cups dried pinto beans
1 teaspoon salt
1 1/3 cups sugar

Dough:
Your own favorite recipe for
sweet yeast dough

Sauce:
1 quart half-and-half (or mix
2 cups milk with 2 cups
cream)
1 cup sugar
3 tablespoons cornstarch

Cook dried beans; drain and mash. Stir in salt and sugar.

When dough is ready to shape, form it into 48 balls the size of a large walnut. Let rise about 10 minutes. One by one, pull balls apart. Place 1 rounded teaspoon bean mixture on half the dough; reseal with other half by pinching edges together. Place in greased pans; let rise about 30 minutes. Bake in moderate oven about 25 minutes.

Prepare sauce by cooking half-and-half with the sugar and cornstarch 2 to 3 minutes, or until thickened. Serve hot over the beroggae.

Makes 4 dozen

Mid-Kansas MCC Relief Sale, Hutchinson

Raspberry Cobbler

2/3 cup sugar
1 tablespoon cornstarch
1 cup boiling water
2 cups raspberries, blueber-
ries, or blackberries
1 3/4 cups flour
2 teaspoons baking powder
1/2 teaspoon salt
1/4 cup soft shortening
3/4 cup sugar
1 egg
3/4 cup milk
1 teaspoon vanilla

In a small saucepan, mix together the 2/3 cup sugar and the cornstarch. Add the boiling water; boil 1 minute. Spread berries over bottom of baking pan; pour mixture over berries.

Mix together flour, baking powder, and salt. Add shortening, the 3/4 cup sugar, egg, milk, and vanilla; beat with beater or spoon until well combined. Spoon dough over berries.

Bake at 350°F for 25 to 30 minutes. Serve warm, with or without milk.

Grace Cable, Hollsopple, Pennsylvania
MCC Quilt Auction and Relief Sale, Johnstown

Strawberry Pizza

Crust:
1 cup butter, softened
2 cups flour
1/2 cup powdered sugar

Topping 1:
1 package cream cheese,
softened
1 cup powdered sugar
1 package Dream Whip
whipped topping mix
(prepared according to
package directions)

Topping 2:
1 pint strawberries, crushed
1 cup granulated sugar
4 teaspoons cornstarch
1/4 cup water
1 pint strawberries, sliced
(reserve a few whole
strawberries for garnish)

Prepare crust by mixing together butter, flour, and powdered sugar. Press into pizza pan. Bake at 350°F for 20 minutes. Cool.

Prepare Topping 1 by combining cream cheese, powdered sugar, and most of the whipped topping (reserve some to garnish top of pizza) until smooth. Spread over cooled crust. Chill.

Prepare Topping 2 by combining *crushed* strawberries and granulated sugar. Bring to a boil; add paste of cornstarch and water. Cook until thick and clear. Cool thoroughly. Spread *sliced* strawberries over cream cheese layer. Pour cooled strawberry sauce over. Chill.

Garnish with whipped topping and reserved whole strawberries before serving.

Serves 16

Bernice Lehman, Johnstown, Pennsylvania
MCC Quilt Auction and Relief Sale, Johnstown

Fruit Pizza Dessert

Crust:
1/2 cup margarine
1/2 cup solid vegetable
    shortening (Crisco)
1 1/2 cups sugar
2 eggs
2 teaspoons cream of tartar
1 teaspoon baking soda
1/4 teaspoon salt
2 3/4 cups flour

Topping 1:
1 package (8 oz) cream
    cheese, softened
1/2 cup sugar
2 tablespoons fruit juice

Topping 2:
1 can pineapple chunks
1 can mandarin orange
    segments
2 bananas, sliced
Fresh strawberries, sliced
3 tablespoons cornstarch

Make crust by mixing shortenings, sugar, and eggs. Add remaining ingredients. Mix thoroughly. Press into large jelly-roll pan. Bake at 400°F for 8 to 10 minutes. Cool.

Make Topping 1 by beating all ingredients together. Spread on cooled crust.

Make Topping 2 by draining canned fruits; reserve juice. Arrange canned and fresh fruit over cream cheese layer. Combine a little of the fruit juice with the cornstarch to make a smooth paste. Bring reserved juice to a boil, add cornstarch paste, and cook until thick and clear. Cool; then pour sauce over fruit layer. Chill pizza before serving.

Serves 12 to 16

Janice Mendel, Freeman, South Dakota
Minn-Kota MCC Relief Sale, Sioux Falls,
South Dakota

Rhubarb Dessert

5 cups rhubarb
1 package (3 oz)
    strawberry-flavored
    gelatin
1 cup sugar
1 packaged yellow or white
    cake mix
2 cups miniature marshmal-
    lows

Mix rhubarb, gelatin, and sugar. Spread *half* the mixture in a greased 9x13-inch pan. Prepare the cake mix; pour batter over rhubarb mixture in pan. Top with marshmallows. Spread remaining rhubarb mixture over. Bake at 350°F for 1 hour.

MCC Quilt Auction and Relief Sale, Johnstown,
Pennsylvania

Cookie Salad

This dessert can be made a day ahead and refrigerated until serving.

1 package instant pudding
   mix
1 cup buttermilk
1 small can crushed pine-
   apple
1 container (8 oz) nondairy
   whipped topping,
   thawed
Half a package
   fudge-striped cookies,
   broken into small pieces

Mix ingredients in order given. Chill.

SERVES 8

Mrs. Arthur (Beverly) Carlson, Odin, Minnesota
Minn-Kota MCC Relief Sale, Sioux Falls,
South Dakota

Four-Layer Dessert

1 1/2 cups flour
3/4 cup soft margarine
1 cup chopped nuts
1 package (8 oz) cream
   cheese, softened
1 cup powdered sugar
2 containers (8 oz each)
   nondairy whipped
   topping, thawed
2 packages (3 1/2 oz each)
   instant chocolate or
   lemon pudding mix
3 cups milk

Prepare crust by combining flour, margarine, and 3/4 cup of the chopped nuts. Press over bottom of a 9x13-inch pan. Bake at 375°F for 15 to 20 minutes. Cool.

Combine cream cheese and powdered sugar. Mix in 1 container of the whipped topping. Spread over crust.

Prepare pudding mix using the 3 cups milk, as directed on package. Pour over cream cheese layer.

Spread remaining container of whipped topping over dessert. Sprinkle with remaining 1/4 cup chopped nuts. Refrigerate.

SERVES 12 TO 15

Mrs. Allan (Doris) Bachman, Putnam, Illinois
Willow Springs Mennonite Church, Tiskilwa
Illinois MCC Relief Sale, Peoria

Cream Cheese Grapes

1 package (8 oz) cream
    cheese, softened
1 1/2 cups powdered sugar
1 cup sour cream
1 tablespoon lemon juice
1 container (8 oz) nondairy
    whipped topping,
    thawed
4 pounds seedless grapes
2 bananas, sliced (optional)

Mix cream cheese, sugar, sour cream, and lemon juice thoroughly. Add whipped topping; mix well. Then add grapes (and bananas, if desired). Chill.

Serves 6 to 8

Ann Goossen, Beatrice, Nebraska
Nebraska MCC Relief Sale, Aurora

A volunteer serves the ice cream as fast as others scoop it at the Ohio Mennonite Relief Sale in Kidron.

Frozen Dessert

Base:
1 cup flour
1/2 cup margarine
1/4 cup brown sugar
1/2 cup chopped nuts

Topping:
1 package (16 oz) frozen
    strawberries, thawed
1 cup sugar
2 egg whites
1 tablespoon lemon juice
1/2 teaspoon vanilla
1 cup whipping cream,
    whipped

Prepare base by combining all ingredients and placing in a 400°F oven for about 15 minutes, stirring regularly, until brown. Sprinkle the crumbs over the bottom of a 9x13-inch pan, saving some of them to top the dessert. Do not press the crumbs down.

Prepare topping by beating strawberries, sugar, egg whites, lemon juice, and vanilla for 10 minutes. Fold in whipped cream. Spoon topping over crumbs; garnish with reserved crumbs. Put in freezer. Thaw slightly and cut in squares to serve.

Anne Neufeld, Coaldale, Alberta
Alberta MCC Relief Sale, Coaldale

Strawberry Chantilly

1 cup flour
1/4 cup brown sugar
1/2 cup margarine
1/4 cup ground nuts or
    Grape-Nuts cereal
2 egg whites
2/3 cup granulated sugar
2 tablespoons lemon juice
1 pint strawberries, sliced
1 container (8 oz) nondairy
    whipped topping,
    thawed

Combine flour and brown sugar; cut in margarine until blended; stir in nuts. Spread on a rimmed cookie sheet. Bake at 325°F for 20 minutes, stirring three or four times; cool. Reserve 1/2 cup crumbs; pat remainder over bottom of 9x13-inch pan.

Beat egg whites, granulated sugar, and lemon juice until stiff. Add strawberries and beat until blended. Fold in whipped topping. Spread over crumbs in pan; top with reserved crumbs. Freeze. Let thaw for 20 minutes before serving. Cut in squares.

Bernice Lehman, Johnstown, Pennsylvania
MCC Quilt Auction and Relief Sale, Johnstown

During the 1993 MCC Alberta Relief Sale, a Montana family on vacation saw the MCC SALE sign and decided to drop in. The brief stay included a barbecue supper, the teen joining in the evening youth activities, an overnight stay at a local home and enjoying food and fellowship at the auction the following day. It was the highlight of their trip.

Zesto Cracker Dessert

40 Zesto crackers
1/2 cup melted butter
4 egg whites
1 cup granulated sugar
Pinch salt
1/2 teaspoon vanilla
1 can pie filling (cherry, blueberry, or raspberry)
1/2 pint whipping cream
2 teaspoons powdered sugar

Crush crackers; mix with butter to form crumbs. Reserving 1 tablespoon crumbs to top dessert, press remainder over bottom of a 9x13-inch pan.

Beat egg whites until stiff, gradually adding granulated sugar, salt, and finally, vanilla. Spread over cracker crumbs in pan. Bake at 325°F for 10 to 15 minutes. Cool.

Spread pie filling over cooled crust. Beat the whipping cream and powdered sugar. Spread over pie filling. Sprinkle reserved cracker crumbs over top.

Ila Mae Miller, Pekin, Illinois
Bethel Mennonite Church, Pekin
Illinois MCC Relief Sale, Peoria

Strawberry Angel Cake Dessert

Half an angel food cake
1 large package (6 oz) instant vanilla pudding mix
1 cup cold milk
2 cups vanilla ice cream
1 large package (6 oz) strawberry-flavored gelatin
2 cups boiling water
1 large box frozen strawberries, thawed
Nondairy whipped topping

Tear cake into bite-size pieces. Use to line a 13x9-inch glass baking dish. Whip together pudding mix and milk. Add ice cream; whip until smooth. Pour over cake in pan. Refrigerate 2 to 3 hours.

Thoroughly mix gelatin and boiling water; let cool. Stir in strawberries. Pour mixture over pudding-topped cake in pan. Refrigerate until set. Spread with whipped topping before serving.

Mary Ann Cashdollar, Morton, Illinois
First Mennonite Church, Morton
Illinois MCC Relief Sale, Peoria

Refrigerator Dessert

This no-cook dessert is served at the kick-off dinner for the Minn-Kota Relief Sale in Sioux Falls, South Dakota.

2 cups graham cracker
    crumbs
1 cup soda cracker crumbs
1/2 cup melted butter
2 packages (each 3 1/2 oz)
    instant vanilla pudding
    mix
2 cups milk
1 quart ice cream
1 package (4 1/2 oz) whipped
    topping mix (prepared
    following package
    directions)
2 Butterfinger candy bars

Mix crumbs with butter. Spread two-thirds of the crumbs over bottom of a 9x12-inch pan; reserve remaining crumbs.

Combine pudding mix, milk, and ice cream; blend very well. Pour over crumbs in pan. Chill at least 1/2 hour. Then spread whipped topping over top. Crush the candy bars; mix with reserved crumbs. Spread mixture over top of dessert. Refrigerate until serving time.

SERVES 12 TO 15

Sarah Buller Hofer, Freeman, South Dakota

Butterfinger Dessert

This is a slightly different version of the no-cook dessert served at the annual kick-off dinner for the Minn-Kota Relief Sale.

2 1/2 cups graham cracker
    crumbs
1 1/2 cups crushed Rice
    Krispies
1/2 cup melted margarine
2 packages (3 1/2 oz each)
    instant vanilla pudding
    mix
2 cups milk
1 quart vanilla ice cream
1 container (8 oz) nondairy
    whipped topping,
    thawed
2 Butterfinger candy bars

Combine crumbs, crushed cereal, and margarine. Spread two-thirds of the crumbs over the bottom of a 9x13-inch cake pan; reserve remaining crumbs.

Combine pudding mix and milk; mix until smooth. Blend in ice cream. Pour mixture over crumbs in pan. Let set in refrigerator. Spread whipped topping over top. Crush candy bars; mix with remaining crumbs. Sprinkle mixture over whipped topping. Serve chilled.

Note: This dessert keeps well frozen; thaw before serving.

SERVES 12

Marie Hofer, Freeman, South Dakota

Creamy White Fudge

2 tablespoons butter
3 cups sugar
1 1/4 cups milk
1 cup black walnut meats
1 1/2 teaspoons vanilla
1/2 cup candied cherries

In a heavy 3-quart saucepan, combine butter, sugar, and milk. Cook over medium heat until candy reaches the softball stage, stirring all the time. Remove pan from heat and let stand at room temperature until cooled to warm.

Stir in walnuts, vanilla, and cherries; beat until creamy. Pour into buttered 9x5x3-inch bread pan. Let stand at room temperature until cool. Then wrap pan in foil and let stand overnight or until ready to use.

Bernice Schroll
(submitted by N. Elizabeth Graber, Wayland, Iowa)
Iowa MCC Relief Sale, Iowa City

Shanty Candy

This is a very old family recipe. Its contributor, whose mother prepared it each year at Christmas, describes the candy as "delicious." Mrs. Kauffman carries on her mother's tradition and hopes that one of her daughters will continue to do so in the future. No one knows where the name came from—unless the candy was taken to the shanty to cool after it was cooked.

2 cups granulated sugar
3/4 cup molasses
1/4 cup water
Whites of 2 eggs
Vanilla
1/2 cup chopped English
    walnuts
1/2 cup dates

Bring sugar, molasses, and water to a boil. Boil until it reaches hardball stage on a candy thermometer (or until it is crisp when a small amount is dropped into cold water).

While syrup is cooking, beat egg whites until very stiff. When syrup is ready, pour it slowly into beaten whites. Beat candy until too stiff to work, mixing in vanilla, walnuts, and dates just before it stiffens up. Pour into buttered pan. Cut into squares before it hardens.

Mrs. Aaron Kauffman, Cochranville, Pennsylvania
Gap Relief Sale, Pennsylvania

  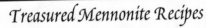

Candy Crunch

1 1/2 cups Cap'n Crunch's
    peanut butter crunch
    cereal
1 1/2 cups Rice Krispies
1 1/2 cups unsalted peanuts
1 1/2 cups thin stick pretzels,
    broken into small pieces
A 1-pound block white
    chocolate

Combine cereals, peanuts, and pretzels. Melt chocolate; pour over dry ingredients and mix thoroughly. Spread candy on foil-covered cookie sheets. Refrigerate. To serve, break sheet of candy into pieces.

Lena Sala, Hollsopple, Pennsylvania
MCC Quilt Auction and Relief Sale, Johnstown,
Pennsylvania

Relief Soap Making

Relief Soap Recipe

1 1/2 gallons water
3 1/2 pounds lye
24 pounds grease

The day before you want to make soap, place the water in a large plastic or stainless steel *(do not use aluminum)* container. Carefully pour lye into water; stir with a wooden spoon or spatula until lye is dissolved. Let mixture cool.

The next day, heat clean grease to 110°F in a large stainless steel *(not aluminum)* container. Carefully add lye solution, stirring with a wooden spoon or spatula until soap begins to thicken like honey. Pour into a heavy 5x16x22-inch cardboard box lined with plastic. Let set several hours until firm but not solid; cut into 4-inch squares. Let set in box for 3 to 4 days. Remove, dry, and cure. Soap will be ready to use in about 4 to 6 weeks.

MAKES 40 TO 50 POUNDS OF SOAP

Mary Wenger
Missouri MCC Relief Sale, Harrisonville

◆ Index ◆

A

Abbotsfordd, viii
Akron, Pa., xii
Albany, Ore., xxiii
Alberta, v, 212
Amish-style Deviled Eggs, 3
Angel Food,
    Supreme Cake, 164; Cake, 165
Anhaltskuchen, 167
Apple,
    Overnight Salad, 83; Tasty Salad,
    84; Cider Butter, 97; Hot Spiced
    Cider, 111; Froese-Fritz Fritters,
    141; Oppel Kuchen, 142; Tart Pie,
    151; Cookies, 194; Danish Squares,
    197; Dumplings Deluxe, 204; Crisp,
    205; Rolls, 205
Arkansas, xviii
Arthur, Ill., xii 132
Augusta Relief Sale, xxviii
Aurora, Neb., xix
Arthur Mennonite Relief Sale, xii

B

Baked Beans, 73, 74
Banana Cake, 166
Barbecued Kraut, 64
Bar cookies,
    Poor Man's, 198; Mabel's Marble,
    199; Swirl Chocolate, 199; Oh
    Henry, 199; Layer, 200
Bath Fair Grounds, xix
Bath MCC Relief Sale, xix
Bean Salad, Emma's, 89
Bean Soup, 11-13
Beef, Cabbage Soup, 18;
    Best Ever Stew, 34; Swiss Steak, 34;
    Meat Loaf, 35; Meatballs, 36-38;
    Barbecue, 38; Sloppy Joes, 39;
    Haystacks, 40; Cabbage Rolls, 41;
    Stuffed Eggplant, 42; Dried Hot

Dish, 42; Hamburger-Corn Bake,
43, Green Bean Casserole, 43;
Zucchini Casserole, 44; Impossible
Cheeseburger Pie, 44; Quick Italian
Bake, 45; Vegetable Pasties, 55
Beverages,
    Spicy, 110; Rhubarb Juice, 110;
    Golden Punch, 111; Lemonade, 111;
    Swiss Tea, 111; Hot Spiced Apple
    Cider, 112; Pineapple Punch, 113
Bierocks, 57
Biscuits, Cheese, 136
Black Creek, B.C., vii
Black Creek MCC Relief Sale, vii
Black Creek Pioneer Village Relief
    Sale, xxi
Blueberry Rhubarb Jam, 95
Bohne Beroggae, 206
Borscht, 7-10
Boysenberry Pie, 152
Brandon Relief Sale, xvi
Bread,
    No-Knead, 114; French, 115;
    Honey-Whole Wheat, 115; Sesame
    Multigrain, 116; Pilgrims', 117;
    Farm, 118; White, 119; Raisin, 119;
    Cinnamon, 120; Christmas Braid,
    121; Kringel, 122; Sour Cream
    Twists, 123; Mak Kuchen (Poppy
    Seed Rolls), 123; Orange Butter
    Rolls, 124; Hot Cross Buns, 125;
    Semmel (German Crusty Rolls),
    126; Dampfnoodles, 126; Refrigera-
    tor Rolls, 127; No-Knead Refrigera-
    tor Rolls, 127; Zwiebach, 128-131;
    Zucchini Orange Coconut, 132;
    Rhubarb, 132; Pumpkin, 133; Dale
    High Nut, 133;
Bread-and-Butter Pickles, 104
British Columbia, vii, viii
Broccoli,
    -Cauliflower-Cheese Soup, 19;

Index

Hot Dish, 77; Sauce for, 78; Delight Salad, 90; Raw Cauliflower and Salad, 90;
Brownies, 200, 201
Butter Tarts, 161
Buttermilk,
Cake, 165; Brownies, 200
Butterscotch,
Curls, 192; Brownies, 201

C

Cabbage
Beef Soup, 18; Cheese Soup, 6; Rolls, 41; Sweet-Sour (Gadaemftes Kraut), 77; Quick 'n Easy Sweet-Sour, 78; Napa Salad, 86; Oriental Salad, 87.
Cake,
Sour Cream Coffee, 137; Fruity Coffee, 137; Quick Coffee, 137; Lazy Daisy Duff, 138; Sour Cream Cocoa, 162; Down-Side Up Fudge, 162; Wacky, 163; Miracle Whip, 163; Schichtkuchin (Layer Cake), 164; Angel Food Supreme, 164; Angel Food, 165; Buttermilk, 165; Banana, 166; Cranberry, 166; Anhaltskuchen (Loaf Cake topped with Almonds), 167; Chocolate Applesauce, 167; Granny, 168; Poor Man, 169; Texas Chocolate, 169; Great-Grandmother Troyer's Eggless Wonder Spice, 170; Karovei, 171
California, x,
Calzone, 58
Candy,
Shanty, 214; Crunch, 215
Carmel Popcorn, 93, 94
Carrots,
Glazed, 75; Casserole, 75
Cass County, Mo., xviii

Casselton, N.D., xix
Casseroles, 27, 29, 30, 31, 36-38, 43, 44, 46, 50-53, 58-60, 67, 75, 76, 79, 87, 88, 91
Cheese,
Ball, 4; Cabbage Soup, 6; Biscuits, 136
Cherry,
Moos, 25; Ground Pie, 151;
Chicken
Borscht, 7; Corn Soup, 11; dumplings with wild rice soup, 20;
Chili, 19; Filled Shells, 26; and Dressing Casserole, 27; Bean Casserole, 27; and rice (Plou), 28; baked with rice, 28; Broccoli Casserole, 29; Vegetable Casserole, 29; Quick Saucy Casserole, 30; Festive Mexican, 30; Casserole, 31; Macaroni Casserole, 31; Brunswick Stew, 33; Turkey Salad, 80.
Chili, 14
Chili Sauce, 106, 109
Chinese Chow Mein Dinner, 32
Chocolate,
Applesauce Cake, 167; Texas Cake, 196; Best Ever Chip Cookies, 196; Cookies, 196; Swirl Bars, 199
Christmas Braid, 121
Chronology of histories, iii
Clearbrook Mennonite Relief Sale, vi, viii
Cobbler, Raspberry, 206
Cocoa, Sour Cream Cake, 162
Coconut Fruit Bowl, 82
Colorado, xi, 142
Congerville, Ill., xii
Cookie Salad, 209
Cookies,
Sugar, 182-185; Molasses Crinkles, 186; Ginger Snaps, 186; Ginger, 187; Honey, 187, 188;

Lemon Poppyseed, 190; Peppermint, 190; Refrigerator Norwegian, 191; Mexican Wedding Cakes, 191; Butterscotch Curls, 192; Swedish Creams, 192; Kifli, 193; Oatmeal, 193; $250, 194; Apple, 194; Monster, 195; Pride of Iowa, 195; Best Ever Chocolate Chip, 196; Chocolate, 196
Corn,
    Chicken Soup, 11; Hamburger Bake, 43; on the cob, 79; Casserole, 79; Heather's Muffins, 135.
Cornbread Salad, 88
Cranberry,
    Fruit Medley, 83; Cake, 166
Cream Cheese Grapes, 210
Cupcakes, Never-Fail "Seven Ones", 173
Custard,
    Pumpkin Pie, 154; Grandma's Egg Pie, 157; Pie, 157.

D
Dampfnoodles, 126
Daviess County Relief Sale, xiii
Dessert,
    Fruit Pizza, 208; Rhubarb, 208; Four-Layer, 209; Frozen, 211; Zesto Cracker, 212; Strawberry Angel Cake, 212; Refrigerator, 213; Butterfinger, 213
Dill Pickle Spears, 102
Dip,
    Apple, 4; Ham, 5; The Best You Ever Had, 5;
Doughnuts,
    Ruth Ellen, 143; Berliner Pfannkuchen (Prune-Filled Doughnuts), 144;
Downsview, Ont., xxi

Dressing,
    Salad, 91, 92; Creamy Cole Slaw, 91; Homemade French, 92
Dutch Potato Soup, 13

E
Easy Garden Vegetable Pie, 65
Eggs, Deviled, 3
Elkhart County Fairgrounds, xiv
Elverson, Pa., xxiv
Expoland, xxviii

F
Fairview, Mich., xvii
Fairview, Okla., xxi
Favorite Sweet Pickles, 102
Fisherville, Va., ii, xxviii
Food Grains Bank Sale, xxv
Fresno, Calif., ii, 179
Fritters,
    Froese-Fritz Apple, 141; Oppel Kuchen (Apple Fritters), 142; Raisin (New Year's Cookies), 180;
Frosting, "Baked-on" for an Applesauce Cake, 168
Fruit Pizza Dessert, 208
Fruit Salad with Sweet Dressing, 81
Fudge,
    Down-Side Up Cake, 162; Creamy White, 214
Funnel Cakes, 143

G
Gap Relief Sale, xxiii
Ginger,
    Snaps, 186; Cookies, 187
Goshen, Ind., xiv
Grandma Hannah's Ready-to-Eat Pickles, 98
Green Bean,
    Soup, 15; Hamburger Casserole, 43; Barbecued, 76; Au Gratin, 76;

Index

Guelph, Ont., xxii
Guernsey Sales Barn, xxiv

H

Hague, Sask., xxv
Ham,
    Balls, 2; Baked Balls, 2; Dip, 5;
    and Bean Soup, 18; Loaf, 48; and
    Wild Rice Casserole, 52; Potato,
    and Cheese Casserole, 52; and
    Noodle Bake, 53.
Hamburger,
    Corn Bake, 43; Green Been Casse-
    role, 43; Impossible Cheeseburger
    Pie, 51;
Harrisburg, Pa., xxiv
Haystacks, 40
Henderson, Neb., xix
Herb Shaker, 26
Hillsboro, Kansas, xv
Honey Cookies, 228, 229
Hot Cross Buns, 125
Hot Sauce, 108
Houston Mennonite Church, xxvii

I

Idaho, xxviii
Ikra, 107
Illinois Mennonite Relief Sale, xii
Imam Bayildi, 42
Intercourse, Pa., xxiv
Iowa Mennonite Relief Sale, xv, 97,
    158, 174

J

Jam,
    Rhubarb, 95; Blueberry Rhubarb,
    95; Zucchini, 96.
Jefferson County Fairgrounds 4-H
    Activity Center, xxix
Jelly,
    Turtle Brand Dandelion, 96;

Roll 172
Johnstown, Pa., xxiv, 165, 217

K

Kansas, xxi, xxii, 124
Karovei, 171
Kelowna, ix
Kelowna Curling Rink, viii
Keystone Centre, xvi
Kidron, Ohio, xx,
Kielka, 66
Kitchener, xxi
Knie Blatza, (Nothings), 141
Kraut Runza, 56
Kringel, 122
Kuchli (Nothings), 140

L

La Junta, Colo., v
Lancaster County, Pa., xxiii, xxiv
Lemonade, 111
Lime Pickles, 100
Lime Stick Pickles, 104
Linn County Fairgrounds, xxiii

M

Mak Kuchen, 123
Manitoba, xvi
Meatballs
    Soup, 31; barbecued, 36; Saure
    Klops, 37; Hamburger Balls with
    Sweet-and-Sour Sauce, 38.
MCC Alberta Relief Sale, v
MCC Oregon Fall Festival, ii, xxiii,
    191
MCC Quilt Auction and Relief Sale,
    xxiv,
Mennonite Central Committee 75th
    anniversary, i
Mennonite Country Auction, xxviii
Michiana Mennonite Relief Sale, xiv,
    112, 145

Mid-Kansas MCC Relief Sale, xv
Mince Meat, 159
Mincement Muffins, 136
Minnesota, xx, xxvi
Minn-Kota Country Auction and Fair, xxiv, xxvi, 189
Minot, N.D., xix, 217
Missouri Mennonite Relief Sale, xviii
Molasses,
   Sugar Cookies, 185; Crinkles, 186
Montana, xix, 212
Montgomery, Ind., xiii
Morgantown, Pa., xx, xxv
Morris MCC Relief Auction Sale, xvi
Muffins,
   Morning Glory, 134; Pumpkin 'n' Spice, 134; Heather's Corn, 135; Rhubarb, 135; Mincemeat, 136
Munch Mix, 94
Mushroom Salad, Hot, 89

N

Napa Cabbage Salad, 86
Nebraska Mennonite Relief Sale, xix, 160, 181, 197
New Year's Cookies, 178-182
North Dakota, xx
Northern Michigan Relief Sale, xvii, xviii
Nothings, 140, 141

O

Oatmeal Cookies, 193
Ohio Mennonite Relief Sale, , xx, 184, 210
Okanagan Valley Fall Relief Sale, viii
Oklahoma Mennonite Relief Sale, xxi
Onion Rings, Crispy, 73
Ontario Heifer Sale, xxii
Ontario Mennonite Relief Sale, xxii, 150
Oppel Kuchen, 142

Oriental Salad, 87

P

Pancakes,
   Buckwheat, 145; Russian, 146 Pflinzen, 146; All Over the Pan (Russian Crepes), 147; Kirschen Pflinzen, 148; Noni Snicki or Nolles Nicki, 149.
Paradise Sales Barn, xxiii
Pasties, Savilla's Beef-Vegetable, 55
Pastries, meat filled,
   Savilla's Beef-Vegetable Pasties, 55; Kraut Runza, 56; Bierocks, 57; Calzone, 58; Samosa, 59
Peanut Butter Pie, 158
Pennsylvania Heifer Relief Sale for MCC, xxiv
Pennsylvania Relief Sale, xxiv
Peoria, Ill., xxiii, xxix
Peppermint Cookies, 190
Peppernuts, 174-177
Perischke, 160
Pflinzen, 146
Pickled Beets, 105
Pickles,
   Refrigerator, 98; Grandma Hannah's Ready-to-Eat, 98; "Heinz", 99; Lime, 100; Red Cinnamon, 100; Sweet-Sour Dill, 101; Crisp Slices, 101; Favorite Sweet, 102; Dill Spears, 102; Sweet Gherkins, 103; Bread-and-Butter, 104; Lime Stick, 104
Pie,
   Brownie, 150; Ground Cherry, 151; Tart Apple, 151; Boysenberry, 152; English Walnut, 153; Poppy Seed, 153; Diabetic Pumpkin, 154; Custard Pumpkin, 154; Pumpkin, 155, 156; Pumpkin or Squash, 156; Sour Cream Raisin, 157;

Index

Grandma's Egg Custard, 157; Custard, 157; Peanut Butter, 158; Creamy Butter Pecan, 159; Strawberry Parfait, 159; Perischke, 160
Pineapple Punch, 138
Plou, 28
Pluma Moos, 25
Pluma Mos, 23
Pluma Mose, 22
Plumi Moos, 21
Plumamousse, 24
Poppy Seed,
Rolls,123;
Pie, 153; Lemon Cookies, 190
Pork,
Breakfast Casserole, 46; Breakfast Bake, 46; Roast Pig, 47; Smoky Country-Style Ribs, 47; Chalupa, 48; Black Beans Brazilian Style, 49; Stir-fry, 50; Chinese Casserole, 51; Dutch Goose Casserole, 51; Fettucini Casserole, 53; Barbecued Kraut, 64; SEE ALSO HAM.
Portzilka, 178
Potato,
Dutch Soup, 13; Hamand Cheese Casserole, 52;Make-Ahead, 66; Mashed, 66; Hash Brown, 67; Hash Brown Casserole, 67; Super Duper, 68; New Idea in Scalloped, 68; Scalloped, 69; Amish, 69; Patties, 70; French Fried Mashed Balls, 70; Baked with Choice of Topping, 71; Apricot-Glazed Sweet, 72; Apricot Sweet, 72; Salad, 87, 88;
Pretzels, Little Twister Flavored, 93
Prince George Mennonite Relief Sale, ix
Pudding,
Steamed, 202; Date-Nut, 202; Ye Olde Date-Nut, 203;

Pumpkin,
Bread, 133; 'n' Spice Muffins, 134; Diabetic Pie, 154; Custard Pie, 154; Pie, 155, 156; or Squash Pie, 156; Roll, 172

Q

Quiche, Zucchini, 64
Quick Italian Bake, 45

R

Raisin,
Fritters (New Year's Cookies), 178-182; Sour Cream Pie, 157
Raspberry Cobbler, 206
Reedley, Calif., x, xxiv
Red Cinnamon Pickles, 100
Relish, Country-Style Hotdog, 105
Rhubarb,
Jam, 95; Blueberry Jam, 95; Juice, 110; Bread, 132; Muffins, 135; Squares, 198; Dessert, 208
Richland Mall, xxiv
Richreall Fairgrounds, xxiii
Ritzville, Wash., xxviii
Riverview Curling Club, xv
Rocky Ford, Colo., v, xi
Rocky Mountain Mennonite Relief Sale, v, xi,116
Roderkuchen, 182
Roll Kuchen, 139, 140
Rolls,
Mak Kuchen (Poppy Seed Rolls), 123; Orange Butter, 124; Hot Cross, 125; Semmel (German Crusty Rolls), 126; Refrigerator, 127; Jelly, 172; Pumpkin, 172; Apple, 205
Rosthern, Sask., xxv

S

Salads, 80-92

Salsa, 108
Sandwich Spread, 106
Saskachewan, xxv
Saskatoon Mennonite Relief Sale, xxv
Schichtkuchin, 164
Semmel, 126
Sioux Falls, S.D., xxvi, 128, 189
Slaw,
 Hot, 84; Cole, 85; Tangy, 86;
 Creamy Cole Dressing, 91
Sloppy Joes, 39
Soap, Relief Recipe, 216
Soups, 6-25
 Cabbage, 6; 18; borscht, 7-10;
 chicken corn, 11; bean, 11-13;
 potato, 13; chili, 14; green bean, 15;
 vegetable, 16-17; broccoli, 19;
 zucchini, 19; wild rice, 20; meat-
 ball, 21; moos, 21-25.
Sour Cream,
 Twists, 123; Coffee Cake, 137;
 Raisin Pie, 157; Cocoa Cake, 162
South Dakota, xxvi, 128
Spaghetti with Zucchini Sauce, 64
Squares,
 Danish Apple, 197; Rhubarb, 198
Strawberry,
 Parfait Pie, 159; Pizza, 207;
 Chantilly, 211; Angel Cake Dessert,
 212
Sweet Gherkins, 103
Sweet-Sour Dill Pickles, 101

T

Taco Salad, 80, 81
Tarts, Butter, 161
Texas MCC Relief Sale, xxvii

Tri-County Relief Sale, xxv

U

Upper Mid-West Relief Sale, xx

V

Vancouver Island, vii
Vegetable
 Soup, 16-17; Beef Pasties, 55; Easy
 Garden Pie, 65; Casserole, 76;
Verenike, Verenika, Veranika,
 Vereneki, 60-63
Vietnamese Spring Rolls, 1
Virginia Relief Sale, xxviii

W

Waldorf Salad, Creamy, 82
Walnut Pie, English, 153
Washington, Iowa, xv
Waterloo, xxii
West Coast Mennonite Sale and
 Auction for World Relief, x, 151,
 189
W.H. Lyon Fairgrounds, xxvii
Wild Rice Soup with Chicken Dump-
 lings, 20
Winnepeg MCC Relief Sale, xvii
Wisconsin Mennonite Relief Sale and
 Benefit Auction, xxix

Z

Zucchini,
 Soup, 19; Casserole, 44; Spaghetti
 with sauce, 64; Quiche, 64; Cres-
 cent Pie, 65; Jam, 96; Orange
 Coconut Bread, 132.
Zwieback, 128-131

Order Form

Yes, please send the following:

____ copies of Treasured Mennonite Recipes @ $11.95   _____

____ copies of More Treasured Mennonite Recipes – #2 @ $12.95   _____
                 (Available Fall 1995)

(Please add $2.00 per book to a maximum of $4.00)   _____

                                         TOTAL   _____

Please send check or money order to:

Fox Chapel Publishing
Box 7948M
Lancaster, PA 17604-7948

Order Form

Yes, please send the following:

____ copies of Treasured Mennonite Recipes @ $11.95   _____

____ copies of More Treasured Mennonite Recipes – #2 @ $12.95   _____
                 (Available Fall 1995)

(Please add $2.00 per book to a maximum of $4.00)   _____

                                           TOTAL   _____

Please send check or money order to:

Fox Chapel Publishing
Box 7948M
Lancaster, PA 17604-7948